CAMBRIDGE STUDIES IN ECONOMIC HISTORY

PUBLISHED WITH THE AID OF THE ELLEN McARTHUR FUND

GENERAL EDITOR
J. H. CLAPHAM, Litt.D.
Professor of Economic History in the University of Cambridge

THE ORDINANCE BOOK OF
THE MERCHANTS OF THE STAPLE

T0381799

The
ORDINANCE BOOK OF THE MERCHANTS OF THE STAPLE

WITH AN INTRODUCTION

BY

E. E. RICH

Fellow of St Catharine's College and
Lecturer in History in the University of Cambridge

CAMBRIDGE
AT THE UNIVERSITY PRESS
1937

CAMBRIDGE UNIVERSITY PRESS
Cambridge, New York, Melbourne, Madrid, Cape Town,
Singapore, São Paulo, Delhi, Mexico City

Cambridge University Press
The Edinburgh Building, Cambridge CB2 8RU, UK

Published in the United States of America by Cambridge University Press, New York

www.cambridge.org
Information on this title: www.cambridge.org/9781107677357

First published 1937
First paperback edition 2013

A catalogue record for this publication is available from the British Library

ISBN 978-1-107-67735-7 Paperback

CONTENTS

ACKNOWLEDGMENTS

My thanks are due to Mr G. T. Legg, Merchant of the Staple of England, and to Mr G. J. Freeman, Clerk to the Merchants of the Staple, for their kindness in placing their knowledge of the Staple Company at my disposal and in allowing me to consult and transcribe the Company's documents.

To the General Editor of this series I am deeply indebted for much advice and many valuable suggestions in preparing the manuscript for the press.

E. E. R.

EDITOR'S PREFACE

The Staple Company of England from its earliest days—when that name had not yet taken shape—was so closely linked to the government of England, the trade of its members was so vital to the prosperity of England, that most of what historians and economists can want to know about it may be learnt, and the greater part during the Company's most prosperous days has already been learnt, from the Public Records. Even for the later years after it lost its headquarters at Calais and—with the decline in the export of wool—most of its importance, the Public Records are a primary source of our knowledge, as Mr Rich's use of them to illustrate this period of struggle and decay shows. But the loss of Calais meant the loss of the Company's own copies of its charters and of domestic documents such as Ordinances and Minutes which did not concern the Crown and so are not to be found at the Record Office. About all this side of the life of the Staplers we have hitherto been rather ignorant.

The discovery of the Ordinances of 1565 here edited takes us inside the Company at a critical date. Driven from Calais and domiciled uneasily at Bruges, it tried "to reconstitute the conditions of its trade" (p. 4) as they had been in the old days, with a minimum of adjustment to new circumstances and interpretation of uncertain rules and traditions. We may be sure that the formalities of apprenticeship and election, the ordinances for general shipping, "stint" of apprentices, "the olde order for dayes of shewes and tymes and places of sales" (p. 155), and the rest, reproduce faithfully traditions at least of early Tudor, and often of much more remote, times. For these things the memories of senior officials were not likely to be at fault, and we know (p. 104) that they did "serche oute copies of our auncient lawes and orders aforesaiede suche as coulde in any wise be obteyned".

Mr Rich has taken the opportunity to sketch the history of the Company's decline in the sixteenth century and transformation in the seventeenth, and has given us a close and most satisfactory account of the critical years 1561–7, in the midst of which this Book of Ordinances was compiled, years in which trade and religion, wool and heresy, William Cecil that "homme bas et rusé, versé dans la connaissance des lettres grecques et latines" and Cardinal Granvelle who so described him, high politics and mistaken economic calculations, all jostle one another, reminding us that there is no such thing as economic history *in vacuo*. Among them the boat of the export trade in English wool that carried the fortunes of the Staplers, bound for the shallows and the miseries in any event, was lamentably tossed about. Of how the Staplers tried to get a footing in other trades, and how they finally broke their own rules to occupy themselves in wool dealing at home, something was already known; but Mr Rich with the Jacobean Minute Book before him, has added to our knowledge. He is the first to make use of either the Minutes or the Ordinances, which but for him might have remained unknown or inaccessible.

J. H. CLAPHAM

THE ORDINANCE BOOK OF
THE MERCHANTS OF THE STAPLE

❖

INTRODUCTION

Chapter I

THE BOOKS OF THE STAPLE COMPANY

In 1887 the Staple Company of England was brought to the notice of a public which had forgotten the very existence of this once powerful corporation. Their Clerk had embezzled the funds of the Company, £4,250 in three per cent. Consols standing in the Company's name in the books of the Bank of England. Since the Clerk had been given no power of attorney the Company sued the Bank for handing over the stock to him and, in the course of a very important action, attracted much attention to itself.

Gross, who was at that time engaged on his *Gild Merchant,* tried to find out more about the Company, and was particularly anxious to discover whether it still had any of its ancient records. In this he was unsuccessful and could find out no more than was divulged at the trial.[1] There it was stated that "the Company had no address, nor any office or place of business where persons having to transact business with them could apply. And they had no banking account and no minutes books of any kind except a minutes book which was kept by Drew, their Clerk, who was a solicitor, and members of whose family had for generations been members of the corporation and had preceded him in the office of Clerk".

At the trial it was also stated that "their original objects and purposes having long ceased to exist, the corporation dwindled

---

[1] Gross, *Gild Merchant,* I, p. 145, n. 4.

down into something like a family party, the members whereof belonged to three or four families only . . . and the chief, if not the sole, business of the corporation was to dine together once every half-year at the Albion Tavern and the Trafalgar Hotel alternately".[1]

Of such a corporation Gross prophesied that "Now that its funds have been embezzled, this spectre of a once-powerful organisation will probably soon vanish". But although its funds had been embezzled, the Company's case against the Bank was a good one and the Bank was compelled to refund the full £4,250. This may explain why the Company did not hasten into its grave with the speed which Gross anticipated. Up to 1914 it still flourished as a family party and some effort was even made to bring it once more into real contact with the wool trade. But the wool merchants of the Midlands and the North who were approached seem to have relished the Company's hospitality when they attended the dinners as guests and prospective members but balked at the heavy entrance hance which they were expected to pay.[2]

So the Company remained an exclusive family affair. By 1928 the membership was very limited indeed. In that year the remaining members agreed to terminate the Company. Having taken counsel's opinion, they voted against surrendering their charter since that would give Chancery control over the possessions of the Company at the time of the surrender. Instead, they decided to call no further meetings, owing to the difficulty of finding a quorum, and to distribute the funds of the Company among the few remaining members. The name of the Company was perpetuated by setting aside the sum of £500 as a gift to the Royal Agricultural Society of England. From the interest on that sum two special cash prizes, known as the "Merchants of the Staple of England Prizes", are awarded at the Society's annual show for the best fleece taken from any long-woolled breed of sheep and for the best fleece taken from any

[1] *Law Times Reports*, LVI, pp. 666 et seq.
[2] For the system of hances *vide infra*, pp. 132 et seq.

short-woolled breed of sheep.[1] Some small sums appear to have been set aside for charity, but the rest of the funds the members divided amongst themselves. Those who were members of the Company at the time of this resolution are members for the rest of their lives,[2] but there has been no meeting of the Company since 1928.

When the Company thus decided to end itself, its records, about which so much reticence was observed at the trial in 1887, were lodged for safe custody at the British Museum. They were not made the property of the Museum and so were not given numbers or catalogued. By a fortunate chance the writer was able to find the solicitor who was Clerk of the Company in 1928 and so to find the records. Steps have now been taken to make these valuable documents the property of the Museum and they have been numbered and catalogued.[3]

At a meeting of the Company on St George's Day 1914, the Clerk reported that the Company had certain money and government bonds, the charter given by Charles II, "The Old Book of the Ordinances", three Minutes Books beginning in 1619 and going down to date, and the common seal of the Company. There was yet another most valuable book in the possession of the Company, which must have escaped the Clerk's attention. This was a Register of royal grants to the Company up to the year 1619. The Register begins with the grant of privileges to the English merchants at Bruges of 1341[4] and continues down to the charter given by James I in 1619. This Register is similar in appearance to and partly contemporaneous with the Ordinance Book. Much of it is written in a good Elizabethan hand, and possibly represents an attempt on the part of the Company to provide a substitute for the actual

[1] Royal Agricultural Society of England, *Annual Report*, 1928, p. 8.

[2] At the moment of writing, spring 1935, there are three survivors, to one of whom, Mr G. T. Legg, I owe much of the above information.

[3] The numbers which the Museum authorities have assigned to these documents are: Additional MSS. Nos. 43847–43852 and Additional Charter 70834.

[4] *Vide* Rymer, *Foedera*, 1816 edition, II, ii, p. 1172.

documents which were lost in the fall of Calais.[1] There is little or nothing in this Register which is not available elsewhere, in the Patent Rolls, the Close Rolls, Rymer's *Foedera*, or the Gascon Rolls, but it must none the less rank as a valuable compendium of the documents dealing with the Staple Company at a time when it was the most important trading organisation of England, and possibly of Europe.

The book which is here printed is "The Old Book of the Ordinances". Like much of the Register of royal grants, this book is written in a good Elizabethan hand on parchment.[2] Whilst the Register reproduces the documents lost in the fall of Calais, the Book of Ordinances is an attempt to commit to writing the customs under which the trade at Calais had flourished, and to adjust them to the changed conditions of 1565, the year in which this book was drawn up.

The Register and the Ordinances are therefore both parts of an attempt by the Staple Company to reconstruct the conditions of its trade as it had been at Calais. But whereas the royal grants contained in the Register are all available elsewhere, the internal arrangements of the Company (both in 1565 and in former times) can be considerably clarified by this Book of Ordinances.

[1] In 1565 the Staplers said that they had lost all of their documents with the fall of Calais (*infra*, p. 104). There can, however, be no reasonable doubt that the Register was begun in the late fifteenth century, and that at least the first seventy pages were written during the English occupation of Calais. Pages 68d–70 contain "The true Copie of a decree late made between the Maior and feliship of the Staple at Caleis and the Maior and his brethren alderman of the same". This decree was made in 1525 and the copy in the Register was collated with the original decree by the Secretary of the King's Council at Calais, Adrian Dyer.

[2] The book was re-bound by an order of the Company of 29 April 1859 (Staple Company Minutes Book).

Chapter II

THE STAPLE AT CALAIS

The importance of the Staple Company was based on its control of the export trade in English wool. "The speciall gift of the fynes and goodness of the staple wolle, which Godd by his first day of everlastyng light by vertu of his holy spirit gaff into the erth for the comon welth of Englande" made English wool inimitable, and essential for the making of fine cloths.[1]

This vital export trade had been placed entirely in the hands of alien merchants by the great Statute of the Staples of 1353. The wealthy English exporters were then for the moment unable to finance Edward III, and so the aliens and the small "upland" merchants (who were still of potential value to the Crown) were allowed to dictate the trade policy of the kingdom. A series of English towns was therefore nominated as "Staples": there alone could wool, fells or hides be sold. The English merchant was to have the business of collecting the wools in the upland districts and was to carry them to these Staples, but the alien alone (who paid the King higher customs than the English exporter, and who paid the upland merchant a good price for his wares) was allowed to buy the wools for export. But certain English merchants were already so committed to this trade, and so certain of their markets and their profits, that they suborned aliens to "colour" their exports for them. Then, in 1359, they agreed to pay as much customs as the aliens. In return they were allowed to export their wools in their own names and to set up their organisation to control the trade. This organisation was set up at Bruges in 1359, but

[1] For the peculiar merits of English wool see *A Treatise Concerning the Staple*, ed. R. Pauli, reprinted in Tawney and Power, *Tudor Economic Documents*, III, pp. 90 *et seq.*

Bruges very soon proved unsatisfactory as a mart, and in 1363 the trade was transferred to Calais, to which town alone could English wools be exported.[1]

"The New Company of English merchants dwelling nowe at Calais", as it was called in 1363, was not originally a clearly defined company. It consisted of a group of English merchants who had lent the King money and had received privileges in return. They were wool merchants, who had been transferred to Calais from Bruges and were in many respects the successors of the Estate of "Merchants of the Realm" of the earlier years of Edward III's reign. This Company controlled the trade to Calais, and merchants from London and from provincial ports who wished to engage in that trade had to join the Company. Such merchants seem to have gained admission either by purchase or by apprenticeship and they, and not the Company itself, then carried on the actual trade. During the fifteenth century the Company numbered between three and four hundred members, and although there was certainly a constant tendency to place the interests of the few great merchants above those of the many lesser men,[2] yet to the end of the Middle Ages it remained open to individual merchants to buy and sell their wools as best they could, subject to the rules of the Company.

When exactly "The New Company of English merchants dwelling nowe at Calais" came to be called the Staple Company of England is not certain: they were in effect the Staple Company from the beginning, as they included all the English merchants who wished to share in the trade to Calais.[3] The Company does

[1] For the origin of the Staple at Calais see *Cambridge Historical Journal*, 1933, pp. 135–8. The setting up of "home staples" instead of a foreign one was often discussed; cf. *infra*, p. 26 and p. 53.

[2] For a discussion of the dissensions within the Company, and especially of the Partition Ordinance of 1429, which gave the wealthier merchants dominance until 1442, see Power and Postan, *Studies in English Trade in the Fifteenth Century*, pp. 82–90.

[3] Officially there had been a "Gouvernour et Compaignie en la dite ville de Bruges" as early as 1359. By 1369 they were a "Communitas

not seem to have been given a direct control over the wool trade as such, but it controlled the trade to Calais, and in normal times English wools (with one great exception)[1] could only be shipped to Calais after 1363. So the Staple Company controlled this vital trade. Thereon it founded its greatness as a corporation, and thereby it enabled its members to gather such wealth that they might rightly declare to Elizabeth that they were such a Company "as no other prince in Europpe had the like, and eny prince wolde be glad to embrace".[2]

Such a corporation could not remain aloof from the political struggles of fifteenth-century England, and the Staplers were largely embroiled in the financial expedients of the English governments, both as individuals and as a Company. The importance of the customs which they paid, and their ability to raise loans for the government, placed them in a strong position, and their privileges in the wool trade were confirmed by Yorkists and Lancastrians alike.

Even this control over the wool trade was not always enough to ensure power for the Company or wealth for its members. Calais had many advantages as an entrepôt for the trade, but it had disadvantages also; indeed, one of the almost insuperable difficulties in the whole system of forcing trade to go to one compulsory staple was that it was almost impossible to choose a staple which answered all the needs both of buyers and of sellers.

The chief disadvantages of Calais were that it was very badly placed for one of the greatest manufacturing areas, that of North Italy, and that it was too near the war zone of North-

mercatorum Stapule" at Calais, and officially they were the Mayor and Company of the Staple *at Calais* until Elizabeth's charter of 1561. Then they became "Maior, constabularii et societas mercatorum *stapule Anglie*".

[1] For this exception, the Italian trade to the Mediterranean, *vide infra*, p. 8. The wools of the North were also largely exempt. It has been reckoned that about four-fifths of the wool export was in English hands in the fifteenth century (Power and Postan, p. 12).

[2] State Papers, Public Record Office, S.P. 12, Vol. 15, No. 61.

west Europe. In addition, it was itself a garrison town and so to some extent unsuitable for trade.

The first of these disadvantages, the distance from the weaving centre of North Italy, caused a considerable breach in the Staple Company's control of the wool trade. Some few wools found their way to Italy by passing through Calais. They were then either carried through the Netherlands and over the Alps or else were shipped again, to complete their journey by sea. But many of the wools for Italy were shipped by royal licence direct through the "Straits of Marrock". So the Staplers not only found their control over wool export diminished but also found in the Italians persistent rivals for the purchase of wool from the English growers.[1] From time to time the Company complained of such licences, averring that they were ruining Calais,[2] but the fees from the licences and the complaisance of the dependent Italians were so valuable to the royal finances that the permits for shipments direct to Italy continued.

The second disadvantage of Calais, its position near the war zone of North-west Europe, was increased during the fifteenth century by the alternate belligerency and incapacity of the English governments. The Staplers suffered much from "the contynuall debate contention and warre, that hath bine in many yeares past, which hath stayed not onely the emperors subiectis and Frenchmen to come to Caleis to buy the said staple-merchandises, but also hath stayed the said staplers to adventure their goodes into their handes".[3] At the same time the poverty and uncertainty of the English governments tended

[1] For a study of the wool trade to Italy see Power and Postan, pp. 43 *et seq.* As late as 1551 the Staplers complained of licences to ship wools through the Straits of Marrock instead of to Calais, where they should have been sold to Italians. They alleged that the Italians not only defrauded the customs by paying only on the best wools, but also only paid the customers "after longe dayes". P.R.O. S.P. 10, Vol. 13, No. 80.

[2] *E.g.* Rotuli Parliamenti, v, p. 149.

[3] Schanz, *Englische Handelspolitik gegen Ende des Mittelalters*, II, p. 567.

to thrust the burden of defending both their own goods and the whole town of Calais on to the Staplers.

The safeguarding of Calais was obviously vital to the Staplers, and in the early days of the English occupation the Company itself seems to have acted at times as a garrison. When the Captain was absent from the town on a foray the Company provided a hundred billmen and two hundred archers from among the merchants and their servants.[1] Later, the inability of the government to pay the garrison, and the raids which the soldiers were apt to make on the goods of the merchants, led the Company to make itself responsible for the regular payment of the garrison's wages and so to play an even greater part in the fiscal machinery of the Crown than before.[2]

By the end of the Middle Ages, then, the Staple Company was still controlling the wool trade (not without some rivalry from licensees, and especially from Italians[3]) but was heavily committed in its responsibilities to the government; for if the Company got its privileges confirmed by both sides in the Wars of the Roses it likewise advanced money to both sides. Later, it lent largely to the Crown during Henry VIII's reign,[4] and with both Henry VII and Henry VIII it entered into engagements. By these "Acts of Retainer" the Company agreed to make itself responsible for the payment of the Calais garrison and to recoup itself from the customs due on the wool exported by members.[5]

Although the Company was obliged to undertake these duties in the sixteenth century it lacked its former confidence. By about 1527 it was complaining that it was reduced from four hundred to a hundred and forty shippers, whilst "the

[1] Rot. Parl. II, p. 358.

[2] For the Staplers' embroilments in governmental finance see G. A. C. Sandeman, *Calais under English Rule*, pp. 23–5 and 68–73, and the chapter by W. I. Haward in Power and Postan. *Vide* also Schanz, II, pp. 16–17.

[3] *Supra*, p. 7, n. 1.

[4] *Cal. Letters and Papers, Henry VIII*, IV, 3, p. 3090, and Schanz, II, p. 564.

[5] *E.g.* S.P. 12, Vol. 15, No. 57.

poore and middle sort be decayed and declyned and the best and richest dayly decay and declyne after all".[1] The members had found themselves unable to carry out the Act of Retainer into which they had entered in 1515; they could not pay the garrison of Calais and did not know when they would be able to pay,[2] and in order to be excused from their obligations they had had to give Henry VIII their lands to the value of £40 a year, to let him off £10,000 which he owed to the Company, and to pay him an additional £10,000 over a set period.[3] A generation later the Company ruefully remembered that its inability to fulfil its commitments had "coste theym £20,000 and more, over and above their place called the Staple Inne with all their landes and tenementes beyng within the Towne of Caleis and marches of the same", and that by reason thereof many merchants "were brought into such decaye and povertie that they were never since able to occupie".[4]

Many of Henry VIII's actions show an unscrupulous political ability, but there can be no doubt that this fierce amercement of the Staplers must rank along with his debasement of the coinage as a major economic blunder, in which he allowed his genius for spoliation to upset trade. But that the Staple Company should fall into Henry's clutches was as much the outcome of a decline which had already set in as a cause of future decline. For it was its inability to fulfil its commitments which placed the Company at the King's mercy. The Company itself advanced many reasons for its decay, and, true to the type of the Regulated Company of the sixteenth century, saw the chief reason for its failure in the existence of competition. The licences to export, particularly those granted to the fraudulent Italians, were a special grievance.[5]

[1] Tawney and Power, II, p. 26.
[2] *Cal. Letters and Papers, Henry VIII*, IV, 2, pp. 2116, 2201.
[3] S.P. 12, Vol. 15, No. 57.
[4] S.P. 10, Vol. 13, No. 80. The "Staple Inn" here mentioned was in Calais, not in London. It was restored to the Company in 1550. *Cal. Acts of Privy Council*, 1550–1552, p. 80. Cal. Patent Rolls, 1550–1553, p. 15.
[5] S.P. 10, Vol. 13, No. 80.

It was not only the existence of competition which was up-setting the staple trade. It was being subjected to more heavy taxation than it could bear. The customs and subsidy payable on a sack of wool amounted to forty shillings, and the average price of a sack of wool in England seems to have been about £8, so that a merchant would consume his original trading capital in customs payments in four shippings. This might have been borne if the trading profits had been exceptionally high. But the Staplers maintained that the profits of the trade bore no relation to this heavy toll. "He that buyeth any wolles or felles in Englande at the best fardell he can (as the price goeth) and selleth the same in Caleis at the full price of the Staple, yet shall not he gayn viii li. in the C li."[1] These figures, it must be admitted, were produced in controversy, and in controversy the Staplers sometimes produced such accounts that they felt bound to apologise for presenting them. "All-thoughe yt maye seeme that the Reconnynge ys untrewe by Reasone of the apparent losse yt may please ye too be advertysed that yt ys made as the Comen price of Woulles goethe" they felt bound to add to one such account.[2] More soberly, they tried to show that they made profit only by the exchange of their Flemish money into sterling.[3]

[1] S.P. 10, Vol. 13, No. 80.

[2] S.P. 12, Vol. 15, No. 58. Recent bankruptcies are adduced as evidence.

[3] The system of allowances by which the Staplers managed to make a profit despite their heavy tolls is analysed in Schanz, 11, p. 569, and in Power and Postan, pp. 70–2. The arguments of the Staplers, demon-strating that, in the conditions of 1560, they were unable to make any profits, are in State Papers 12, Vol. 15, Nos. 53, 55, 56, 58, 62, 63. Both sides "wrested truth" shamelessly. The opponents of the Company omitted the canvas in which the wool was wrapped from their account and asserted that the Staplers bought their wool "by the Great Parcell" and so got an overweight allowance from the grower of a half-pound in every tod of twenty-eight pounds. They said, too, that the Staplers bought their wools after the rate of three sacks of good wool to one sack of middle quality. All of this the Staplers denied. They said (untruly) that the canvas cost them as much as the wool. They denied that they bought wools sorted and graded into good and middle qualities (but

Even had the rate of profit been enough to clear the legal customs duties and leave a working margin, the trade would have been sorely hampered by the conditions of the sixteenth century. For by the Acts of Retainer[1] the Company made itself responsible for a fixed sum each year. Consequently a cycle was set up. The less wool the merchants exported in any one year, the more they had to pay the Crown on each sack and the less money they had to trade with in the next year. The buyers knew, moreover, that the Staplers had to provide this ready money for the King and that therefore they could not afford to hold their stocks and wait for good prices.[2] So, the Staplers said, the selling-price of the wools declined and they asked that they should pay customs and subsidy only on those wools which they actually exported.

Nor was excessive taxation the only trouble. The Staplers had been accustomed since their earliest days to the competition

were prepared to believe that the Italians did so) and they said that they bought their wool only by the half-sack, standing weight. By so doing they never got more than a fleece or so extra, and they lost at least that much by the drying of the wool as it awaited shipment or sale. None the less their account, in which they made out that they got a profit of only £5. 19s. 8d. on a capital outlay of £129. 12s. 8½d., was based on "Three Sarplers of Cotswold bought in the country, to pack 2 sarplers of good wool and 1 sarpler of middle", and elsewhere they reckoned on the basis of "one sarpler of Cottswold woull Bought in the Countrey to pack ii sackes good woull and one myddell woull" (S.P. 12, Vol. 15, No. 58). The Staplers also reckoned (in these accounts) on having to pay £13 a sack for Cotswold wool. Elsewhere they admitted that at this time the normal price for wools was little more than £8 a sack (S.P. 12, Vol. 15, No. 54): that Cotswold wools, even with the rise in prices which had occurred, cost perhaps a little more than £10 a sack (S.P. 12, Vol. 15, No. 53, No. 55). £13 or more a sack would be the price which they paid for the best Lymster wools (Schanz, II, p. 571, Power and Postan, p. 71). For wool weights see *infra*, p. 20, n. 1.

[1] For which *vide supra*, p. 9.

[2] Schanz, II, pp. 567–8. *Vide* also S.P. 10, Vol. 13, No. 81 (1551), where the Staplers argue that by the "appresting" of money to the Crown their stock, which is "only money", is diminished and they are driven out of trade.

of the Italians, riding about in the upland districts and bidding
against them for the wools. Now another and more formidable
rival had arisen. Since the last years of the fourteenth century
the native clothing industry had been absorbing ever more and
more of the wools of the land, and by 1551 the Staplers were
pointing out that the English drapery had so increased (thanked
be God) that if the progress of the next twelve years equalled
that of the last twelve a dearth of wool would be inevitable
and even the native clothiers would have to go short.[1]

It is in this situation that we may see the essential cause of
the decline of the Staplers. Excessive taxation, wars, greed and
inefficiency on the part of the Company,[2] might all have been
sustained, the flaws in the position of Calais might have been
overlooked, but for the fact that the staple trade in wools was
itself steadily becoming less and less important. Whereas in
the early fourteenth century our exports of wool had exceeded
30,000 sacks a year and our cloth exports had been only about
5,000 cloths, by the middle of the sixteenth century our wool
exports were down to 4,000 sacks a year but our cloth exports
had risen to well over 100,000 cloths.[3]

This change in the nature of England's exports reacted in a
double way on the Staplers. On the one hand they found wool
less plentiful, and on the other hand they found the continent
a less willing buyer. For as the English cloths poured into the
continent "as it were an inundation of the sea" they took the
market from the Flemish weavers who had formerly bought

[1] S.P. 10, Vol. 13, No. 80.

[2] The critics of the Company alleged that the Staplers made new
members of the Company daily, and that they had been doing so over
a period of years, that they took from each such new member £150
"unles they make some for frendshipp", and that these new members
shipped more wools in one year than all the licensees did in six years
(S.P. 11, Vol. 13, No. 50). See also the strictures in the *Treatise concerning the Staple* (Tawney and Power, III, pp. 90 *et seq.*).

[3] H. L. Gray, "Production and exportation of English woollens in
the fourteenth century", *E.H.R.* 1924; Power and Postan, pp. 10–11;
Tawney and Power, I, pp. 178 *et seq.*; Schanz, II, pp. 15–20.

most of the Staplers' wools. The heavy taxation to which the wool was subject placed the Netherlanders at a grave disadvantage, for whereas they got their wool after the English Crown had subjected it to a duty which amounted to about twenty-five per cent. *ad valorem,* the English weavers got it duty-free and the duties on cloth export were not at all comparable with those on wool. The Staplers were not slow to point out by how much the revenues would benefit if export of wool once more took pride of place. They estimated that the 100,000 cloths which the Merchant Adventurers exported annually consumed 24,000 sacks of good wool. If this were exported as wool it would yield £48,000 in customs and subsidy; exported as cloth it produced but £5,833. 6s. 8d.[1]

A further disadvantage from which the Netherlanders suffered was that their industry was still trammelled in the sixteenth century by those municipal and gild regulations from which the English clothing trade had largely escaped by settling in the country villages rather than in the corporate towns. This was clearly seen by Thomas Hall, Cecil's factor, who pointed out to his employer that the English cloths were taking the market from the Netherlanders and that the latter were therefore ceasing to drape English wools and, turning to the draping of Spanish wools, were producing an inferior article and seeking a new market. The Netherlanders were constantly supervised, from the spinning of the yarn through all the processes, and they worked by hand, whereas the English clothier used a mill, "and howe the Englishe clothier is overseene is welle knowne".[2] In similar vein the Staplers themselver aver that the increase of clothiers is the cause of the troubles which beset the whole realm, and not only the Staple Company, vouching as proof the fact that since clothiers have been over-much cherished the statutes of the realm show that there have

[1] S.P. 12, Vol. 15, No. 54. On this point *vide infra,* pp. 25, 39.
[2] S.P. 12, Vol. 34, No. 51. The "mill" here spoken of was the gig-mill, for "raising a nap" on cloth. It had been forbidden by statute in 1552 (St. 5 and 6 Ed. VI, c. xxii), but had none the less persisted.

been continuous complaints in Parliament and the towns of the land have bewailed their great ruin, poor estate, and desolation. They joined in the general accusations that the clothiers were the ultimate causes of rural depopulation and the decay of husbandry and added that "though there be clothes made in such nombre as may seame rather to be cast in mouldes, then to have any tyme of workmanshippe", yet the workmen were very poor. The remedy which they suggested was to subject the English clothier to the same municipal restraints as the Netherlander suffered from by ordering that no white cloths be woven save in a city, borough or town corporate, and that no person take benefit of or occupy more than one process in clothmaking.[1]

Neither Hall's memorandum nor the Staplers' complaint affected the situation: England's wool exports remained diminished and her cloth exports remained swollen. One result mentioned by Hall, the substitution of Spanish wool for English by the Netherlands weavers, was to a certain extent offset by the fact that "the wolles of Spayn are of such kynds withowt the wolles of England be myxed with, it can make no cloth of it self for no durable weryng, to be nother reisid nor dressid", whereas when mixed with English wools it could be made into "such cloth that will tak a shynyng glosse with forcibly pressing, plesaunt to the jie, by cause the Spaynysh heyry woll will kepe the pressyng, wher English woll of fyne staple will not"—a saleable, if inferior, commodity. The fact that "in short tyme the wolle shall were awey unto the likness of worstedd",[2] and that these cloths could not compare for quality with the English broadcloths, did not prevent this "New Drapery" from springing up in the progressive town of Antwerp and in many villages of the Netherlands. In these places little or no attempt to restrain enterprise was made, so that whilst the old corporate towns which had absorbed the

[1] S.P. 12, Vol. 15, No. 54 (1560).
[2] Tawney and Power, III, pp. 102, 114; *Libel of English Policy* (Rolls Series, *Political Poems and Songs*, II), pp. 161–2.

bulk of the Staplers' wools were decaying,[1] there was growing a new, but limited, market for the Staplers in supplying the modicum of English wool necessary to make the Spanish wool workable.

Even this sop of comfort was peculiarly liable to be soured by political difficulties or by the murrain, which seems to have attacked England's flocks with increasing frequency at this time.[2] The Spaniards took advantage of any uncertainty in the supply of English wool to further the sale of their wares, and it was reckoned, for example, that the breach with the House of Burgundy under Henry VIII caused English wool to be abandoned by the towns of Ghent, Ypres, Armentières, Isell, Amsterdam, Rotterdam and Poperinghe.[3] At a time when English wool was becoming scarcer and scarcer on the continent, the Spaniards had ample chance to push their wares. There can be no doubt that the system of stapling English wools at Calais had for long been disliked by the Netherlanders. Calais was not really near enough to them. Only the great merchants frequented the Staple at Calais, and the mass of the clothiers and weavers had to buy from them at enhanced prices when they had transported the wool to their own towns.[4] The Italians, with their knowledge of the machinery of credit, had made a rich profit out of this trade in earlier times.[5] It

[1] For the rise of the "New Drapery" in the Netherlands and the decay of the old towns see Pirenne, *Histoire de Belgique*, III, pp. 215 *et seq.* Bruges had been feeling the rivalry of English cloth and the scarcity of English wool since the beginning of the fifteenth century (*Inventaire des Archives de la ville de Bruges*, first series, V, p. 10), her trade steadily declined (Schanz, I, pp. 7, 25–6, 45), and it was not until 1534 that, with English wool getting dearer day by day, the weavers of Bruges began to drape Spanish wools (Delepierre, "Renseignements sur la fabrication des draps à Bruges", *Annales de la Société d'émulation de la ville de Bruges*, I, iii, p. 240).

[2] Tawney and Power, II, p. 27; Schanz, I, p. 450, II, pp. 15, 568.

[3] S.P. 12, Vol. 15, No. 61.

[4] *Inventaire des Archives de la ville de Bruges*, I, vi, p. 143; S.P. 12, Vol. 15, No. 52, Article 3.

[5] *Libel of English Policy*, p. 176.

was their practice to buy on credit from the Staplers at Calais and then to sell the wools at Bruges for "redy money in honde", making a handsome living out of the trade which they conducted on this capital until their day of settlement at Calais came round. The difficulty and expense of getting the wools from Calais distributed to the actual weavers were recognised, and some of the weaving towns of Holland even sent municipal buyers to Calais to bring home wools on which their weavers might work at a reasonable price.[1] In the sixteenth century not only was there this practice of sending communal buyers, but it seems to have become easier for the ordinary clothier to go and buy his wools at Calais. The result was that wools were a little cheaper both at Calais and in the Netherlands than they had been when the trade had been in the hands of the great buyers, who paid good prices (on credit), bought large consignments, and trusted to make their profit out of their control of the trade.[2]

Even so, although Calais was "a place nerest the merchaunte buyers, aswell of woulles as felles",[3] yet the slight distance which separated it from the weaving centres involved some difficulties and some expense. Moreover, the whole system of concentrating the wool trade into a staple mart irritated the Netherlandish peoples. The restraints on trade which the staple system involved were brought forward as part of the reasons for the embargo which Maximilian placed on English trade in 1494,[4] and the Calais Staplers were reported to be quarrelling with the Flemings in the Intercursus Magnus in 1496.[5]

---

[1] Delepierre, *Annales de la Société d'émulation de la ville de Bruges*, I, iii, p. 241; cf. Power and Postan, p. 61.

[2] S.P. 12, Vol. 15, No. 52.

[3] S.P. 12, Vol. 37, No. 32.

[4] Tawney and Power, II, p. 7.

[5] *Ibid.* p. 15. The malpractices of the Staplers were a constant source of grievance. *Vide* Power and Postan, pp. 61–2 and 83–5, and *Rélations politiques des Pays-Bas et de l'Angleterre*, III, pp. 61–2.

Whilst thus the English system of trading counted against the Staplers the Spaniards took a step in the right direction when they made Bruges the staple for their wool in 1494.[1]

It must be admitted that the Spanish wool-traders also suffered some disadvantages and that the English Staplers were not driven right out of the market. Apart from the excellence of their wares, the Staplers scored because "the Spanysche flete many tymes by Reson of longe viage and contrary wyndes Dysapoynteth the Drapers".[2] But even this was but a meagre set-off to the cheapness and plenty of the Spanish wool. Moreover, the Staplers had to make some pretence of observing the English government's bullion regulations by bringing to the mint at Calais actual bullion in return for their sales.[3] By contrast "Nothing cawseth the Spanishe wulles to be so well and so abondantly uttered as dothe that the Spaniardes use to take cloth in paiement for their wulles."[4] Even the suggestion that the Staplers should export baser wools, as well as the staple wools, at a less customs duty, so that "syche townes as drape spanysche wolles may by thys menes fynde in the kynges staple at Calleys as good pennyworths as they do of spanysche Wolles"[5] would not have overcome this difficulty, for England would never be a large consumer of Flemish cloths again.

With all these disadvantages, by the middle of the sixteenth century the Staple Company was still toiling valiantly to maintain its position. Only the great wealth which it and its members had won in previous good times enabled it to continue, and there was justification for the Company's claim that "their is no fellowship of merchandes under any christian

[1] Pirenne, *Histoire de Belgique*, III, p. 236.
[2] S.P. 10, Vol. 13, No. 81.
[3] For a discussion of the bullion regulations as they affected the Staplers *vide* Power and Postan, pp. 80 *et seq.*, and Tawney and Power, III, pp. 93–6.
[4] S.P. 12, Vol. 15, No. 52.
[5] S.P. 12, Vol. 13, No. 81.

prince that could so long have sustayned like burden and damage".[1]

True, their trade was not utterly gone from them: they still had a limited *clientèle*. But since they had fallen into the hands of Henry VIII by failing in their Act of Retainer,[2] their trade had been allowed to continue only by reason of a series of more or less temporary licences. Their forfeitures in 1525 allowed them to trade up to 1534 (the period to which their Act of Retainer would have run) but after that year their licences seem to have been for a year or two years only.[3] Such a basis was too insecure for confident and successful trade, and the Company naturally tried to reach some more permanent understanding. In 1551 they asked for a charter allowing them to ship for the next thirty years. They were willing to pay £1,000 for such a charter, but they only got liberty to ship for one year, as before.[4]

Such temporary licences were bad for trade, but they were better than the Acts of Retainer which they replaced. The fact that during these last years at Calais the Company was being used by the debt-ridden government to pay its dues to the international financiers of the Netherlands[5] gave the Staplers a certain amount of political power, and they did at least manage to stave off any further commitments. They were thus able to sell their wools at remunerative prices, instead of having to provide a definite sum for the government by a fixed day, and trade increased accordingly with this returning freedom. The result was that during these years the shipments made by members of the Company rose by well over a hundred per cent., from 2,300 pockets in 1551 and 2,340 in 1552 to 6,300 pockets in 1553, 5,400 in 1554, and 4,700 in 1555 from the port

[1] Tawney and Power, II, p. 26.

[2] *Vide supra*, p. 10.

[3] *E.g.* Nicolas, *Proceedings of the Privy Council*, VII, pp. 86, 109, 307; *Cal. Acts of the Privy Council*, 1552–1554, p. 274.

[4] *Cal. S.P. Dom.* 1547–1580, p. 37; *Cal. Acts of the Privy Council*, 1550–1552, p. 241; S.P. 10, Vol. 13, No. 80.

[5] *Cal. Acts of the Privy Council*, 1552–1554, pp. 267, 275, 278.

of London,[1] whilst the payments in customs reflected the renewed prosperity.[2]

Even this return to the normal standards of the shipments of the fifteenth century bore no promise of a revival of the greatness of the fourteenth century. Nothing could alter the fact that the growth of English weaving had undermined the Flemish industry and had robbed the Staplers of their market. This was the ultimate reason why, in 1551, it was alleged that "at thys Day the hoole felyschyppe be so Dyscomfortyd that they are mynded to forsake the staple for to seke theyre poore lyvynge some other Way".[3]

---

[1] S.P. 11, Vol. 13, No. 49. A pocket of wool was normally 48 nails, or cloves, of 7 lbs. each (*infra*, p. 30 and p. 146). The specimen accounts of the wool trade leave the impression that the woolsack of 364 lbs. was rather a term of accountancy than an actual sack of wool. The "sack" was used for reckoning, and we are told ("Nombre of Weyghts", Brit. Mus. MS. Cotton. Vesp. E. IX, fo. 87) that "Amongyst husbondes in the Countrie [wool] is most used to be sold by ye Stone and by ye Todde. And betwixt gaderers of ye countrie and ye merchauntz it is most used to be sold by ye Sakke." The "sack" was used for answering the export duties, but the merchants usually bought their wools by the tod of 28 lbs., and shipped and sold them by sarplars and pockets—both terms which mean a bundle rather than a specific weight (*supra*, p. 11 n.). The pocket naturally varied a little in weight. Usually it was slightly less than the standard sack: thus in 1559 a London merchant twice shipped 25 sacks of wool in 30 pockets (E. 122/88/4, fo. 1). But the Staplers' Ordinances of 1565, whilst accepting the pocket of 48 nails as the normal (p. 146), admitted that sometimes a pocket might weigh as much as one sack and four cloves (p. 147), *i.e.* 56 nails. This would appear to be the pocket which alien wool-merchants used (S.P. 12, Vol. 56, No. 66). It was during the period 1540–1560 that the Staplers took to shipping in pockets rather than in sarplers, which contained about three pockets, *i.e.* 2½ sacks and 10 nails (*ibid.*).

[2] S.P. 10, Vol. 13, No. 80.   [3] S.P. 10, Vol. 13, No. 81.

Chapter III

THE LOSS OF CALAIS

If the Staple Company was struggling in vain against economic developments during the last years of the English occupation of Calais, the loss of that town to the French made its position desperate. Grievously the Staplers moaned that "the losse of Callice, being most lamentable to this hole state, was neither at the present surprice thereof so hurtfull, nor yet hath bynne synce that tyme so great a hynderaunce to anny privat parte of this Realme, as to us, your Majesties faithfulle and obedient subiectes the ffellowshipp and Company of the Merchauntes Staplers, ffor we did not only lese than presently such a masse of goodes as no other Subiectes did, but also synce that tyme our hoole trade to lyve is cut away from us, our lawes established for that only place beinge nowe by the losse thereof quiet disannulled and made of non effecte".[1]

From the days of Richard I, English monarchs had from time to time forbidden the export of wool as a means of bringing pressure to bear on the princes of the Netherlands, and in later times the policy had been continued with the object of giving English weavers first choice of the wools and yarn. Under Henry VI, Edward IV, Henry VII and Henry VIII there had been such embargos,[2] but Edward was apt to turn them to his own advantage by selling licences to export during the embargo.[3]

The trade of the Staplers to Calais had never been entirely

---

[1] S.P. 12, Vol. 15, No. 50, cf. S.P. 12, Vol. 114, No. 29.

[2] Statutes 8 Henry VI, c. 17; 18 Henry VI, c. 15; 3 Edward IV, c. 1; 1 Henry VII, c. 10; 22 Henry VIII, c. 1; Schanz, I, pp. 445 *et seq.*

[3] Schanz, I, p. 448.

stopped by these regulations,[1] although it suffered in the quarrels of which they were sometimes a part. The staple trade to Calais was treated more as an internal than as an export trade and was specifically exempted from the embargos so that, diminished though they might be at times, the shipments were allowed to pass.

Comparatively immune as the Company had been so long as Calais was English, when that town was lost it immediately felt the full force both of the embargos and of all previous statutes enforcing the Staple. The policy had been summarised in the statute of 1552,[2] by which the purchase of wool save for the purpose of manufacture within the realm or for merchants of the Staple to ship to Calais was forbidden. Calais being closed to the Staplers after 1558, this statute meant that they were committing a crime whenever they bought wool.

The last months of Mary's reign were occupied in negotiations between the government and the Company, and the Staplers, assured of kindly consideration and confident of the issue, bought wool freely. But before any definite arrangement had been made Mary died. The immediate difficulty was overcome by the grant of a licence to export. In August 1559 Elizabeth granted pardon for the forfeiture which the Staplers had incurred by buying wool for export and allowed the wools already purchased to be shipped to Bruges from London, Hull or Boston, subject to the payment of an "increment" of a mark on each sack so shipped. One hundred and eighty-eight members of the Company were mentioned by name as having incurred forfeiture and as receiving pardon,[3] and under the terms of the grant about a hundred Staplers shipped from London to Bruges 2,341½ sacks, 14 cloves of wool and 170,137 fells.[4] No record of the shipments made from Hull or Boston

---

[1] Power and Postan, p. 22, and the tables of Enrolled Customs, printed *ibid.* pp. 330 *et seq.* and summarised pp. 402–6. *Vide* also Schanz, II, pp. 15–17, 46, 84.   [2] Statute 5–6 Edward VI, c. 7.

[3] Staple Company, Register of Royal Grants, fo. 76d *et seq.*

[4] P.R.O. E. 122/88/4, fos. 3 *et seq.*

is preserved, but merchants from those ports are mentioned in the grant of pardon.

The respite which the Staplers had thus won by an increment in their customs payments was but a precarious one, and until another Staple should be set up they could only buy wools at their peril and ship them by special licence. Their trade had already been very heavily taxed and they found the greatest difficulty in paying, in addition, the new increment. Their case was made more difficult by the fact that the Company was now so dispersed that the officials found it hard to charge the members their quota.

The extremely penurious position of the new government did indeed make the plight of the Staplers somewhat better, for the government realised that the "forberinge" of the Company from trading was "not only to their greate detrement hinderance and hurte but to our greate losse and decaye of our costome which was wonte to be received for shippinge and transportinge of the same".[1] Moreover, the government was not content merely to try to raise revenue, it had to raise loans also. For these loans both the Merchant Adventurers and the Staplers were mulcted, and the Staplers, despite their plight, did their share.[2] Accordingly, in the autumn of 1560, they were again licensed to ship contrary to the terms of the Statute of 1552. Once more Bruges was to be the port of unlading, but this time the Staplers were to pay an increment of twenty-six shillings and eight pence on each sack so shipped.[3] They tried to get permission to pay their dues in Flemish money, but they ultimately agreed to pay in sterling in order to help the Queen, provided that the exchange were taken into account.[4]

In 1560, therefore, the Staplers shipped from London a total

[1] Register of Royal Grants, fo. 79.
[2] W. R. Scott, *Joint Stock Companies*, I, p. 28. They had made a similar loan to Mary: Burgon, *Life of Gresham*, I, p. 288; cf. *supra*, p. 19, n. 5.
[3] Register of Royal Grants, fos. 79 d and 80. *Vide* p. 32, n. 2.
[4] Manchester to Cecil, S.P. 12, Vol. 6, No. 53.

of nearly 2,000 sacks of wool with 187,953 fells,[1] whilst from Boston sixty-eight and a half sacks, fourteen cloves of wool and 40,599 fells were shipped.[2] These were fair shipments, but by no means large, and the advantage for which the Staplers were paying so heavily was offset by the fact that they were not the only shippers to whom the Queen was willing to extend her favour. Against other licensees than themselves the Staplers railed in vain, though they attributed to the existence of the court favourites all the major evils of the times, the decay of husbandry, the depopulation of villages, and the rise in prices. Nor were other licensees their only rivals: owing partly to the disorganisation of the Company itself,[3] smuggling was rampant—"Others by no Lawe, without order, agaynst all conscience, bothe to our utter undoinge and to the greate dymynishinge of your Majesties Custom and Revenew at manny secrett and dead Creekes convey craftely into other Countries a greate quantitie of the Woll of this Realme."[4]

Against these two rivals the Staplers could find no remedy. The licensee was safe because he was too mighty; the smuggler because he was too elusive. But, seeing that they commanded a certain amount of public sympathy, and hoping to make capital out of the Crown's needs, they tilted at this time against the real and underlying cause of their decay, the growth of the English clothier. Here they were able to take up an orthodox and patriotic position, showing that the growth of the clothiers caused the decay of husbandry, and that they engrossed all occupations belonging to clothing without knowledge, number or rule. They said that our purchases of foreign commodities were steadily rising and so our own artificers were losing employment and our bullion was being exported, that the actual weavers were sadly poor, and that the country was running a grave danger in allowing so many of its artificers to become dependent on a foreign mart which could be closed by the whim or cunning of an alien prince. The Merchant

[1] E. 122/88/5.
[2] E. 122/14/5.
[3] S.P. 12, Vol. 15, No. 61.
[4] S.P. 12, Vol. 15, No. 50.

Adventurers also came in for a share of the blame, and here once more the Staplers showed themselves indiscriminate in their choice of weapons. The oligarchy of the Merchant Adventurers had been to some extent broken down by the Statute of 1496,[1] which ordered that any merchant might become a member of that Company and share in the lucrative business of cloth export on payment of an entrance fee of ten marks, but now the Staplers complained that since that statute the numbers of Merchant Adventurers had greatly increased, "and specyally of unskillfull and unable marchaunts", any one of whom might ship as much as £5,000 worth of cloths in a single year.[2]

For remedies the Staplers suggested that the clothing industries should be confined to corporate towns and that the statutes forbidding the export of unshorn and unrowed[3] cloth should be enforced. But although they could show the penurious government that wool paid about ten times more customs if exported raw than if exported as white cloth, yet their attack on the clothing industry substantially failed,[4] and they had to be content to purchase licences to export their wools by the payment of extra customs. With this arrangement they were by no means satisfied, and they pointed out that the uncertainty and risk of forfeiture involved in the purchase of the wool pending the royal pardon was upsetting their trade. Many great merchants now bought no wools for shipment,

---

[1] Statute 12 Henry VII, c. 6.   [2] S.P. 12, Vol. 15, No. 54.
[3] *I.e.* without its nap having been raised.
[4] The Staplers were but one element in a very general attack on the clothing industry at this time, and much legislation was directed against clothing in the country districts. The attack failed, since so many areas were exempted from the statutes as to make them ineffective, but perhaps some connection may be traced between the Staplers' complaints and the clause in the Statute of Artificers which prevented children of rustics from being apprenticed to weaving (Statute 5–6 Eliz. c. 4, s. 25). On the whole the reign of Elizabeth saw the vindication of the clothier rather than his restriction. *Vide* Unwin, *Studies in Economic History*, pp. 187, 318, 319, and Lipson, *Economic History*, I, pp. 422, 442, II, p. 39.

and many others were afraid to trade on as large a scale as they would like.[1]

The need for some sort of order in the trade, and for the setting up of the Staple somewhere, was generally admitted, but the difficulty was to decide on a port. As was to be expected, the project of setting up Staples in England and of making aliens come to English ports for their wool was again mooted at this time. Cecil seems to have been prepared to bring such a project before Parliament. He thought that to have the Staple abroad was only for the advantage of the Staple Company and of that foreign prince who happened to be favoured, whereas to have a series of staple marts in England, after the model of 1353, would lead to the repair of the English ports, the increase of the customs (since the alien exporters would pay heavier customs than natives), and the prosperity of the whole realm. The opposition of the Staplers was discounted in advance. "Rather than the reformation should come to pass the Staplers will shrine some solicitors in gold to take upon them to abuse the Queen. Merchants have grown so cunning in the trade of corrupting, and found it so sweet, that since 1 Henry VIII there could never be won any good law or order which touched their liberty or state; but they stayed it, either in the Commons or higher House of Parliament or else by the Prince himself, with either *le roy non veult* or *le roi s'advisera*, and if they get the Prince to be advised they give him leave to forget it altogether."[2]

Whether the Staplers indulged in corruption or not, they certainly opposed the project and they had all the stock arguments of mercantilism ready to hand. The scheme would involve the dependence of the trade on foreign shippers and foreign

---

[1] S.P. 12, Vol. 15, No. 61.

[2] Historical MSS. Commission, 1883, Part I, p. 164, "Considerations delivered to the Parliament, 1559". The scheme was to remove the Staple "from Middleburgh where it is now newly erected, into England". There is no other evidence that the Staple was taken to Middleburgh in 1559.

princes; English shipping, already in a parlous state, would decline still more; treasure would cease to be brought into the realm and it would prove impossible to prevent the aliens from exporting our bullion; the price of English commodities would therefore abate, that of foreign commodities would soar, the exchange would react against England, and the great peril of the whole realm could be clearly foreseen.[1]

These were reasons which appealed alike to the popular imagination and to the prejudices of statesmen. But the Staplers had much yet to do before they could reckon that they had achieved their objective. The home-staples idea was argued before the Council, and many of the Staplers' arguments were subjected to searching criticism. It was pointed out that their trade was but a small help to the navy of the realm, for they largely used Flemish ships, that in the present state of the trade "if the freight of all the wulles and ffelles caried over in one year come unto one thowsand powndes it is moche", and that the proposed system would allow the Queen to reform the abuses in packing and to bring down the prices for the continental buyer and so to put English wool into sale again.[2]

Unabashed, the Staplers continued to petition Elizabeth to remedy their "wofulle case and myserye". They asked for the renewal of their ancient privileges "with our most humble sute and request to have certen Statutes and Actes dispensed withall, which doe referre our hole trafick only to the Towne of Callice". They therefore rehearsed the constitution of their Company, organised under a Mayor and two Constables. They summed up its privileges and asked for their renewal, but asked that "the Staple of woll and felles to be transported may be kepte at Bridges, Middilborough or Barges,[3] or in anny other place in the lowe Countrey or in anny other partes beyond the seas of amytie, or in England wheare it shalle seme good to the Quenes highnes hir heires and successours by thadvise of the said Merchaunts to be most for their benefite, that the

---

[1] *Cal. S.P. Dom. Add.* 1547–1565, p. 497.
[2] S.P. 12, Vol. 15, No. 52.   [3] *I.e.* Bergen-op-Zoom.

same Staple to be ordered and ruled in suche manner and forme as it was at Callice".

They wanted not only permission to buy wools to ship to this Staple (wherever it might be) but also to sell to the Italians or other aliens who proposed to ship it direct to the Mediterranean, whilst the Company's complete control of the trade was to be confirmed by the grant to the Mayor of the Company of power to search out and punish smugglers. The Company was to meet from time to time, in London or elsewhere. They wanted power to bring back their money from the Netherlands "by exchange" and not in bullion, and they asked that each merchant travelling to the Staple might take with him "foure poundes for his reasonable expences and his Rynges and signettes of golde upon his fingers".

The removal of the Staple would almost inevitably involve troubles with the rival organisation of the Merchant Adventurers,[1] so the Staplers now asked that they should "be exempted from the governmente rule or punyshment of the governor of the Merchaunt Adventurers trafeckinge into the lowe Countries. This graunt and every Article therin to be construed most favorable for the said Compeny of the Staple". By these means the Staplers hoped that "olde rightes shalbe iustly renewed, newe unlawfull attempts orderly stopped, your Majesties Custome muche increased, and your hole ffellowship and Company conteyning a greate nombre of faithfull subiectes to your Majestie shalbe therby most bounden contynewally to pray to allmighty god to send you longe yeres, with most prosperous Reign, to your highnes hartes desire and to all your Subiects greatest compforte and Joye".[2]

This weighty petition was referred to a committee consisting of the Marquis of Northampton, the Earl of Pembroke, Sir William Cecil and Sir William Peter. They investigated the history and claims of the Company very thoroughly and decided that the scheme for the organisation of the Company

[1] For the relations between the Staplers and the Merchant Adventurers *vide infra*, pp. 71 *et seq.*   [2] S.P. 12, Vol. 15, No. 50.

under a Mayor and two Constables was both justified by history and helpful in practice. They also acquired a knowledge of the English trade with Bruges from the time of Edward III and decided that a staple in that city or elsewhere in the Netherlands would stand a much better chance of preventing the sale of Spanish wools and of resurrecting the English trade than would a system of staples in England.

But they were by no means inclined to grant all of the demands of the Staplers, although they were in favour of a staple in the Netherlands. They advised that the Staplers should be allowed to buy wools for transport and that they should be allowed to sell their refuse wools in England, but they thought it better that they should not be allowed to sell their wools within England to aliens to ship to the Mediterranean, contrary to the Statute of 1429.[1]

As for the Staplers' request that they should be allowed to bring their monies home again by means of exchange and not in bullion—a request in strange discord with their appeal to the bullionist doctrines when they were decrying the alien shippers—the committee thought that the request should not be granted "saving that the new prohibitions of the duke of Burgundie for carieng out of bullion be so straight as it is doubtfull whether this may be executed, and therefore it seemith reasonable that they may be dispensed withall in that pointe during some reasonable tyme". They thought that forty shillings, rather than four pounds, was enough for a merchant to carry abroad for his personal expenses, and they were obviously much concerned to prevent bullion from leaking out of the realm even by this comparatively insignificant means.

A clash of jurisdictions, the committee agreed, might easily arise when both the Staplers and the Merchant Adventurers found themselves in the Netherlands, and they thought that it would avoid confusion if the Staplers were exempt from the jurisdiction of the Adventurers, but they thought, also, that

---

[1] Statute 8 Henry VI, c. 17. This statute was not intended to interrupt the Mediterranean trade, but merely to confine it to the Italians.

it was unnecessary to insert a clause stating that this item was to be interpreted "most favorable for the Compeny of the Staple".

The committee then went on to consider the difficult problem of the weights and measures which the Staplers should use, and so of the customs which they should pay. They suggested that the Company should pay customs at the rate of £3 a sack until they had shipped 3,000 sacks in any one year; on any sacks shipped over that amount they should pay 53s. 4d. They pointed out that the Staplers were accustomed to ship their wools in pockets containing forty-eight nails of seven pounds each. One of these nails the customers allowed free for the canvas in which the wool was wrapped, and the Staplers paid customs on the remaining forty-seven of actual wool as though they were only thirty, being allowed the odd seventeen nails as an "overdraught" by the customers. This "overdraught" the committee thought excessive and proposed that it should be reduced to seven nails in each sack.[1]

The result of these considerations, and of Cecil's championship of the Staplers' claims,[2] was that the Queen inclined favourably towards them, and in May 1561 they at last received their coveted charter. They were now to be "in re facto et nomine unum corpus incorporatum per se in perpetuum...et quod habeant successionem imperpetuam et commune sigillum rebus et negociis suis deserviturum", and were to elect their officials either in London or in their staple city abroad. The Staple was to be at Bruges, Middleburgh or Bergen and was to be removable to England at nine months' notice. As the committee had suggested, the Staplers were to pay £3 customs duty on each sack up to a total of 3,000 a year, and 53s. 4d.

---

[1] S.P. 12, Vol. 15, No. 51. This "overdraught" or "luste" had been severely commented on during Mary's reign. It was then acknowledged that the "luste" had been given "of longe tyme", but it was proposed that it should be restricted and that the customers should be appointed by the Crown instead of by the Staplers. S.P. 11, Vol. 13, Nos. 49, 50.

[2] Winchester to Cecil, S.P. 12, Vol. 16, No. 58.

for each sack above that total, but the committee's suggestions for the drastic diminution of the "overdraught" were miti-gated. This point was at first left open for discussion and in a brief summary of "The effect of the newe Patent for the marchaunts of the Staple"[1] the actual number of nails which was to be allowed in each sack was still left a blank, but later it was agreed that on each sack of good wool only seven nails should be allowed, but that on coarse and middle quality wools the Staplers should have an allowance of ten nails on each sack. Finally, in the charter, the "overdraught" allowed was a little greater than this, nine nails in a sack of good wool and twelve in a sack of coarse or middle wool.[2] This allowance was to include the allowance for the canvas packing.

Thus the Staplers, after three years of uncertainty, had once more established both their trade and their Company on a regular footing. The charter was above all things valuable to them because it allowed them to buy their wools for export despite the terms of the Statute of 1552, and it was sedulously quoted in the returns of the customs officials for many years to come. Although the charter was not granted until the 30th of May, by the middle of June the shipments under its terms were well under way. From London some ninety members of the Company shipped a total of 1,482½ sacks, 5½ cloves of wool and 299,585 fells in a fleet of thirty-two ships, each member dividing his shipment up amongst as many vessels as possible, according to the normal custom in a regulated com-pany.[3] At the same time, from Boston thirty-five merchants shipped a meagre 44½ sacks, 10 cloves of wool and 69,137 fells,[4]

---

[1] S.P. 12, Vol. 15, No. 64.

[2] The charter is printed in Jenckes, *Origin, Organisation and Location of the Staple of England*, pp. 66 *et seq.*, but this clause is omitted. *Vide* also the copy preserved in the Staplers' Register, fos. 70 *et seq.*, and Patent Rolls, C. 66, No. 964, m. 27–30.

[3] Queen's Remembrancer's Accounts, E. 122/88/10. *Vide* also E. 122/171/3 and E. 122/198/1.

[4] E. 122/14/5 and E. 122/171/3.

whilst from Hull there went a total of $54\frac{1}{2}$ sacks, 4 cloves of wool and 28,989 fells.[1] These shipments were average ones for these times and shew neither a recovery of confidence nor any great decline as compared with the shipments of the previous year.[2] In terms of sacks of wool they total nearly 3,239 sacks, counting 240 fells to the sack.

Under the terms of their new charter the Staplers could set up their Staple at Bruges, Bergen or Middleburgh; actually they do not seem to have given much serious consideration to the other ports open to them but to have continued almost automatically to ship to Bruges.

Bruges, above all other cities of the Netherlands, had seen her prosperity diminish as the Middle Ages gave way to modern times. Her weavers were by 1511 in such a state of decay that they had to double their membership fee;[3] even so they were barely solvent and they had to sell their plate in 1544 in order to keep their hall and chapel in repair.[4] The setting up within the city of the "New Drapery" of Spanish wools did something to relieve their plight. Encouraged by the remission of the duty of a "preuve",[5] by 1546 there were over twenty establishments engaged in this business, whilst the "Oude Draperie" of weaving English wools had sunk from the five hundred looms which it had once boasted to some five or six establishments.[6] But these beginnings of a new industrial activity were offset by the transference of Bruges' mercantile activity to new centres, especially to Antwerp.[7]

[1] E. 122/171/3.

[2] Under the licence of 1 September, 2 Eliz. (*vide supra*, p. 23) the Staplers shipped from London, in 1560, $1,908\frac{1}{2}$ sacks, 12 cloves of wool and 187,953 fells (E. 122/88/5), whilst from Boston they shipped $68\frac{1}{2}$ sacks, 14 cloves and 40,599 fells (E. 122/14/5). From Hull none was shipped.

[3] Delepierre, *Annales de la Société d'émulation de la ville de Bruges*, I, iii, p. 239.   [4] Pirenne, III, pp. 224–5.

[5] Delepierre, *Précis analytique des documents à Bruges, seizième siècle*, II, p. 78.   [6] Delepierre, *Annales*, III, p. 240.

[7] *Vide* Ehrenberg, *Capital and Finance in the Age of the Renaissance*, pp. 233 and 255 *et seq.*

Deserted even by their own *banlieues*, watching their access to the sea becoming ever more and more difficult owing to the silt deposited by the Zwyn and the increasing cost of dredging,[1] the citizens made great efforts to recapture prosperity by making their city an emporium for the purchase of raw wool. Since 1494 the staple for Spanish wools was settled at Bruges, and in 1545 an embassy was sent from Bruges to Scotland to seek the staple of Scotch commodities.[2] Now, with the English trade to Calais interrupted, Bruges set itself out to offer a home to the English Staplers, and to Bruges the Staple Company quite naturally turned after the loss of Calais. A port in close proximity to the weaving centres of the Netherlands was essential for them, and their first interim shipments by special licence went almost automatically to Bruges.

Bruges did her utmost to grasp this trade. But although the Staplers were seeking a home and Bruges offered a welcome, it took them some years to arrange their terms. The Staplers knew exactly what privileges were necessary for them at Bruges, whilst the city archives contained records of the grants which had been made to the English when they formerly stapled their wools there. A long correspondence was begun between the Company and the city, of which the outcome was that the Staplers received a grant of privileges.

The summary of this grant, which is filed at the Record Office, bears no date, and it has been roughly dated in 1559. But as late as 1562 the Regent in the Netherlands was writing to Cadiz to explain that "Il y a quelque temps que aucuns marchans anglois ont négocié avec ceulx de Bruges, pour y faire venir la négociation des laines, que cy-devant soulloit estre à Calaix, et sont entrez en grandes communications et par plusiers fois, sur quelques franchises et privilèges qu'ilz desireroyent y avoir."[3] It is therefore certain that the negotiations

[1] Pirenne, II, pp. 396 *et seq.*, and III, pp. 216–19.
[2] Davidson and Gray, *The Scottish Staple at Veere*, pp. 169–70.
[3] *Cal. S.P. Dom. Add.* 1547–1565, p. 496; S.P. 15, Vol. 9, No. 47; *Rélations politiques des Pays-Bas et de l'Angleterre*, III, p. 21, n. i;

dragged on at least until 1562, whilst the Staplers meantime shipped their wools to Bruges on sufferance.

The charter which the Company got from Bruges, when it did come, was a fitting complement to the generous charter which Elizabeth had by then given them. They were to have a house rent free, were to be excused from all municipal imposts, and were to be allowed to appoint their own English head porters, warehousemen and packers. They were to have their own innkeepers, were to be protected in their persons and property, and were to be given special facilities for the fresh-water passage from Sluys to Bruges.

In addition, the city promised to use its influence with the King of Spain and with the Regent to secure that the Staplers should be allowed to elect their own officials, to hold their courts and assemblies, and to punish offences among themselves. They hoped that it would be possible that the offences of a servant should not be visited upon the goods of his master, and that the Staplers would be allowed to use their accustomed weights and to deal direct with their customers without the intervention of municipal brokers.[1]

This generous treatment added to the natural advantages and the traditional connection with Bruges to make it quite certain that of the three cities mentioned in Elizabeth's charter of 1561 it should be Bruges, and not Bergen or Middleburgh, at which the Staple should be set up.

The precarious licensed shipments of 1561 and 1562 were therefore succeeded by regular shipments under the terms of the charter. To Bruges these shipments must have been particularly welcome at this time, for a sudden growth in the weaving industry in Spain had diminished the supplies of Spanish wool for the Netherlands and made Bruges' Staple of this commodity much less valuable.[2]

Gachard, *Correspondance de Marguerite d'Autriche avec Philippe II*, II, pp. 200–1.
    [1] *Cal. S.P. Dom. Add.* 1547–1565, p. 496.
    [2] Tawney and Power, III, p. 172.

Although Bruges was now apparently certain of receiving confident and consistent shipments from England, any dreams of reviving the greatness of the fourteenth century were to prove empty: for nothing like a return to the shipments of the fourteenth century was ever approached. The commissioners who had drawn up the Staplers' new charter in 1561 seem to have gauged the possible volume of the trade very accurately. They agreed to allow the Staplers a rebate of customs duty on every sack shipped in excess of 3,000 a year, and this seems to have been about the maximum volume which the trade could now reach. Guicciardini, describing the Netherlands in 1560, reckoned that at least twelve hundred sarplars[1] were annually exported to Bruges. A sarplar might contain only two and a half sacks, but it was usually reckoned as three, so that Guicciardini here overestimates slightly, for even including the fells (at the current rate of 240 to a sack) the shipments which now went to Bruges barely reached the 3,000 mark upon which the charter was based.

[1] Tawney and Power, III, p. 173.

Chapter IV

THE STAPLE COMPANY AND ENGLAND'S QUARREL WITH SPAIN

No doubt after the charters of 1561 and 1562 the citizens of Bruges hoped that the English Staple had come to a permanent rest in their city, but the members of the Company can never have been so sanguine. Even their new royal charter made allowance for changing times, and the possibility of having to move to Bergen, to Middleburgh, or even to England, must have been ever present. Seeking stability and a settled trade, the Staplers must have felt that all of the new arrangements were but temporary and unstable. For to the ordinary Englishman of the early years of Elizabeth's reign it was only a matter of time until Calais should be restored—and then the whole of the staple trade would return to its accustomed paths.[1]

Nor was Calais the only alternative site for the Staple. In Elizabeth's intrigues with the Huguenots of the years 1562 and 1563 she spent much time and zeal in trying to secure possession of Le Havre. The English occupation of that port proved one of the chief difficulties in the way of the conclusion

---

[1] By the terms of Cateau Cambrésis Calais was to be restored to the English in 1567 at the latest (*Cal. S.P. Foreign*, 1566–1568, p. 195), and English policy was constantly directed to expediting that return. During the negotiations for the Treaty of Edinburgh Elizabeth suggested that the French should pay her 500,000 crowns as damages and should restore Calais (*Hist. MSS. Comm.* 1883, I, p. 240). At the time of the Treaty of Troyes she was equally eager (*Cal. S.P. Foreign*, 1564–1565, p. 59) and Calais runs through all her diplomacy at this period (*vide Cal. S.P. Rome*, 1558–1571, *passim*). Even after she had renounced her claim under the terms of Cateau Cambrésis (at the Treaty of Troyes, *vide* p. 37, n. 1, *infra*) she still showed that she had by no means given up all hope of recovering the town (*e.g. Cal. S.P. Rome*, 1558–1571, p. 319, and *Cal. S.P. Foreign*, 1566–1568, pp. 195–6).

of the Treaty of Troyes and was ultimately used by the French as a pretext for not restoring Calais to the English.[1] Elizabeth certainly wanted Le Havre as a bargaining asset to use for the recovery of Calais,[2] but in itself Le Havre was a potential rival to Bruges for the English trade with the continent. Should it ever become English and be included within the English customs system its natural advantages would be greatly enhanced. A move in this direction was made in 1563, when the Earl of Warwick suggested that Le Havre should be made a staple for Newcastle coal.[3] But the Treaty of Troyes ended any such ideas. Disappointing as this treaty was to England, it is a landmark in the history of the English Staple at Bruges. Elizabeth renounced both Calais and Le Havre, and Bruges was therefore destined to be for some years the seat of the Staple.

Despite the changes which the new industrial conditions had brought in the nature of England's principal exports, England and the Netherlands were still very closely dependent on each other, and both the Spanish and the English governments realised this bond. The Spaniards, for example, had stipulated at the time of Cateau Cambrésis that Calais should ultimately return to England. Later they opposed its return from fear that it would mean that the Staple would be set up there instead of at Bruges.[4]

By the sixteenth century the English were not concerned only for the market for their wool; in the new industrial conditions any breach with the government of the Netherlands meant that the artisans who were engaged in making cloths for export would be thrown out of work, and the English government had had some experience of unemployment of this nature. In

---

[1] *Cambridge Modern History*, III, p. 6.

[2] *Cal. S.P. Rome*, 1558–1571, pp. 107, 125.

[3] *Cal. S.P. Foreign*, 1563, p. 13.

[4] *Cal. S.P. Foreign*, 1562, p. 516, and *Rélations politiques des Pays-Bas et de l'Angleterre sous le regne de Philippe II*, Commission Royal d'histoire: Académie Royale de Belgique, ed. Kervyn de Lettenhove, III, p. 305.

1527 and 1528, when Henry VIII and Wolsey had caused an interruption of our trade with Flanders, the discontent had been so great that the governments were forced to reopen trade relations although England and Spain were at war.[1] This was the only remedy: the discontent and famine had not been really affected by the King's commands that the London clothiers should buy the cloths on pain of his high displeasure, or by Wolsey's threats that the King would take over the industry himself,[2] and the governing classes remembered the riots and unrest long after the artisans had forgotten the penury. As late as 1560 the disorders of 1527 were quoted in a minute to the Council.[3] Even the wise Cecil, fully aware of the danger which such a breach would entail, could only hope that "if men of discretion and creditt wer appoynted to see therto ther might be devisees to kepe that multitud occupyed", whilst as a last expedient the sturdier and stronger of the unemployed might be sent to Ireland.[4]

England was, therefore, very dependent on the Netherlands and, on the whole, English statesmen realised this fact. Although there were many who deplored the reliance upon a single vent for our staple commodities, yet there were none anxious for a breach. The chief source of information which the Council had at this time was Challoner, writing from Brussels or Antwerp; an apt and shrewd man, despite his modesty and his garrulity. He wrote almost verbatim reports of his interviews and sent his letters off with the utmost speed: "Hast, hast, post hast, with all possible diligence, cito, cito, cito, cito"[5] —and he stressed the need for keeping in friendship with the Spaniards. In this he was not swayed purely by economic considerations; the low estimation in which our army was held on the continent undoubtedly affected his judgment at a time

[1] *Cambridge Modern History*, II, pp. 429–30.
[2] *Vide* Unwin, *Studies in Economic History*, pp. 267–8.
[3] S.P. 12, Vol. 15, No. 54.
[4] Tawney and Power, II, p. 47.
[5] *Rélations politiques des Pays-Bas*, I, pp. 579, 591.

when he wrote: "As for our souldiours count them good for a weke, but the next instede of a sallade to wrap their head in a kercher." Still, whatever his reasons, Challoner advised Cecil that "If very necessite seme to offer the breache, for Gods love reteyne the amitie of theis menne".[1]

But despite this attitude amongst the English governing class, both the government and individuals paid but little attention to Spanish feeling, and much was allowed to happen which inevitably roused the wrath of the Spaniards.

For most of the provocation offered by the English government sheer poverty was the reason. Under Edward VI, Gresham had done something to pay off the debts of the English Crown to the international financiers at Antwerp and to restore the royal credit.[2] But Mary was forced to borrow again, and the penury of the early years of Elizabeth's reign must rank as a major political factor. She borrowed both in Antwerp and from her own English merchants, and Cecil was of necessity so keen in his search for money that he was prepared to allow aliens to drive Englishmen out of the wine trade, sacrificing even shipping to keep money in the country.[3]

It is not surprising, therefore, that Elizabeth should have followed Mary's precedent in levying impositions in addition to the ordinary customs dues. Mary had attempted to make raw cloth bring in as much revenue as would have been received if the wool had been exported unwrought.[4] In this she met much opposition, but the Merchant Adventurers, who were chiefly concerned, having fought an obscure case which is of considerable importance in English constitutional history, agreed to pay the new impost "without empeachement"[5] and

[1] *Rélations politiques des Pays-Bas*, II, pp. 85, 108.

[2] For a destructive criticism of the part played by Gresham in this affair *vide* Unwin, *Studies in Economic History*, pp. 149–67.

[3] *Hist. MSS. Comm.* Hatfield House, I, pp. 163, 165. He aimed at discouraging this trade, convinced that it produced an adverse balance, and that "no country robbeth England so much as France".

[4] *Vide supra*, pp. 14, 25.

[5] Gras, *Early English Customs Systems*, pp. 91–3, 129.

Elizabeth, fortified both by precedent and by merchant opinion, could hardly be expected to renounce so opportune an increase in her revenues. Thus, whilst the fall of Calais enabled her to mulct the Staplers for infringing the law, she was also enabled to exact additional customs from their rivals, the Merchant Adventurers.

English law and the opinions of English merchants, however, were not the only matters of importance. The Intercursus Magnus had stipulated that trade between England and the Netherlands should take place according to the established customs, and the Flemings felt themselves aggrieved by the innovation. In point of fact, it is obvious that it was their trade which ultimately bore the impost, for the English merchants would inevitably pass it on to their customers, and the impost amounted, on the average, to an increase of some 400 per cent. in the English customs payable.

To this grievance was added the fact that Elizabeth and her advisers were trying to build up the strength of England by the amassing of bullion within the realm, the encouragement of English shipping, and the fostering of key industries such as fishing and agriculture. It was the attempt to encourage English shipping which first brought the Netherlands into conflict with this English policy. English merchants were ordered either to ship their goods in English ships or else to pay customs as though they were aliens. This rankled with the Netherlands shippers, and the further order that such commodities as tin, lead, leather, bullocks, steers, brass, copper, beer, herrings and, above all, bullion should be conserved within the realm[1] brought forth further expostulations.

In the Netherlands there was a certain amount of sympathy for Elizabeth's penury,[2] and the manipulation of trade so as to achieve independence and power was a policy with which

[1] *Cal. S.P. Foreign*, 1560–1561, pp. 91–2, 1564–1565, p. 313, No. 6; British Museum, Egerton MSS. 2790, fo. 165; *Cal. S.P. Foreign*, 1563, pp. 608–9.
[2] *Hist. MSS. Comm.* 1911, Pepys, pp. 58–9.

the whole of Europe sympathised. So far, therefore, the Netherlands were prepared to expostulate but were not feeling outraged. But the situation was rendered almost impossible by the irrepressible piracy of the English. Even Egmont and Orange, who were suspected (not without cause) of conspiracy with Elizabeth, emphatically declared that Elizabeth would have to suppress her pirates actively, and not merely to utter edicts against them, whilst the enemies of England could not contain their wrath. "O Lord God," exclaimed Viglius to the English envoy, "we live in peace, but we sustain more damage than we should do if we had open war. . . . The pilleries do continue still. There is no justice executed."[1] The negotiations between the two countries were constantly being interrupted by "new miserable complaints" of English piracy; Elizabeth's protestations and proclamations were but too obviously ineffectual, and there was ample justification for Councillor d'Assonleville's statement that "Il n'y a nul fin a leurs larrecins",[2] when even the English envoy, Sheres, was forced to admit that English piracy might well give rise to complaints.[3]

There can be no doubt that England was giving ample cause for a breach with the Netherlands. And there were those in the Netherlands who were willing to take up the gage. There was clearly a small group of manufacturers who hoped that they would find a better sale for their wares if English manufactures were forbidden. Some such feeling had always been present under the surface, and there had always been Flemings who would gladly have seen the end of their dependence on England. This feeling had been increased by the irresistible influx of English cloth. As Hall wrote to Cecil, "The number of Englishe clothes which went then [in Henry VIII's reign]

[1] *Hist. MSS. Comm.* Pepys, pp. 16–17; cf. *ibid.* p. 69.
[2] *Correspondance du Cardinal de Granvelle*, Commission Royale d'Histoire: Académie Royale de Belgique, I, p. 571.
[3] *Hist. MSS. Comm.* Pepys, p. 38. For a catalogue of the English piracies *vide Cal. S.P. Foreign*, 1560–1561, pp. 557–60.

into the lowe countries were a small number to that thei have ben in this our tyme. And the countrie then beinge desierous to banish our clothes, howe much more have thei cause to desier the banishment of them nowe."[1] Sheres wrote from Antwerp that there were, in addition to these manufacturers, certain merchants who were anxious to break the intercourse with England by indirect means. They wanted to share the trade in English cloths on an equal footing with the Merchant Adventurers but, wrote Sheres, the Adventurers might be relied on to oppose this both with words and with money.[2]

Supporting this body of merchants and manufacturers was the weight of the Spanish government in the Netherlands. Spain was perhaps the foremost exponent of that policy of mercantilism which Cecil was pursuing in England. Clashes, with the "countercheck quarrelsome" always lurking near the surface, were bound to occur. Thus, for example, Cecil made Wednesday an additional fish day in order to encourage English shipping (in 1563) specifically as an answer to a Spanish Navigation Act which made English ships return home from Spain in ballast instead of in cargo.[3]

Nor was this the only effect of the prevailing trade doctrines. Not only was each country trying to build up its own strength and independence by measures which caused hostility, not only was it true that nations were taught "the sneaking arts of underling tradesmen,...that their interest consisted in beggaring all their neighbours",[4] but there was also present an elusive converse to the idea of the "Balance of Trade" which is, perhaps, best called the "Balance of Dependence". Mercantilism was in many ways less an economic than a political doctrine: it aimed at independence for a country, and at power in times of war. Any dependence upon another land was therefore to be avoided, whilst domination over the trade

---

[1] S.P. 12, Vol. 34, No. 51, and *Cal. S.P. Foreign*, 1564–1565, pp. 200–1.
[2] *Hist. MSS. Comm.* Pepys, p. 56.
[3] Tawney and Power, II, p. 104.
[4] *Wealth of Nations*, Book IV, c. 3, part II.

of a neighbour was to be exploited diplomatically and politically.

This "Balance of Dependence" occupied much of the attention of both English and Spanish statesmen. True to the tradition of the *Libel of English Policy* and its doctrine that

> The wolle of Englonde
> Susteyneth the comons Fflemmyngis, I understonde.
> Thane yf Englonde wolde hys wolle restrayne
> Ffrome Fflaunders, thys ffoloweth in certayne
> Fflaunders of nede must wyth us have pease,
> Or ellis he is distroyde, wythowght lees,

the English agents and politicians were constantly weighing up the extent to which the Flemings were dependent on their English trade, and they exploited to the full any advantage which they thought they had. On the other hand the Spaniards and their followers in Flanders were convinced that the "Balance of Dependence" lay against England, and they were prepared to exploit that advantage. To Granvelle and his correspondents "Les Pays-Bas sont les Indes de l'Angleterre", and England simply cannot afford to think of alternative markets.[1] "Les Anglais", wrote Granvelle, "voulant faire croire que sans eux les États de Sa Majesté ne pourraient pas vivre, et que eux ils n'ont nullement besoin des Pays-Bas. Pour moi, je pense tout le contraire."[2] In like vein Viglius derisively asked our envoy if England hoped to sell her commodities upon the Alps, as an alternative market to the Netherlands.[3]

Although the Spanish government was thus ready to test the "Balance of Dependence" and the English government was mischievously assuming that it lay with them, there were many on both sides who saw the folly of the whole conception. Adam Smith's day was not yet, and the doctrine of the "Balance of Trade" was not really disputed: there was no

[1] *Correspondance de Granvelle*, I, p. 10; *ibid.* pp. 567–8, pp. 569–70.
[2] *Ibid.* p. 591. I use here the French translation from the Spanish.
[3] S.P. 15, Vol. 9, No. 48.

widespread notion that a regularly conducted trade is always advantageous to both parties. Yet John Sheres did explain to the Prince of Orange that "Flanders and England be unto the seas as the hands and the feet of a man be to the belly; and that even as the belly doing her duty maintaineth both well flourishing and lusty; likewise the seas lying between Flanders and England well aplied by the merchants with the intercourse of merchandise hath maintained both these countries hitherto flourishing and wealthy".[1] In similar vein Guicciardini wrote that hardly could these two countries do without each other, so necessary was their mutual commerce to them,[2] and Montague proclaimed to d'Assonleville that England "no more needeth you than you her. . . . God hath appointed one of these regions to have need of another".[3]

With these views the commons of Antwerp would have been in the fullest agreement.[4] But circumstances were arising which tended to embitter such causes of disagreement as already existed. During Elizabeth's intervention in Scotland against Mary of Guise she had had to borrow money and to buy horses and munitions in the Netherlands, and in so doing she had both to listen to some plain speaking on England's military weakness and to evade or ignore the orders of the Spaniards, who wished to retain their money and munitions within their own grasp.[5] Not only this, but it was clear that Spain was willing to fish in troubled waters by keeping contact with the rebel Irish.[6]

Spanish policy, too, was becoming increasingly subject to religious influences. By 1562 Spain had entered into a league with France to crush heresy in their joint dominions, and she was suspected of concocting a league with France, the Pope,

---

[1] *Hist. MSS. Comm.* Pepys, p. 15.
[2] Tawney and Power, III, p. 173.
[3] *Hist. MSS. Comm.* Pepys, p. 58.
[4] *Vide infra*, p. 48.
[5] *Rélations politiques des Pays-Bas*, II, pp. 6, 29, 51, 139, 143, 200, 201, etc.
[6] *Ibid.* pp. 64, 75, 157. Spain was also intriguing with Norfolk, pp. 131–2.

and the rest of Roman Catholic Europe, to crush England.[1] The "straight amite between the two mighty neighbours" certainly worried Challoner at Antwerp. He wrote off bidding Cecil arm and drill the people "for so shall I trust in myne old dayes to toste a crabbe by the fyre".[2] His fears proved groundless, but none the less it was true that religion was gaining ever more power in directing the policy of the Spanish government in the Netherlands, and was directing it against England.

Trade disputes between the two countries were dawdling on: both England and Spain were pursuing a mercantilist policy, and England was combining with her aggressive trade policy a provocative tolerance towards piracy. But there was little desire for a definite breach until religion entered into the disputes.

It was Cardinal Granvelle who was the force behind this change in Spanish policy. Convinced that in matters of trade the "Balance of Dependence" lay strongly in favour of Spain, he wanted to use the power which he thus imagined to be within his grasp to bring England back to Roman Catholicism —and to humility. To him the blustering arrogance of the English and of their Queen was quite intolerable. In a later letter to Silva, newly appointed ambassador to England, Granvelle warns him of this national trait. "Si les Anglais s'arrogent une fois la supériorité leur insolence est insupportable." De Silva is therefore to praise the scholarship of the English court, but to make it clear that the court of Spain is no whit inferior: in every possible way he is to match arrogance with arrogance, ostensibly in pursuit of "cette égalité qui maintient l'amitie".[3] This is not a spirit in which delicate negotiations can be conducted.

Granvelle, with Viglius and Berlaymont, formed an inner

[1] Ehrenberg, *Hamburg und England im Zeitalter der Königin Elizabeth*, p. 64; Geyl, *Revolt of the Netherlands*, p. 70.

[2] *Rélations politiques des Pays-Bas*, II, p. 85.

[3] *Correspondance de Granvelle*, I, p. 589.

ring which dominated the government of the Netherlands, and Granvelle's opinion was especially weighty in any affairs concerning England.[1] The ultimate object of Granvelle and of his friends was to render the Netherlands independent of England and English trade, their immediate object to reduce that trade to order.[2] So, as they were aiming at a breach of trade, they could not be expected to conduct the negotiations with England in that spirit of compromise which is essential in these matters.

Circumstances were now to add a personal hatred of the English to the mistrust which Granvelle already felt towards them. The Spanish governors in the Netherlands had always feared that the English merchants there might form and encourage groups of heretics. To this suspicion the Staplers were particularly open. Much earlier, before 1440, they had been granted their own confessor by the Pope,[3] but by the early sixteenth century they were already tainted with heresy. At a time when Henry VIII was still a sturdy supporter of the Papacy the Staplers' chaplain, Sir Philip Smith, was found to own many heretical books and to be preaching Lutheran doctrine.[4] Their reputation for Protestantism seems to have stuck to them, and when they were negotiating for the renewal of their former privileges at Bruges Margaret of Parma exerted herself to ensure that they should be given no privileges which might lead to the prejudice of religion.[5] None the less, the Staplers were bound to sympathise with the Netherlanders in their religious troubles—as, indeed, did most of the foreign merchants who frequented those regions.

[1] *Cal. S.P. Spanish*, 1558–1567, p. 351.
[2] *Correspondance de Granvelle*, I, pp. 567–8.
[3] *Calendar of Papal Letters*, 1431–1447, p. 111.
[4] *Calendar of Letters and Papers, Henry VIII*, IV, 2, pp. 1902, 1926, 2064.
[5] Gachard, *Correspondance de Marguerite d'Autriche*, II, p. 201. In 1568 the Spanish governors renewed the charter of the Scottish Staple and shewed a similar spirit in their insertion of a clause that the Scots must "live and behave themselves as good Catholics" (Davidson and Gray, *The Scottish Staple at Veere*, pp. 175–6).

The first serious revolt against the religious policy of Spain followed on the changes brought about in 1561. As a result of those changes Granvelle had enhanced his own position considerably. He had become Archbishop of Mechlin, Primate of the Netherlands Church and a cardinal, and it is not surprising that a good deal of the outcry which followed the changes should have been directed against him personally. In this outcry many of the groups of foreign merchants seem to have taken their part, and Antwerp (which harboured most of them) had been a cause of special anxiety to Granvelle before the changes were introduced. The city petitioned against the changes on the ground that they would upset her population of foreigners, but Philip overrode the objection; yet Granvelle was chiefly worried about the cosmopolitan population of Antwerp, and it was in fact in that city that the opposition to the changes came to a head.[1]

Other cities besides Antwerp took part in the riots against the religious changes of 1561 and in the personal abuse of Granvelle—Bruges amongst others. Here the Merchants of the Staple, barely settled in their new haven, gave their support to the Brugeois in their resistance to the introduction of a bishop[2] and so roused to action Granvelle's suspicion of the English. Apart from his feelings about English trade policy, English piracy, and English arrogance, Granvelle was also profoundly suspicious of Cecil, "homme bas et rusé, versé dans la connaissance des lettres grecques et latines, grand hérétique, orgeuilleux comme ceux de sa nation, neuf dans les affaires et les traitant d'après les doctrines de Machiavel". The copious mixtures of surmise and suspicion which he received as dispatches from London led him to conclude that Cecil was "homme dangéreux qui, par ses intelligences avec les prédicateurs de la hérésie, dirige toute la politique dans le but d'enraciner et étendre les opinions erronées".[3] Granvelle knew

---

[1] Weiss, *Papiers d'état du Cardinal de Granvelle*, VI, pp. 612–15.
[2] *Cal. S.P. Foreign*, 1562, p. 3; cf. *Rélations politiques des Pays-Bas*, III, p. 21, n. 1.   [3] *Correspondance de Granvelle*, I, p. 589.

that Throckmorton was helping the Huguenots in France, so he was prepared to believe that the English were planning a protestant league and were ready to help the discontented Netherlanders.[1] Consequently, when the Staplers at Bruges gave their sympathy to the natives in resisting his religious policy, he became convinced of the danger of harbouring English heretics and took steps against the Merchant Adventurers at Antwerp.[2]

It was at Antwerp that the English merchants were most numerous and it was, also, the English trade in cloths to Antwerp which he most wanted to destroy, not the less important trade in wool to Bruges. Antwerp, too, was the spot on whose loyalty in a struggle with England Granvelle could least count. The people there felt an almost excessive reliance upon England. Years ago they had seized their burgomaster by the beard, growling, "You rich villains, you do undo us, our wives and our children, by your pride and glory, striving with the Englishmen, by whom we must live, by whom we get more in a month than by you in seven years."[3]

This feeling that the interests of Antwerp were bound up with those of England was quite undiminished by the time that the religious troubles came to estrange the citizens still more from their governors. The inhabitants perceived that the movement against England was "for religion's sake and because they withstood having a Bishop in Brabant". Our envoy reported that "the English have no better friends on this side than the magistrates of Antwerp" and that "The first worker for the keeping of Englishe cloth out of the country is said to be the Cardinal",[4] whilst Gresham wrote that the dispute

[1] This fear, ultimately justified, runs through the Spanish correspondence of this time and figures largely in the dispatches of Aquila from London (*Relations politiques des Pays-Bas*, III, pp. xv, xxvii *et passim*); cf. his denunciation of Elizabeth for fomenting heresy in the Netherlands (*ibid.* pp. 14 *et seq.*).

[2] *Cal. S.P. Foreign*, 1562, p. 3.

[3] *Cal. S.P. Foreign*, 1564–1565, p. 172.

[4] *Cal. S.P. Foreign*, 1564–1565, pp. 191, 197.

was held to be "the practice of Spaniards and priests" and that "the States of the land here will never consent to have ware with the Quene's Majestie".[1] Egmont, also, told Sheres that it was Granvelle who had brought the disputes with England into an actual quarrel[2] and, as the quarrel ran on, Windebank wrote that "All men saving the Papists do wishe the Quene's Majestie to make her profit, thinking it shuld be ye proffit of all Christendom". Elizabeth's popularity was rising, whilst there were grumblings against "the practyse of the Cardenall here, whome ys hattid of all men".[3] As long as Granvelle remained in power it was chiefly he who drove on the quarrel against England, and it was only after his withdrawal from office that the nobles of the land knew what steps against England were being taken.[4]

Consequently, although Granvelle alleged trade disputes as the cause of his increasing bitterness against England, no one was deceived. Both the English and the Flemings knew that their trade was being involved in a religious struggle, whilst the Roman Catholics knew quite well that Granvelle did not want the trade disputes to be satisfactorily settled, "la Reine étant en religion telle qu'elle est".

The policy which was dominating the situation and leading to a definite quarrel between the two countries is best summarised from Granvelle's letter of instructions to Guzman de Silva. Here Granvelle implies that he is really interested in trade and wants to revive the weaving of Flanders. He appears to desire nothing but fair trade between Flanders and England and to want England to amend her Navigation Laws, her imposts, her embargo on Flemish manufactures and her piracy. Trade is to be re-established on a basis of treaty obligations. Yet this letter reveals an intense distrust of England and a feeling that the Netherlands can dominate not only England's trade policy but also her internal and religious policy by

[1] *Rélations politiques des Pays-Bas*, II, pp. 332, 333.
[2] *Hist. MSS. Comm.* Pepys, p. 16.
[3] *Rélations politiques des Pays-Bays*, III, pp. 100, 104.
[4] *Cal. S.P. Foreign*, 1564–1565, John Fitzwilliams to Cecil, p. 197.

means of that "Balance of Dependence" which Flanders possesses. He mistrusts England and holds that the English think of nothing but their own good and he rejoices to think of the misery which a breach with Flanders would bring to London. Elizabeth's poverty he rejoices at: it must be prolonged as long as possible. She is (he says) in desperate fear of seeing her export trade in cloth upset and her most important source of customs revenue diminished, and it is Spain's business to maintain this fear. Thus Elizabeth may be brought both to indemnify the Flemings and to re-establish trade on a reasonable footing. This would be good, but in addition she may, if kept thus penurious, and dependent on Spanish goodwill for her revenue, be compelled by the aid of her Roman Catholic subjects to restore religion "sur un pied convenable"—a matter of high importance for the service of God as well as for the good of the Netherlands, and since His Majesty is determined to achieve this result, a matter deserving the attention of de Silva.[1]

Against such authority and determination the inarticulate masses were powerless, and the breach with England came.

The plague that raged in London in 1562 furnished the first pretext for interrupting trade. English cloth was forbidden in the Netherlands from fear of infection,[2] and the result was such confusion in England that Granvelle quickly realised that he had touched her on the raw. He and his friends now decided that England must come to them cap in hand and accept their terms. They looked forward not only to the political and religious subjection of England but also to the humbling of Antwerp, for Antwerp was both the centre of the resistance to their projects in Brabant and the main seat of the finishing trade in English cloth.

Here again we may see how Granvelle was largely actuated by religious motives even when he was apparently seeking only economic ends. He aimed at the revival of the greatness

[1] *Correspondance de Granvelle*, I, p. 592.
[2] *Cal. S.P. Foreign*, 1564–1565, pp. 36, 52.

of Flemish weaving, for that would mean the return to Flanders of those who had fled to "corrupt their religion" in England. He reckoned that during the year's embargo on account of the plague the county of Flanders alone had woven sixty thousand cloths more than she had woven in any year for thirty years.[1] Confirmatory evidence is given by the Englishman Gilpin, who wrote that Flanders and other places which wove cloth had found such gain in the utterance of their products since the restraint began that, if they might have English wools come to them, they would wish English cloths banished out of all places in the Low Countries.[2]

The embargo was therefore continued under pretence of the pestilence, but it was obvious to all that the pestilence was but an excuse, and that the embargo was being used as a means of bringing pressure to bear on England. Elizabeth then sent an envoy over to try to open up the markets once more. She was secretly ready to drop her Navigation Act and her embargo on imports from Flanders in order to further the discussion, but in an act of typical bravado she tried to ride the high horse and forbade all Flemish imports on pain of confiscation—a gesture which intimidated a few Flemings but which was "chose risible" to Granvelle, who saw in it merely "une de ces bravades, de ces forfanteries habituelles à son pays".[3]

In reply, the Spanish government, in December 1563, refused to allow English woollen manufactures to enter the Flemish ports, forbade the export to England of steel, latten, copper, iron, wire, thread, morocco leather and silk, and prohibited the lading of all English ships in Flemish ports.[4] This was one of Granvelle's last acts before, as a concession to public opinion, he was withdrawn from the government of the

[1] *Correspondance de Granvelle*, I, p. 591; *Rélations politiques des Pays-Bas*, IV, p. 111. [2] *Cal. S.P. Foreign*, 1564–1565, p. 201.
[3] *Cal. S.P. Foreign*, 1564–1565, pp. 52–3; *Correspondance de Granvelle*, I, p. 590.
[4] *Cal. S.P. Foreign*, 1563, pp. 608–9, 1564–1565, p. 5; Tawney and Power, II, pp. 43–4; Pirenne, *Histoire de Belgique*, III, p. 429; *Cal. S.P. Spanish*, 1558–1567, p. 356.

Netherlands, leaving Viglius behind as his spiritual legatee to carry on the feud with England. Granvelle felt that England must soon come to heel, and that any talk of alternative markets for her products was idle bravado. The trade dispute on which he had embarked was to test the soundness of his judgment.

Within the toils of this web of commercial and religious diplomacy the Merchants of the Staple continued to exercise their trade. They could not help being involved to some extent, and it was their sympathy with the Bruges protestants which had fired Granvelle's suspicions. But the quarrel went on very much over their heads, none the less. In their desire to revive the greatness of Flemish weaving the Spaniards realised the need for English wool, and it was part of their plan that the embargo on the import of English cloth should throw the English weaving industry out of gear, so that, in order to get a market for their wools, the English wool-growers and merchants would be forced once more to supply the looms of Flanders.[1] Consequently the Staplers were welcomed even by the enemies of England, and at the height of the quarrel, in May 1564, Philip himself ordered the magistrates of Bruges to protect and encourage the Merchants of the Staple there,[2] and the city of Bruges felt so unconcerned with the quarrel which was raging with Antwerp and its trade as focus that it tried to get Burghley to make the Merchant Adventurers hold their marts at Bruges instead of at Antwerp.[3]

True, the Staplers were not altogether scathless. In 1564, immediately after the declaration of the Spanish embargo, the only shipment which they appear to have made was a miserable ten sacks and twenty-one cloves from London to Bruges,[4] but the spring shipping of the next year was well up to their usual standard of this time and the outports of Boston and Hull

[1] *Correspondance de Granvelle*, I, pp. 591, 592.
[2] *Cal. S.P. Foreign, 1564–1565*, p. 129.
[3] *Cal. S.P. Foreign, 1564–1565*, p. 254.
[4] E. 122/89/5 and Enrolled Accounts, E. 356/28. Shipments were still being made under licences granted to Dudley.

once more sprang into activity.[1] Although the Staplers were thus able to trade despite the quarrel with the Netherlands government, the dispute was bound to bring the nature of their business once more into the public eye. Notwithstanding their recent vindication of themselves, and their new charter, they had to defend their traffic before the Council. The Council was bound to consider afresh the advisability of holding both the staple for wool and the mart for cloths in England, and Sir Thomas Smith, our ambassador in Paris, was the spokesman of the adverse party. "If the trade could be removed from Antwerp and settled in England it would be the fairest diamond in the Queen's crown" he wrote to Cecil, whilst he also suggested that, if this should be impossible, it would be better to remove the Staple from Bruges and to have both the Staplers and the Adventurers together at Antwerp. He "mused when he heard, after the fall of Calais, that the staple of their wools should be at Bruges".[2]

The real reason why such projects did not take hold at such a time was that any plan for keeping the marts at home would involve the sacrifice of the shipping trade to the aliens. Such reason might seem to lack force at a time when even the Merchant Adventurers' voyages were rightly described as "these two-day voyages twice a year, where every pedlar may practice, whereby there is scant either a good mariner made or a good ship maintained".[3] At the same time the Staplers were excused from the terms of the Navigation Act of 1558 and there was obviously every reason for their opponents to declare that there were more hoys than good ships used in the trade and that it did no good to the navy.[4]

Unsound though the argument might be, it was none the

[1] E. 122/89/5, E. 122/170/4 and E. 122/89/12.
[2] *Cal. S.P. Foreign*, 1564–1565, p. 172.
[3] *Hist. MSS. Comm.* Pepys, p. 39.
[4] S.P. 12, Vol. 15, No. 52. The permit was first given to the Company on 25 Jan. 1565. It was repeated on 8 April 1570 (Staple Company, Register of Royal Grants, fos. 81, 84).

less adequate to give the Staplers a popular case. Combined with their personal influence and the fact that they were of great use to the Crown (since they could on occasions pay their customs direct to Gresham in the Netherlands[1]), the argument that their trade encouraged shipping enabled them to defeat the proposal that the Staple should be set up within England.

If the Staplers remained comparatively immune during the embargo, their rivals, the Adventurers, bore its full brunt. They were unable to evade it, and many of them suffered severe losses during the first year.[2] Then, with many misgivings, they sent a preliminary surveying expedition to Emden and, the report being favourable, shipped their summer convoy of 1564 to that city. Granvelle and his correspondent d'Assonleville, envoy to England to settle the disputes, refused to take the threat to ship to Emden seriously,[3] and the fate of the venture of 1564 amply justified their contempt.

At first enthusiasm on both sides was unbounded. Emden saw visions of herself as the Antwerp of the future. The Countess Anna and the Earls Ertzard, Christopher, and John vied with the burgesses in promising buildings and privileges, neighbouring rulers projected the opening of the waterways for internal communications, and the English dreamed of trading to a merchant's paradise in which there was so little of the commercial spirit that the city boasted but one lawyer, and he was a beggar.[4]

Yet the venture was a failure. The "Burgundish people" slandered the English to the natives, and Philip ordered the Netherlanders neither to trade with England nor with Emden.[5] The Hanse merchants had anticipated great wealth from carrying on the cloth trade whilst the dispute raged but, finding their

[1] *E.g.* E. 122/88/5.

[2] *Cal. S.P. Foreign*, 1564–1565, pp. 18, 19, 141.

[3] *Correspondance de Granvelle*, I, pp. 568, 570.

[4] *Cal. S.P. Foreign*, 1564–1565, pp. 58, 105; *Hist. MSS. Comm.* Pepys, pp. 22, 23, 39.

[5] *Hist. MSS. Comm.* Pepys, p. 23; *Cal. S.P. Foreign*, 1564–1565, pp. 138, 141.

right to export cloths abrogated by Elizabeth, they opposed the English with all their power.[1] Moreover, the English found that the air of Emden was "not good, for they keep many beasts in the town and do not remove the straw and litter, and their canals have no current".[2] The Adventurers were therefore reduced to writing to England to explain that "the practices are marvellous" to keep the merchants from them. No Dutch or Italian merchants came to buy,[3] and the great convoy of forty-eight merchant vessels and four royal ships sold but 14,000 cloths in the first flush of enthusiasm. Then sales fell off, and the commercial and geographical isolation of Emden became so apparent that within a year the Adventurers carried their goods first to Cologne and then to Frankfurt. There they disposed of them at last.[4]

The Emden trouble had come upon the Adventurers at a time when they were already in difficulties, accused of breaking their charters, exceeding their licences to export, and defrauding the Queen's customs.[5] Their troubles were increased, but they managed to survive and even won a new charter on the 18th of July 1564; indeed the political situation helped them in this, for they were able to point out that they had always been assistant to the Crown and that they held bonds for large sums loaned to Elizabeth. The situation in Flanders also lent point to their statement that a corporation is necessary to prevent wrongs being done to English traders beyond the seas, and that without such a corporation our commodities would decay, foreign goods would be daily brought into the land, and many injuries be done to us by strangers.[6] Never was it more

[1] *Cal. S.P. Foreign*, 1564–1565, pp. 164, 191.
[2] *Hist. MSS. Comm.* Pepys, pp. 22–3.
[3] *Cal. S.P. Foreign*, 1564–1565, pp. 164, 198.
[4] *Cal. S.P. Foreign*, 1564–1565, p. 215; Ehrenberg, *Hamburg und England*, pp. 69–75; Unwin, *Studies in Economic History*, p. 199.
[5] *Cal. S.P. Dom. Add.* 1547–1565, pp. 519, 542.
[6] *Cal. S.P. Dom. Add.* 1547–1565, pp. 541–544; *Cal. S.P. Foreign*, 1564–1565, p. 529; Lingelbach, *Merchant Adventurers in England*, pp. 228 *et seq.*; Heckscher, *Mercantilism*, I, pp. 422, 449.

obvious than in 1564 that trade was a weapon in diplomacy: it therefore followed that trade must be organised, that it might come easily to the diplomat's hand, and the charter which the Adventurers won in 1564 unified the export trade in cloths in a most marked manner. The suspension of the Hanse merchants' right to export cloths, in 1563, had for the moment given the Adventurers the monopoly as against aliens: now their new charter specifically incorporated them as the Adventurers *of England* and gave them control over the admission of new members to their privileges and confirmed their control of the trade as against "interloping" Englishmen.[1]

Although the Adventurers themselves deserted Emden, and most English correspondents could see "small likelihood of amendment" there,[2] yet there were those who thought the connection a valuable one. If the contact were maintained "it shall always be a bridle to the other if they begin to wax insolent again".[3] There can be no doubt that it caused considerable discontent around Antwerp. Many merchants withdrew from that city to Emden[4] and the magistrates tried to use their influence both with Cecil and with Gresham to turn English policy in their favour, although they knew that their "Prince and council bear them little goodwill of this persuading". The desire for a resumption of trade with England was general. Trade was at a standstill, "their merchants break every day",[5] towns where weaving still continued were "at a stay" for lack of wool,[6] and Fitzwilliams wrote from Antwerp that "they of this town would spend a good piece of money to have the traffic between the two countries in the old order again".[7]

The interruption seems chiefly to have resulted in French

---

[1] Ehrenberg, *Hamburg und England*, pp. 69, 73; Lingelbach, p. xxxi; Unwin, *Studies in Economic History*, pp. 170–1.

[2] *E.g. Cal. S.P. Foreign*, 1564–1565, p. 191.

[3] *Ibid.* p. 296.   [4] *Ibid.* p. 249.

[5] *Ibid.* pp. 84–5.   [6] *Ibid.* p. 249.

[7] *Ibid.* p. 125. Granvelle gives his opinion of this covetous spirit in *Correspondance de Philippe II sur les affaires des Pays-Bas*, I, p. 324.

smugglers carrying on the trade at enhanced prices,[1] so that the Spanish Council of Regency alone felt that the breach with England was supportable. With the withdrawal of Granvelle from active domination sager counsels began to prevail even there, especially as Egmont, Horn, Orange and other nobles of the country began to take a more active part in affairs of state.[2]

The "Diet of Bruges" was accordingly arranged. Both the Regent and Elizabeth were anxious for a settlement,[3] but the latter, although willing to yield most points, was adamant on the question of her right to poundage. On this there could be no agreement. So the Diet dragged out an intermittent existence until 1567, delayed by Spanish obstructiveness, enlivened by "new miserable complaints" of English piracy, but not made cogent even by the plan that the English should "send some of their cloth to other places and make a countenance as though they would traffic elsewhere". It ultimately ended in deadlock and prorogation, with "no great hope of any good end of these matters".[4]

Although the diplomatists were unable to arrive at a settlement at Bruges, the needs both of the English and of the Flemings had made necessary a series of interim permits for the resumption of trade. This, in the opinion of Granvelle, was an irremediable mistake for the Netherlanders to have made. He had anticipated some such step and was convinced that it was the worst resolution possible, and was due to the rising interest in the Council of those who sympathised with England.[5] Certain Englishmen also thought that trade should not have been resumed until the disputes had been settled,[6] and it was

[1] *Cal. S.P. Foreign*, 1564–1565, pp. 201–2, 249.

[2] *Cal. S.P. Foreign*, 1564–1565, pp. 141, 169, 191, 197, 285; *Hist. MSS. Comm.* Pepys, p. 28.

[3] Pepys, p. 17; Burgon, *Life of Gresham*, II, pp. 60–71, 88–103.

[4] *Cal. S.P. Foreign*, 1564–1565, pp. 251, 289, 303, 313, 323, 330, 337, 351, 363, 379, 450; *ibid.* 1566–1568, pp. 32–3, 49, 52, 55, 61–3, 75, 93, 131.

[5] *Correspondance de Philippe II*, I, pp. 324, 339.

[6] *Cal. S.P. Foreign*, 1564–1565, p. 252; Tawney and Power, II, p. 45.

probably this resumption of intercourse which was answerable for the failure of the Diet. At all events, such trade was almost certain to be bad trade. The English, fearful for the future, both bought and sold wildly,[1] and the Netherlanders bought with equal abandon. It was reckoned that 24,000 cloths were brought back from Emden and sold at Antwerp, and that a further 80,000 or 90,000 cloths were ready for shipment from England,[2] whilst the English bought so much on credit in Flanders that the Flemings were in mortal fear lest trade should again be interrupted.

English cloths were once more flooding into Flanders, and any hope of restoring Flemish weaving (and with it the greatness of the Staple Company of England) was steadily vanishing. True, the Adventurers themselves were even better informed than the Spanish government, and they realised that the revival of their trade would prove to be but temporary. To them the religious troubles boded no good for traders, and Gresham, sent to the Netherlands at this time, found "not a penny to be had" of all the rich merchants of Antwerp. He advised Cecil that "I like nothing here of these proceedings; therefore your honour shall do very well in time to consider some other realm and place for the utterance of our commodities that is made within the realm: whereby her Majesty's realm may remain in peace and quietness, which in this brabbling time is one of the chiefest things your honour hath to look to, considering in what terms this country doth now stand in, which is ready one to cut another's throat for matters of religion".[3]

The Adventurers therefore began to seek new marts. Of Emden they had already had experience, and they had left bitter feelings behind them when they withdrew from that city in 1565. One contemporary wrote of them that their thankless conduct was like that of a sailor who vows a wax candle the

[1] *Cal. S.P. Foreign*, 1564–1565, p. 348.
[2] *Correspondance de Philippe II*, I, p. 345.
[3] Burgon, *Life of Gresham*, II, pp. 159–60.

size of his mast when he is in danger, but forgets his vow when he sights land again.[1] It was, therefore, not to Emden but to Hamburg that the Adventurers now turned and, despite the opposition of the rest of the Hanse League, Hamburg gave them, in 1567, a charter of privileges for ten years which won for that city the trade in English cloth.[2]

The charter which Hamburg gave not only terminated the age-old loyalty of Hamburg to the Hanse League,[3] it also brought to a definite conclusion the dependence of the Merchant Adventurers on the Netherlands. In their new mart they were to find both merchants and artisans in abundance: at the end of their ten years of privilege they left Hamburg very reluctantly, to return as soon as they could again win suitable terms from the Senate, and never again did the Netherlands act as the chief outlet for English cloths.

For the Staplers the situation was far different. They had not been vitally affected by the quarrel of Granvelle with England, and when trade had been resumed they had hoped for great prosperity, since the Netherlands princes were then planning to restore their weaving industry by forbidding the import of English cloths.[4] But the religious troubles were showing signs of interrupting their trade in a much more serious way than had the diplomatic disputes, and they reluctantly looked round for alternative marts.

[1] Ehrenberg, *Hamburg and England*, p. 74.

[2] *Ibid.* pp. 90–100, 312.

[3] Hamburg had not always submitted unquestioningly to the dictation of Lubeck (cf. Power and Postan, p. 131) nor did she now persist in sheltering the Adventurers. She returned to her allegiance to the Hanse League in 1577, and not until 1611 did the Adventurers settle there again (Lipson, *Economic History*, II, pp. 204–11). Yet the discussions which preceded this charter and the attitude which Hamburg then adopted make it "a permanent renunciation of the Hanse by Hamburg" (Ehrenberg, pp. 87–9).

[4] *Rélations politiques des Pays-Bas*, IV, p. 518. *Cal. S.P. Foreign*, 1564–1565, p. 390. Although the magistrates returned a most satisfactorily gloomy answer to "What damage might follow" (*ibid.* p. 397), yet this enquiry disquieted the Adventurers.

In answer to the demands of the Council, the Staplers in September 1565 submitted a memorandum dealing with the possible alternatives to Bruges. They considered that there were but three, Calais, Emden, and a home port. Calais they found quite unsuitable as being a "Towne of warre planted with soldiers of another nation", whilst Emden was not only too far a voyage from England but was also too far removed from our buyers, and there was no drapery near at hand to consume the wools. The notion of an English Staple, involving the sacrifice of the shipping trade and the relinquishing of the Netherlands market to the Spaniards, was considered as already exploded, and no time was wasted on it.

The Staplers, conducting an already declining trade, realised that their only hope of survival on an important scale lay in maintaining contact with the Netherlands at all costs. "And fynally wee doubt not but that youre Honours dothe right well consider that yf upon suche alteracion of place king Philipp shuld inhibit his Subiects there to buy our commoditie as of late at Empden hathe bene practised then were wee utterly destitute of eny our accustomed traffique. Neverthelesse as it shall please your honours to Appoynte Soo shall wee most willingly obey youre order."[1]

It was obvious that the Staplers would leave the Netherlands only with the most extreme reluctance, and events proved the wisdom of their conservatism. In July 1566 Elizabeth forbade wool to be transported. A recent proclamation had extended the previous permission for trade to be resumed,[2] but the Council decided that a shortage of wool might bring the Diet of Bruges to a more sensible frame of mind. It therefore became necessary to find some other mart for the Staplers, and so clear was it that on the continent their mart lay in the Netherlands alone that the government had to forgo its customs, renounce its policy of denouncing wool-brokers, and

[1] S.P. 12, Vol. 37, No. 32.
[2] Steele, *Tudor and Stuart Proclamations*, I, pp. 64, 65.

allow the Staplers to sell their wool within the land [1] to clothiers and manufacturers. That this gesture failed to bring the Diet to a satisfactory conclusion may be ascribed to the fact that within a month of its issue the Staplers were petitioning to be allowed once more to export in the accustomed manner, and although they were not immediately successful, yet they had won permission by the 21st of July.[2]

Their trade continued throughout the deliberations of the Diet as it had continued throughout the embargo, but once more they had to run the gauntlet of some pertinent criticism. At the Diet the Spaniards produced a heavy indictment of the Staplers' methods of doing business. They stated that their subjects of Holland were denied the right to traffic in wools and that the Staplers did not bring their wools regularly. When the wools arrived, it was found that the English packers had used fraud, whilst the purchasers were forced to pay tolls to the Company and to employ the servants of the Company. For some years, the men of Holland, now the chief customers of the Company, had demanded more fells and less wool.[3] They stated that the Staplers mixed the qualities of their fells, exported only the worst qualities of fells, compelled buyers to take one-third of their requirement in old and evil fells,[4] and insisted that the buyers should take at least one sarplar of wool with each fifteen hundred fells.[5]

To these complaints the Staplers prepared their answers. They rightly replied that the Netherlanders had no right to share in the wool trade, for no such right had been given by the Intercursus. Wars and disputes were apt to interrupt their trade and they could not always be answerable for delays in shipment. They alleged that they bought the best fells available

[1] Staple Company, Register of Royal Grants, fo. 82.
[2] S.P. 12, Vol. 40, No. 31.
[3] Power and Postan, pp. 60–1.
[4] Cf. the complaints of 1478, *ibid.* p. 62.
[5] *Cal. S.P. Foreign*, 1564–1565, pp. 303–4; cf. the similar complaints of June, 1562. *Rélations politiques des Pays-Bas*, III, pp. 61–2. *Vide infra*, p. 157. Malden, *Cely Papers*, p. xii.

and sold them as they bought them, according to the scale of prices in the Intercursus, without purposely intermingling them. Sometimes the fells were damaged in transit, but no more old fells were forcibly sold than had been the custom at Calais. "Time out of mind", they said, it had been the custom of the Company that one sarplar of wool must be sold with each fifteen hundred fells. Any purchaser who found he had been deceived in the packing had the right to return the deceitful goods and obtain both costs and damages from the seller. As for weights, the Senate of Bruges had been given the standard weights and allowed to share the oversight of weights, and as for exactions, their customers now paid less than they had paid at Calais, for they now paid in Flemish florins instead of in sterling.[1]

These answers were about as effective as anything else which happened at that most ineffective conference. The Staplers continued their trade, and it is to be assumed that they did not greatly mend their ways. They did, however, realise that in appealing to their practice at Calais they were appealing to a past of which the records had been taken from them.

Ever since their departure from Calais they had tried to replace the documents there lost and now they searched out copies of their privileges and charters and entered them in a book—the Register of Royal Grants.[2] Here, however, there was little mention of that internal organisation of the Company, or of its rules for trade, to which they were now referring. Such things were probably largely matters of tradition and hearsay, and a committee which had sat at Bruges to draw up the copies of the charters and to reconstruct the customs of the Company had left so many matters open to dispute that now, in 1565, it was felt necessary that a new committee should sit and bring the rediscovered charters and the reconstructed ordinances into conformity with the conditions of trade in 1565 by drawing up a new set of ordinances.

[1] *Cal. S.P. Foreign*, 1564–1565, pp. 303–4.
[2] *Vide supra*, pp. 3, 4 and n. 1. *Infra*, p. 104.

It is this set of ordinances which is here published. The importance of the document lies not in the rules which it set up for a Company already decayed and in imminent danger of losing its only real mart. It is the retrospective light which the ordinances cast on the former practices of the Company which is valuable. For the ordinances were drawn up at a time when the Staple Company was being compelled to defend itself by reference to those practices, and when it was sadly bemoaning its former greatness at Calais. It was attempting to reconstruct and interpret the customs of the Company as they were when it dominated the trade not only of England but of much of Europe as well. This document, therefore, is part of an effort to recapture that greatness as a corporation which had once marked the Staplers' organisation.

Chapter V

THE LAST OF THE STAPLE

It was perhaps as well that the Company consolidated its organisation at a time when, although trade relations were rocking all round it, it had found a momentary security at Bruges in the midst of the storm. For but few shipments had been made under these rules when, in January 1569, came hasty reports from refugee Staplers and Merchant Adventurers that their goods had been confiscated at Bruges and themselves misused.

The cause of this harsh treatment was that Elizabeth had arrested a shipment of bullion which had fled to Plymouth.[1] Most of the bullion was not Spanish property but was a loan to Spain from Genoese bankers, destined for Alva's troops in the Netherlands: Elizabeth took the treasure first of all into protective custody and ultimately negotiated with the Genoese for the loan of it. Legally her action was defensible, but it had the result of depriving Alva of some £85,000 which he badly needed to pay his troops. Alva therefore made up the deficit in his war chest by sequestrating the goods of English merchants in the Netherlands: this gave him a rough equivalent for the money which Elizabeth was withholding from him. The ultimate diplomatic results of this series of events were to be tremendous. No less important were the immediate commercial results. The religious disputes which the Merchant Adventurers had watched with fear for some years now engulfed English trade to the Netherlands, and the Staple Com-

[1] For an account of this episode *vide* Scott, *Joint Stock Companies*, I, pp. 49–52, and Conyers Read, *Journal of Modern History*, 1933, pp. 443 *et seq.*

pany was to be amply justified in its fear that by the "arrest and trobles not beinge hereafter well appaised youre poore suppliantes are lyke to Sustayne great losses to the utter undoinge of the greatter parte of them".[1]

They knew that the only market for which they cared was now taken from them. Expedients which satisfied the Merchant Adventurers in their trouble comforted the Staplers little. In answer to their plea that the Council should "be good to us the poore merchantes of the staple for other wyse we shalbe all utterly undone", they were allowed to ship their wools to Hamburg, the Adventurers' haven of refuge.[2] But their shipments to Hamburg[3] showed a lack of confidence which was fully vindicated, and they later claimed that they had to ship back to England wools which had lain unsold for five years at Hamburg.[4]

Their plight was made worse by the fact there was an increase in smuggling at this time. Much wool still found its way to Calais, and there was a ready market for any wools which could evade both English and Spanish officials and get into the Netherlands.[5] The real extent of this leakage it is difficult to estimate, for smuggled trade always defies any attempt at accurate analysis, but the Company had enough public feeling behind its complaints to enable it to secure a far-reaching search into the export of wools in the counties of South-east England which were most convenient for trade with France and the Netherlands.[6]

At the same time attempts were made to find some port on the continent which should prove more satisfactory for wool exports than Hamburg. The smuggled trade made it obvious that a French channel port would be admirable, but diplomatic

---

[1] S.P. 12, Vol. 49, Nos. 12, 13, 19.
[2] Staple Company, Register of Royal Grants, fo. 83.
[3] Enrolled Accounts, E. 356/28.
[4] S.P. 12, Vol. 114, No. 29.
[5] *Ibid.*; cf. Tawney and Power, I, pp. 193 *et seq.*
[6] Staple Company, Register of Royal Grants, fos. 84d–85d.

and commercial difficulties brought to nothing all attempts to settle the staple at a French port.[1]

The failure of the attempt to settle the staple at a French port was not due to any lack of eagerness on the part of the French, but to English objections. Sir Thomas Smith, who had already expressed himself so strongly in favour of a system of home staples,[2] was in charge of the negotiations, and he was here as outspoken as ever. "Quoth I, we wolde not have Calais nor Boloigne if ye wolde appoynt them for us, for then wolde the low contrey have thadvantage, and we wolde have them a while fele the smart of their folie,...Nay, quoth I, we are fooles that do offer yt, to put suche a treasure in the power of eny foreign prince, and suche an occasion to enriche his contrey, The daie hath bene, but it is long ago, when we were wise, and then Sowthampton was the porte and Winchester the Staple, Boston the porte and Lyncoln the staple, London the porte and Westmynster the staple, and other suche, which then were goodly and flourishing townes and cities. Now thei are beggeres and we have enriched Briges and Andwerp and ones Calais. Yt is our marchantes that will have it so, becawse thei wolde bring it into a monopoly, and to a few of their hands. But what remedie, Seing our desteny is to play the fooles still, I must be content to be a doer, but I assuer yow, yt is against my will to enriche either yow, or eny other foreyne prince before our selves. But what remedy, and so we lawghed and left of that matter."[3]

Smith did indeed support his own prejudices by taking the opinion of the merchants, but they were afraid that the creation of a staple in France would result in confiscations of their accumulated property. They did not think the trade to France great enough to warrant a staple, and they were not at all satisfied with the justice which the French officials meted out

---

[1] Jenckes, *Origin, Organisation and Location of the Staple*, p. 50; *Cal. S.P. Foreign*, 1572–1574, p. 22.
[2] *Vide supra*, p. 53.
[3] S.P. 70, Vol. 122, No. 34.

to them.[1] The eagerness of the French, and the English desire
to placate them, led to the inclusion of clauses dealing with
this project in the Treaty of Blois in April 1572, but the
English were apparently only consenting to it in order that
the Netherlanders might "fele the smart of their folie", and
these clauses had never even been pertinently discussed by
the time that the Massacre of St Bartholomew interrupted
friendly relations between the two powers.[2]

There was, in fact, but one port to which the Staplers' wools
could be satisfactorily shipped, and by 1573 they were trading
to Bruges once more.[3] Yet although England's relations with
Spain had improved sufficiently to allow trade to flow again,
times were still very troubled. "By gods ordynance" trade
was disturbed throughout the world, and no merchants
were willing to commit themselves to definite plans for the
future.

Uncertainty and experiment are the chief features of the
time. The Staplers, having re-established themselves at Bruges,
may be seen in the very next year shipping both to Bruges and
to Hamburg;[4] yet, even with two ports of destination, the shipments made have by now shrunk almost out of recognition.
The charter for the trade to Bruges had been based on an
estimated annual export of about 3,000 sacks[5] (a sufficiently
accurate estimate for the years up to 1565) but the total
shipments of 1571 amounted only to 751 sacks, 40½ cloves of
wool and 135,331 fells, or, reduced to terms of wool, to
1,315 sacks and 32½ cloves. The opening up of Bruges again
in 1574 brought London's shipments up to over 1,100 sacks,
but in the next year they had dropped to 700, then to 600, and
so to between 100 and 200 sacks in the period 1580–1585. At
the same time the shipments from the outports of Boston and
Hull ceased to be of any importance in a normal year, and the

[1] S.P. 12, Vol. 92, No. 46.
[2] Conyers Read, *Sir Francis Walsingham*, I, pp. 190–3.
[3] Enrolled Accounts, E. 356/29.   [4] *Ibid.*
[5] *Vide supra*, pp. 30, 35.

trade in fells also passed away save for occasional shipments from Hull.[1] There was some cause for the statement that the whole company now shipped less than three merchants would formerly have shipped.[2]

The trade went from bad to worse. In 1579 the Company tried Middleburgh as a mart, but the total shipments for the year from all ports did not amount to more than 356 sacks, 28 cloves of wool and 56,290 fells, a meagre enough total to divide between Hamburg, Bruges and Middleburgh!

A proposal that they might ship to their accustomed marts was then rejected,[3] and in 1580 they were ordered to ship to Brille.[4] This move was against the wishes of the Staplers themselves and proved very costly to them. They protested against the move, bemoaning their "present decaiede estates", and, in actual practice, they do not seem to have made any shipments to that port, their only shipment of this year being a cargo of 184 sacks, 22 cloves of wool and 594 fells from London to Bruges.[5]

In such times it is not surprising that the Staplers should have turned again to bewailing the licences to ship wools to Italy, and should have sought to uphold their monopoly of the export trade in wool against all rivals.[6]

Even had they been able to monopolise this trade com-

[1] Enrolled Accounts, E. 356/29. This may be attributed directly to the establishment of the "New Draperies" in England. The Bayes-makers later pointed out that each of their cloths contained from twenty to twenty-five pounds of wool "pulled off from the felles" and that "before the Baies were made in England the felles with the woole were sent over beyonde the seas by the marchauntes of the Staple" (E. 122/196/7). Later, some bayes were made partly of fleece wool, cf. the Staplers' complaint that the "pulling of fells" in England had greatly decreased their exports, and that the "strangers clothing in England" absorbed 40,000 tods of wool a year (S.P. 12, Vol. 114, No. 29).

[2] S.P. 12, Vol. 114, No. 29.

[3] *Hist. MSS. Comm.* 1888, Hatfield House, II, p. 296.

[4] *Cal. S.P. Dom.* 1547–1580, p. 694; S.P. 12, Vol. 146, No. 21.

[5] Enrolled Accounts, E. 356/29.

[6] *Cal. S.P. Dom. Add.* 1566–1579, p. 504; S.P. 12, Vol. 146, No. 21; S.P. 12, Vol. 146, No. 77.

pletely, it would have provided but scant scope for them, and at this time they were turning ever more persistently to earning their living by broking wool within the realm rather than by exporting it. This they had themselves sternly forbidden in 1566[1] but, having been allowed to dispose of their wools in this way in 1566,[2] they seem to have tended to devote themselves to this business ever since.

In 1577 the Council instituted an enquiry into the reputed decay of the English clothing industry and the high price of English cloths. The reasoned answer, derived from many reports from the counties, was that the chief cause for these troubles was the engrossing of wools by rich men, so that the clothiers were forced to buy their wools at second or third hand. None were more vehement in denouncing this practice than the Staplers: they suggested an enquiry into the licences issued to wool-buyers and a correlation of the statements made by wool-buyers and wool-sellers, so that discrepancies might be revealed and broggers and other unlicensed buyers sought out and punished.[3] They provided the Council with two lists of "common buyers and broggers of wool",[4] and they suggested a house-to-house search of the white tawyers and the glovers, whom they named as the chief offenders.[5]

Perhaps the Staplers protested too much. Perhaps no protestations were necessary to call attention to their own operations. Certainly all of the counties showed a most ready zeal to place the Staplers in the forefront of the iniquitous broggers. "There be Staplers that have bought wolles here in our markets and have sold it in the same market"[6] alleged the clothiers of Gloucestershire, whilst those of Wiltshire said that "Mr. Offlese [Offley] and others of the merchantes of the Staple douthe engrosse...great quantities and Somes of Wolles into their Handes."[7] The Staplers were accused of buying largely on

---

[1] *Vide infra*, pp. 151, 162.   [2] *Vide supra*, pp. 60–61.
[3] S.P. 12, Vol. 114, No. 30.   [4] *Ibid.* Nos. 31, 39.
[5] *Ibid.* No. 39.   [6] *Ibid.* No. 32.
[7] *Ibid.* No. 27. They allege that the practice has grown up since about 1566.

credit and of selling again at much enhanced prices. It must be admitted that the Council delegated the business of making the enquiry to the Merchant Adventurers and that all the witnesses seem to have held it their first duty to clear their own characters, so that the Staplers could hope for but little sympathy in the course of the enquiry. Still, not a single county whose opinion was asked held the Staplers guiltless, and the men of Suffolk said that they bought such quantities of wool "as is not almoste to be believed" and did not ship abroad above one tod in twenty which they bought.[1]

So great was the outcry, and so much truth was there in the complaints, that the Staple Company held a court at Bruges to remedy the situation.[2] They were forced to agree that many Staplers bought wools to sell within the realm by royal licences, and that others did the same having no such licences. Both practices they esteemed "much Contrary to the Auncient order of the staple, who have always abhorred to be broggers of woll, having binne merchauntes of great antiquity and fame, whereuppon is growne such infamy as though glovers Chapmen husbondmen and divers other persons be great buyers and sellers yet is the fault cheifly imputed to the merchauntes of the Stapell."[3] Their remedy was to denounce and fine the Stapler who engaged in unlicensed brogging, but, by setting up a registry at London at which all such licences must be enrolled, they admitted that many merchants would henceforth normally get their living by licensed broking. By means of this registry they hoped it would be possible to prevent the licensee from buying the full amount of wool specified in his grant from each of several growers. The Company also strictly forbade the practice of buying unshorn wool by the payment of an earnest penny, when it would be re-sold later in the year without its having ever left the grower's hands.

[1] S.P. 12, Vol. 114, No. 33.
[2] For the significance of the fact that the court was held at the mart town *vide infra*, p. 96.
[3] S.P. 12, Vol. 113, No. 19.

Much as the Company might regret that its members should forsake their feat of merchandise to become broggers, it hereby recognised that individual merchants would undoubtedly follow that course in the future.

Nor was wool-broking the only alternative open to the Stapler. Members of the Company had for long been finding their way into the trade of exporting cloth to the Netherlands. In the fifteenth century they had been largely content with their trade in wool, although an occasional member had made shipments of cloth,[1] but as the trade in cloth increased on the one hand, and the control of the Merchant Adventurers over the trade became more efficient and authoritative on the other, strife between the two organisations became almost inevitable. Clashes of jurisdiction on the continent were a frequent cause of trouble,[2] but the vital dispute was as to whether the cloth trade to the Netherlands was a monopoly of the Adventurers or was open also to merchants of the Staple.

About the time of the renewal of the Adventurers' charter in 1505 the quarrel became fiercer, and the two companies took their case to the Star Chamber. The verdict of that court brought no real solution, for it was interpreted by the Adventurers to mean that any Stapler trafficking in cloths must pay his hance and become an Adventurer, but by the Staplers and the Crown the verdict was taken to mean that the Staplers must pay the necessary impositions on the actual shipments of cloth which they made, but could not be compelled to pay a hance to the Adventurers' Company.[3] In practice, "wise merchants became members of both Companies",[4] and it was reckoned that although a hundred Staplers not free of the Adventurers' Company could be proved to have shipped cloths in the reigns of Richard II, Henry VI, Edward IV, and Henry VII,[5] yet

[1] Power and Postan, pp. 15–17.
[2] *Vide* Schanz, II, p. 541.   [3] *Ibid.* II, pp. 547–64.
[4] Carus-Wilson, "The origins and early development of the Merchant Adventurers' organisation in London", *Econ. Hist. Review*, 1933, p. 167.
[5] Schanz, II, p. 588; S.P. 12, Vol. 161, No. 26.

in the reign of Henry VIII seventy-three Staplers, of whom fourteen had been Mayors, had become members of the Adventurers and were "Therwith right well contented unto nowe of late dayes".[1]

The Staplers in these early years of the sixteenth century refused a proposal that the two companies should offer reciprocal hospitality,[2] taking the attitude that "No man may nor ought to occupie nor enjoye their said liberties, except he be free of the saide estaple, but the said estaplers may at all tymes occupie and enjoy the liberties of the said merchauntis adventurers according to the liberties and pryvyleges to the said felaship of merchauntis of the staple graunted and made"—an arrogant attitude, in little accord with the development of trade at that time.

For the time being the quarrel was settled on the basis of the King's interpretation of the Star Chamber decree, and the Staplers were free to ship cloths if they liked. Still their knowledge, interest, and trading connections bound them to wool rather than to cloth, and the two organisations remained separate and hostile, blaming each other for the difficulties which beset them in the troubled conditions of sixteenth-century trade.

On the whole, the Staplers seem to have been regarded as the senior organisation, deserving to be protected against the encroachments of the Adventurers. The removal of the Adventurers' mart to Calais in 1527 also served to emphasise the claims of the Staplers to seniority and greater stability.

But when the Staplers were driven from Calais and forced to seek a mart in the Netherlands the tables were turned. The danger that they might be interfered with by the Adventurers was fully realised. Their charter of 1561 carefully exempted the Staplers from the jurisdiction of the Governor of the Adventurers,[3] and when the Adventurers had their charter renewed in 1564, Cecil sent a copy to "My very loving frend Sir Thomas

---

[1] Schanz, I, p. 346, II, p. 559.   [2] Ibid. II, p. 563.
[3] Vide supra, pp. 29–30.

Offeley, Knight, Maior of the Staple" to explain that no en-
croachment on the liberties of the Staple was intended. Cecil
could see nothing in the charter which could be derogatory
to the Staplers, but he suggested for Offley's consideration an
additional clause which should cover them from any uninten-
tional infringement.[1]

During the period when both companies were suffering
from the "stand of trade" with Flanders, relations between
them seem to have been fairly amicable. For example, when
trade was opened up again in 1573 it was the Adventurers who
suggested to Orange that the two companies, each in its
respective trade, should be given a monopoly of it.[2]

Yet the events of this decade, 1560–1570, were making it
quite clear that the cloth trade was now England's chief trade,
and however much the privileges of the Staplers might be
safeguarded in the Adventurers' charter of 1564, the charter
confirmed the Adventurers' grip on that trade.[3] In consonance
with current notions, the government took steps to regulate
so vital a trade and in 1570 Elizabeth volunteered her help to
the Adventurers. They might hale any interloper before the
Privy Council "to thentent we may take suche order with
hym, as may be to the example of anny attemptinge the like".[4]

Comforted by the royal sympathy, the Adventurers seem to
have tightened their regulations against the Staplers at the
very time that the latter were most tempted to encroach on
their trade. By 1579 the situation was such that in the Adventurers' charter of that year the clause, reserving to the Staplers
the right to share in the monopoly of trade to the Netherlands
by shipping wools and fells to the Adventurers' marts, was
cancelled.[5] The Adventurers were now engaged in an attempt
to force all cloth exports to their marts and were meeting

[1] S.P. 12, Vol. 34, No. 21.
[2] *Hist. MSS. Comm.* Hatfield House, II, p. 49.
[3] *Vide supra*, p. 56.
[4] S.P. 12, Vol. 75, No. 101.
[5] *Hist. MSS. Comm.* Hatfield House, II, p. 296.

opposition in this from the clothiers of the North.[1] Their drive against the Staplers was a part of this general move to establish their complete control of the trade. They said that there were now about fifteen hundred Adventurers and that their trade afforded a living only for five hundred, so that they had been forced to "stint" both their apprentices and their shipments. Consequently not only did they neglect the interests of the Staplers when they sought the renewal of their charter, they also turned to the Council and demanded that the Staplers' trade in cloths should be governed by the Star Chamber verdict of 1504, as interpreted by them. They pointed out that when the Staplers' trade had been great the Adventurers had been excluded from it, and they said that the business of finding and establishing a mart was so difficult and expensive that they were not prepared to undertake it unless they could be assured that the Staplers would be prevented from interloping.[2]

The Staplers, shipping almost no wools abroad by this time,[3] and feeling that there was "no hope of amendment of the Staple beyond the seas", owing to the discontents in the Netherlands and to the high prices of English wools, continued to ship their cloths until the Adventurers effectively stopped them through Cecil's intervention. They got Cecil to issue orders to the customs officials ordering them not to allow the Staplers' cloths to pass the ports. This they achieved in August 1580.

The only response which Cecil made to the protests of the Staplers was to allow them to ship their cloths provided they would enter into bonds with the customers to indemnify the Adventurers should it ultimately be proved that they were infringing the Adventurers' privileges by so shipping. The Staplers, obviously lacking confidence in their own case, and feeling that such bonds might hamper their power to dispose of their capital in the actual business of shipping, refrained from shipping under these conditions but concentrated their efforts

[1] S.P. 12, Vol. 146, No. 74.   [2] *Ibid.* No. 76.
[3] *Vide supra*, pp. 67–8.

on getting Cecil to revoke his injunction. At last, by the consent of both parties, the dispute was referred to Cecil's arbitration and he passed it on to a committee consisting of the Lord Chief Justice, the Lord Chief Baron of the Exchequer and the Master of the Rolls.[1] They heard the parties several times each and finally reported that the Staplers had shipped cloths before the Adventurers were ever incorporated, that cloth had been expressly mentioned as an article of staple merchandise in the preambles of several statutes, and that all the matter alleged by the Adventurers contained nothing which should debar the Staplers from this trade.[2]

Cecil therefore revoked his orders to the customers. But the Adventurers subjected the verdict to some pungent criticism. They showed that the Staplers shipping cloths, to whom the committee referred, were either Staplers who were free of the Adventurers also[3] or else were to be dismissed as "but straglinge interlopers, whereof they are and alwayes hath bene divers", many of whom did not ship to the Netherlands at all, and so were outside of the present discussion.[4] Their arguments weighed with Cecil, and he again placed his ban on the Staplers, leaving the matter for the Privy Council to decide.

The Staplers, dwindled now to two hundred householders and a hundred young men, who had "in a maner no trade of any other comoditie", protested vigorously,[5] but the Council asked Cecil to continue his ban on them until the matter should be finally settled.[6] Cecil therefore merely told the Staplers that if they disliked his system of bonds to the customers they might seek their remedy at Common Law.[7]

This the Staplers, seeing that the trial by the Council could

---

[1] This committee and its verdict is mentioned in Malynes, *Centre of the Circle of Commerce*, pp. 86 *et seq.*

[2] S.P. 12, Vol. 161, Nos. 25–6.

[3] They said that sixty-three out of the seventy-seven who had thus shipped under Henry VIII were members of both companies.

[4] Schanz, II, pp. 588–9. [5] S.P. 12, Vol. 161, No. 26.

[6] *Hist. MSS. Comm.* 1889, Hatfield House, III, p. 4.

[7] S.P. 12, Vol. 161, No. 27.

not well end in their favour, were prepared to do, but the Adventurers, submitting a lengthy list of statutes to prove that woollen cloths were not staple merchandise, argued that any rights which the Staplers might claim "that a mere merchaunt of the staple, as in his owne right, might ship wollen cloth into the lowe countries" would appear in their grants and charters and so would be of record and not cognisable by trial by jury.[1]

There was no trial by Common Law. Instead, the quarrel dragged on before the Privy Council until 1586, and meantime the Staplers were forbidden to ship cloths abroad. In 1586 they joined with the artisans and the clothiers who were complaining that the Adventurers had held up their industry by refusing to buy and "creating a stand" of clothing.[2] The Council investigated the complaints and ordered that unless the Adventurers bought more freely they should have the sole right to buy cloths for export only up to Friday noon in each week: then, on Friday afternoon and on Saturday, the Staplers might buy.[3] Since the root cause of the "stand" was the warlike state of the continent and the machinations of the Hanse League, this measure brought little relief to the clothiers. In the next year any merchant, native or alien, was allowed to buy and ship cloths, subject to certain conditions,[4] but even this brought no relief to the clothing industry, or to the Staplers, whom it merely placed on a par with other merchants.

By 1586, therefore, the struggle of the Staplers to get a footing in the cloth export trade had merely resulted in their becoming a bludgeon wherewith the government might beat

[1] S.P. 12, Vol. 75, No. 102. This document is undated and is filed under the year 1570, but it clearly deals with this affair of 1580–1586.

[2] The privileges of the Hansards had not yet been finally abrogated in England, but these complaints make it clear that the opposition which they were meeting from the Adventurers (*vide* Lipson, *Economic History*, II, pp. 204–6; Unwin, *Studies*, p. 203) made them of little account in the eyes of the English clothiers as an alternative to the Adventurers.

[3] Tawney and Power, I, p. 216.

[4] Unwin, *Studies*, pp. 201–4.

the Adventurers into the proper performance of an appointed part in the national economy. They had failed to vindicate their claims.

As an offset to this failure, they could get but small consolation from the fact that in 1584 they had been granted a renewal of their monopoly to export wools for another seven years.[1] As a means of livelihood for a wealthy corporation wool export was valueless; the shipments were minute, and the Company could have no hope of prosperity in the future. This grant must be taken as a tribute to the history and traditions of the Company rather than as a means whereby members might win future wealth. True, they still made occasional shipments beyond seas. Sometimes they shipped to Bruges, sometimes to Hamburg. After 1584 they were allowed to ship "at their pleasure into any place or places beinge in amytie" with England,[2] and there are records of their subsequent shipments to Rouen, Amsterdam, Leghorn, Middleburgh and Venice.[3]

Such diversity really took away all the virtue of a "stapled" trade and turned it into the "straggling" trade which was so contrary to the principles underlying the regulated companies. The Staple Company as an exporting company was henceforth an indefensible anachronism, in theory as in fact. That it survived must be attributed to the fact that, although it had failed to open up for its members one alternative livelihood, the trade in cloth, yet it succeeded in making good the claim that its members should be tolerated as wool-brokers.

Since the Company had set up its registry for licences to broke wools in 1577[4] this business had been a regular and closely supervised part of its affairs. In 1580 the Company had to answer Mr Simon Bowier, a would-be licensee, but one

[1] Staple Company Register of Royal Grants, fo. 86d.
[2] *Ibid.* fo. 85d. A marginal note emphasises the "Clawse of libertye to sell in England", but this clause refers only to the refuse wools; cf. Acts of the Privy Council, 1615–1617, p. 179.
[3] E. 122/88/35, E. 122/90/50–51, E. 122/170/7, E. 122/90/48, E.356/29.
[4] *Vide supra*, p. 70.

who was "nother a Stapler, Clothier or hathe spinners under him, nor knowledge in wolles". He alleged that the Staplers bought fleece wool of good quality and mixed it with the coarse refuse wools which they were allowed to sell in England; they then sold the mixture in England, under cover of the law but contrary to its spirit. The Staplers were probably right in saying that this was an absurd charge: they were certainly right in saying that the practice would be uneconomic,[1] for they knew better ways of circumventing the statutes than by spoiling their own wools.

For the rest of Elizabeth's reign the members of the Company appear to have broked wools within the realm only (legally) by royal licence. But such licences were easily obtained and the statutes against brokers were constantly dispensed with, although the Company as a whole received no general permit to engage in this trade. The increased interest of the Company is none the less apparent: the internal wool trade was becoming its chief business, and it tried to ensure that that business should be conducted according to rules and within certain places only.[2]

No real change in this situation is noticeable until the government of James tried to interfere in the wool business in order to promote the finishing processes for cloth in England.[3] The ultimate outcome of this interference was the suspension of the liberties of the Merchant Adventurers Company and the grant of the export trade in cloths to Alderman Cockayne and his Company, who promised to export dyed and finished cloths.

[1] S.P. 12, Vol. 146, No. 77.

[2] *E.g.* in 1588 they petitioned against the citizens of Lincoln for selling wools outside of the liberties of the city (Lansdowne MSS. 58, No. 74) and in 1590 they asked for power to enforce the statutes against brogging (*ibid.* 66, No. 11).

[3] Efforts to encourage dyeing and finishing had been made previously, and the Adventurers had to export one finished cloth for every nine "raw". For the whole history of this project see Astrid Friis, *Alderman Cockayne and the Cloth Trade.*

The project was further helped by a veto on the export of wools, in 1614,[1] so that English weavers might have a monopoly of the supply. From this embargo dates a change in the official status of the Staple Company. Hitherto Staplers had undoubtedly tended to interest themselves in the business of broking wools within England, but the official business of the Company was to regulate the export trade to the continent. From 1614 to 1825 much wool was smuggled out of England, but throughout the period the export trade was officially forbidden and suppressed.[2] Three years were to elapse before the Company was officially given new functions in conformity with the changed situation, but with the embargo of 1614 ends its history as a regulated company for foreign trade.

The Staplers protested at having their ancient livelihood thus taken clean away from them,[3] but in actual fact the prohibition affected their business at that time but little. A more shrewd thrust at their real trade was made when the clothiers complained that the Staplers, as brokers, bought the wools in such quantities that it was becoming impossible for the small clothier to get supplies except through a Stapler.[4] To this the Staplers returned an answer pointing out their value as chapmen, to carry the wools to the clothiers, and asked that they might be still allowed to serve as brokers.[5] By 1616 so greatly was the Company committed to broking wools within the land, despite its own ordinances[6] and the complaints of others, that it was forced to plead for special treatment in the

---

[1] *Cal. S.P. Dom.* 1611–1618, p. 253.

[2] *Vide infra*, p. 85, n. 5, and Lipson, III, pp. 23 *et seq.* The change in the official duties of the Company was *not* marked by a change in name, for they had been the "Merchants of the Staple of England" since their charter of 1561 (*vide supra*, p. 6, n. 3). The fear of a smuggled trade to France was one of the reasons why the Irish wool trade was concentrated in the Bristol Channel ports instead of at Exeter in the seventeenth century (Hoskins, *Industry, Trade and People in Exeter*, 1688–1800, p. 30).

[3] *Journal of the House of Commons*, I, p. 505.

[4] *Cal. S.P. Dom.* 1611–1618, p. 271.

[5] *Ibid.* pp. 271, 339.　　　　　　[6] *Supra*, p. 69.

enforcement of the statutes against broking, because members were involved "to an exceedinge greate value" and their condemnation would effect "their utter undoenge and overthrowe".[1]

The failure of Cockayne's project brought the whole of the wool trade under the scrutiny of a committee of the Council, and it was in the efforts of the government to reconstruct the cloth trade which it had so seriously interrupted that the Staple Company succeeded in getting a new charter and a new lease of life. First came an experimental year in which the Council recommended that, since the restrictions on brokers were working to the disadvantage of the wool-growers and to the advantage of the clothiers (who had had a practical monopoly since export had been forbidden), it should be ordained that no Staplers or other brokers should buy between shearing-time and Michaelmas. During that period the clothiers were to be the sole buyers, but when Michaelmas was past the Staplers and other brokers, as licensed by the Council, were to buy freely and to take their wools into the industrial areas which needed them.[2]

After this experiment came the new charter to the Staple Company, in March 1617. The government, still trying to remedy the chaos which Cockayne had caused, and to give the English weavers the first choice of the wools, completely abandoned the idea of a foreign staple in any form. There was nothing radically new in this; the embargo of 1614 had killed a system which had long been in a decline and from which the charter of 1584[3] had taken all chance of recovery. But innovation was apparent when, for the principle of a foreign staple, there was substituted a series of home staples. Only at certain towns was wool to be sold, export was to be forbidden, and the Staplers alone were to distribute wools within the realm.[4]

---

[1] *Acts of the Privy Council*, 1615–1616, pp. 512–13.
[2] British Museum Add. MSS. 34,324, fos. 10–13.   [3] *Supra*, p. 77.
[4] Staple Company, Register of Royal Grants, fo. 87d; *Cal. S.P. Dom.* 1611–1618, p. 452. Twenty-three such staples were set up, in which the

By this charter of March 1617, therefore, the Staplers were "made broggers for order's sake", and the membership of the Company for the next few years reflected this change in status. Northumberland, Cumberland and Westmorland complained of the working of the new system; Kendal was the only staple for the whole of these three counties and it could not absorb any large proportion of their wools. Neither were the wools of this district costly enough to make it worth while for the local dealers to pay the Company's hance and to become Staplers, so that they were now prevented from continuing their wool-dealing. In answer to the complaints the Staple Company offered to buy all the wools of these counties and, also, to admit to membership of the Company any men of those parts who wished to join. Despite the pleading of the Northerners that it did not pay them to join, it was shewn in 1619 that by that time forty men from Yorkshire had become Staplers.[1]

With the change of occupation and the admission of the wool men from the North and of some clothiers,[2] there disappeared the domination within the Company of the wealthy London exporter. In other ways London increased its hold on the Company.[3] The minutes book of the Company reveals that this new charter was obtained (as so many Stuart patents were) by a group of "undertakers" who could buy influence at court. The chief of these was Lord Fenton, who had no connection with the wool trade. But the others of the "undertakers" were Staplers and both they and Lord Fenton proposed to recover their outlay in obtaining the charter from the entrance fees of those who subsequently joined the Company.[4] For

Staplers were to exercise all their former liberties, rights and dues (*Acts of the Privy Council,* 1616–1617, pp. 178–80). The charter is given on 24 March 1616–1617, *i.e.* 1617, New Style.

[1] Brit. Mus. Add. MSS. 34,324, fos. 8, 14–21; Minutes of Council Meetings by J. Caesar.   [2] *Vide infra,* p. 82, n. 5.

[3] For a fuller examination of this point *vide infra,* pp. 95 *et seq.*

[4] Minutes Book (Brit. Mus. Add. MSS. 43,849) 19 Jan. 1619, *et passim.* The patent for the erection of staples in Ireland was granted on similar terms, *ibid.* 22 March 1619.

RSC   6

this inner ring of "undertakers" Leadenhall in London was
the centre of the Company's life. Round that centre every-
thing turned, so that the Staplers soon became far more of a
London Company than it had ever been in the days when its
seat was at some foreign port.

The Company is still not entirely reconciled to its new func-
tion, it asserts its right to export lead[1] and other staple wares.
Still in the future lies another unsuccessful attempt to assert
the Staplers' right to export cloths.[2] But from 1617 onwards
it is not really concerned with export: the Company has
turned reluctantly from its former career and is launching on
a new stream, on which it has already stolen some promising
voyages.

Most of the Staplers' work is now done in overseeing the
wool-winders[3] and in sorting and moving wools about the
country. In this they are not without faults, and they do not
escape without blame. In 1619 they made the city of Lincoln
at last conform to their standards in the weighing of wool,[4]
but in 1621 they were the subject of a complaint that they had
conspired with the clothiers to cause a drop in the prices which
the growers could get for their wools and they had to explain
to the House of Commons "why some of the Clothiers were
admitted to the freedome of the Company".[5] Not only did
they buy and transport English wools, they dominated the
increasing trade in bringing Irish wools to the English clothiers,
and although the Irish growers alleged in 1619 that the
Staplers' management of this business was causing men to cease
to nourish sheep and was driving "the new undertakers" back

[1] Staple Company Minutes Book, 25 Feb. 1619.
[2] They tried this in 1621–1622, and again in 1634. *Cal. S.P. Dom.* 1619–
1623, p. 250; *Lords' Journal*, III, pp. 174, 175, 184; Brit. Mus. Add.
MSS. 34,324, fos. 203, 209; *Cal. S.P. Dom.* 1634–1635, pp. 218, 257;
cf. also Staple Company Minutes Book, 1620–1621, *passim*.
[3] *I.e.* packers; *vide infra*, p. 101.
[4] *Vide supra*, p. 78, n. 2; *Cal. S.P. Dom.* 1619–1623, pp. 19, 35.
[5] Staple Company Minutes Book, 21 Feb. 1620 (1621).

into England with their sheep again,[1] yet this was recognised as a part of the services which the Staplers should perform. In 1622–3 a petition was presented to the Council asking that the Staplers should be regulated in their wool-broking so that they should not compete with the clothiers for supplies, and that they should be given the task of importing the wools of Scotland, Ireland, the Isle of Man and the Isle of Wight.[2]

To allow the Company to enjoy its new charter the statutes against wool-broking had to be repealed. This was not done until 1624,[3] but the royal charter and proclamation seem to have protected the Staplers in their broking during the interim.

The new business in which the Company was engaged also made necessary a revision of the ordinances drawn up for the trade to Bruges. Many of those rules, dealing with shippings, responsibility for customs, or residence in a foreign town, now had no meaning, and the part played by the mart town and its assemblies also had now to be cancelled from the rules of the Company. Consequently, in 1619 the Company met in London to draw up new ordinances.[4] Although from 1619 onwards the minutes books of the Company have survived,[5] yet there is no extant copy of these new ordinances and it is impossible to say precisely where they differed from those now printed. Still, order was taken for the new trade, the restrictions against brokers[6] were presumably modified, and the Staple Company entered on a new lease of life, of which the new minutes book is symbolic.

During the third and fourth decades of the seventeenth century the Company applied itself closely to this newly won trade. A delegation was told off to "followe the busines for

[1] Brit. Mus. Add. MSS. 34,324, fo. 23; cf. *Acts of the Privy Council, 1619–1621*, p. 157.
[2] Brit. Mus. Add. MSS. 34,324, fo. 25.
[3] *Statutes of the Realm*, IV, ii, p. 1239.
[4] Staple Company Minutes Book, minute of 1 March 1619.
[5] Brit. Mus. Add. MSS. 43,849–43,852.
[6] *Vide infra*, pp. 151, 162.

the Company and attend the lords from tyme to tyme" in order to defeat the wool-growers' petition for "a tolleracion for every man to buy and sell Woolls, which wilbe the subvercion of the Company" in 1619. Similar zeal was shown in attempts to get better privileges from Parliament and in emphasising the value of the functions now performed by the Staplers.[1] They protested that no members were engaged in exporting wools and, insisting on the payment of their hances, excluding "persons of very mean estate" and inveighing against the broggers, whilst giving membership to certain clothiers, they were building up a close control of wool-broking during these years.[2]

By the middle of the century the Staplers, despite opposition, had built up a tradition for the trade within the framework of the staples ordained in 1617. To the wealthy clothiers, who could travel far afield for their wools and who regarded the Staplers' grading and sorting as muddling and needless, they were mere engrossers. With the lesser clothiers they were unpopular because they took away local supplies to distant markets and could afford to outbid them. They were (probably justly) accused, in 1650, of joining within their Company into a "Joint Stock" to purchase large quantities of wool.[3] They certainly dominated the wool supply, and they had by now half a century of skill in, and attachment to, broking behind them. There was more than sentimental reluctance to change traditions and habits of trade in the insistence of the Staplers of the late seventeenth century on their business as brokers. They were by then thoroughly involved in and committed to this trade, and they even joined with the fellmongers

[1] Minutes of 17 October 1620, 13 Feb. 1620, 21 Feb. 1620, etc.

[2] Minutes of 14 May 1628, 10 May 1626, 30 June 1630, etc. Cf. the complaint to the Privy Council that the Staplers, "for their own private lucre, and to ingrosse all into their own hands, have taken into their Companies many of the best broggers of wool that were wont to be the best chapmen to the wool-growers, and that they either forced the meaner broggers to become Staplers or else suppressed them" (*Acts of Privy Council*, 1619–1621, p. 207).

[3] *Cal. S.P. Dom.* 1650, pp. 406 *et seq.*

to advise the Council that the veto on the export of wools and fells should be continued.[1] By 1651 they were almost prepared to aver that the business of supplying the clothier with his wools had always been a part of their trade. In that year a committee of the Common Council of London had reported that, the export of wools being forbidden, the Staple Company had no legal existence. This report quite ignored the charter of 1617, and the Staplers replied that they had had "a constant allowed trade to buy and sell wools in England and Wales, though not to ship them" and that from the first the Staplers had always been "both merchants and artists, as merchants to buy and transport and as artists to sever and sort wools".[2] They regarded James' charter of 1617, by now, as being simply confirmatory of their ancient privileges, but they none the less got another confirmation from Charles II.[3]

The situation is already substantially that which we meet in the nineteenth century. Then we may see a few Staplers shipping wools abroad,[4] but the majority of the Company is far more intent on supplying the home market and even petitions the government in 1817 and again in 1824 to continue to forbid the export of wools.[5]

[1] *Cal. S.P. Dom.* 1651, p. 248.
[2] *Ibid.* p. 270 and 1651–1652, p. 472.
[3] Brit. Mus. Add. Charter No. 70,834.
[4] Staple Company, Minute of 17 April 1823.
[5] *Ibid.* Minutes of 23 April 1817 and of 19 March 1824. After the veto on wool export of 1614, a series of proclamations continued the veto (*vide* Lipson, *Economic History of England*, III, p. 23). The Statute of 1662 (Stat. 14, Car. II, c. 18) again continued it and, re-inforced by subsequent statutes (*e.g.* 1 Wm & Mary, c. 32, and 4 Wm & Mary, c. 24), remained unrepealed until the nineteenth century. On this subject see Adam Smith, Book IV, chapter 8, and the opinion of the Lord Chief Justice of the King's Bench, delivered to the House of Lords in 1800 (quoted in full in John Maitland's *Observations on the impolicy of permitting the export of British wool*, 1818). The restrictions were removed in 1825 and some of the surviving Staplers became exporters again. For the extent to which the veto had proved effective, and for the part played by the Staplers in the life of eighteenth-century England, *vide* Heaton, *Yorkshire woollen and worsted industries*, pp. 323–32.

The charter of 1617 had merely made more definite and legal tendencies which were already present in the staple trade. It cannot be taken as marking a period in itself, but it does, at least, acknowledge the results of the development of the English clothing industry. Since the end of the fourteenth century the Staplers had fought the clothiers, now they serve them: they are, indeed, accused of entering into conspiracies with them. Such export as takes place after 1614 is haphazard, and dictated by the knowledge or enterprise of individual merchants: there is no longer the least desire for the erection of a staple on the continent.

Probably this was the inevitable end to the Staplers' efforts to maintain their export trade. Their market was in any case disappearing from them and their supplies were being encroached on, and any chance of survival which their trade might have had was crushed in December 1568 and January 1569. With the interruption of their trade to Bruges they lost all hope of ever recovering their position. Marts were always hard to find, but Bruges had answered the necessary conditions. When that trade was overthrown the Staplers never again found a satisfactory home, and the whole train of their later history follows almost inevitably from their emigration from Bruges. The ordinances drawn up for the trade to Bruges therefore represent the last effort which the Company made to preserve the principles of a stapled trade. The next ordinance of the Company which has come to light was that made to regulate the trade of its members as brokers.[1] The Company had decided, as the government was shortly to decide, that never more was the export of wool to figure largely in England's trade.

[1] *Vide supra*, p. 70.

Chapter VI

THE ORDINANCES AND THE TRADE

The technique of wool-stapling in the days of a continental staple mart has already been closely examined and most ably set out. The correspondence of one great family of staplers, the Celys, has provided the practical detail and the personal interest of which the editor of the Cely Papers[1] and Professor Power have made full use in welding a mass of miscellaneous official references and documents into a comprehensive account of the trade.[2] To the work already done on this subject these ordinances can add but little: indeed they lack many items of interest which are available elsewhere. Yet these ordinances have the advantage of being official and authoritative, of revealing the skeleton of which the descriptions of the staple trade are the embodiment.

For the ordinances of 1565 are by no means simply innovations. Throughout the various items is manifest a desire to reaffirm the ordinances of the past rather than to create new ones, and the ordinances are really more valuable for the light which they shed on the contents of the books which were lost in the fall of Calais than for the new ideas which they enforced for the last fifty years of the foreign staple.

The first point which strikes the reader of the ordinances of 1565 is the time which was taken in the compilation of them. The original meeting of the committee appointed *ad hoc* was called at Bruges on the 1st of May 1565, with the object of bringing such ordinances as then governed the trade into conformity with the existing situation.[3] The bulk of the ordinances appears

[1] *The Cely Papers*, ed. H. E. Malden, Camden Society, 3rd Series, Vol. I. Cf. also *Stonor Papers*, Camden Society, 3rd Series, vol. xxx.

[2] "The wool trade in the fifteenth century" in *English trade in the fifteenth century*, ed. Power and Postan, and "Thomas Betson" in *Medieval People*.   [3] *Vide infra*, pp. 104 and 105.

to have been passed on that day, and that fact need not surprise us, for they were already well known to, and approved by, the committee. They were the products of a former meeting at Bruges, which had established the trade to Bruges on the basis of the regulations which had been in force at Calais—a system which now needed adjustment. Such clauses mostly dealt with the organisation and officials of the Company.[1]

But many clauses which dealt with the actual trade were not passed at this first meeting, but at subsequent sessions which were held during the next six weeks. Thus, for example, the ordinance of hances and that setting up the "Stint" for wools was not passed until the 17th of May,[2] the rule for remedying the complaints of purchasers[3] two days later, that against "broggers" also not until the 19th, others on the 22nd, the 24th and the 26th,[4] and that ordering a general search and the control of the wool-winders not until the 5th of June.[5] Possibly these ordinances decreed on the 5th of June were passed by a full assembly of merchants who had journeyed over in advance of their wools, for they were enacted, not by the committee, but by "alle we the bretheren of this our wourshipfulle companie being assembled in ample nombre",[6] and they use a more pompous phraseology than appears in most of the ordinances. The shippings of this year took place in January and February, and then in August, so the long residence of the committee at Bruges probably cannot be accounted for by the fact that they had their own business to attend to. The only adequate explanation is that they were making serious and lengthy attempts to modify in the light of present experience practices which had been successful in the past.

Such an explanation would be amply borne out by the wording of the ordinances. Evidence of retrospection is everywhere. The important ordinance of "hances" begins "The wayes and meanes to attain to the fredome of this estaple are

---

[1] *Infra*, pp. 105 *et seq.*   [2] Pp. 140, 149.   [3] P. 158.
[4] Pp. 163, 167, 170, 193.   [5] P. 193.   [6] P. 196.

and tyme oute mynde of man have ben divers".[1] The equally fundamental ordinance for the general shipping[2] is also obviously merely a summary of the usual procedure: the keeping of attornies appointed to buy and sell in the Staple is now regulated, but is an age-old custom,[3] the "*olde order* for dayes of shewes and tymes and places of sales" is specified and enforced[4]—and so throughout the book. Many of these ordinances are nothing but records of the rules of other times, rules which we can only see elsewhere in practice, not in principle.

Occasionally these former ordinances do not date from the Calais period, but have been made during the period of residence at Bruges.[5] Far more often they transcend the Bruges period and go straight back to Calais. Such—an example of many—is the "Ordenaunce for woulles and felles lost by casualtie of seas", which announces that "Where there was an ordenaunce in the staple at Calles concerninge woulles and woullfelles lost by casualtie of seas the same ordenaunce now being lacking is very necessarie to be revived".[6]

The backward glance so cast reveals above all else the validity of the Staple Company as a "Regulated Company". The publication of the codified rules of later regulated companies has obscured the fact that the Staple Company was the first regulated company: these ordinances show that, at a period when the craft gild was the typical organisation for English industrial life, the Staple Company at Calais bore the marks of the typical regulated company of the sixteenth century. Material already available has shown the outlines (and many of the details) of the system of regulation which the Company enforced during its life at Calais, but in the absence of any code of rules such information has been too haphazard to allow the Staple Company to be taken as the great example of a regulated

---

[1] *Infra*, p. 132.   [2] Pp. 142 *et seq.*
[3] Pp. 118, 152.   [4] P. 155.
[5] *E.g.* p. 140.   [6] Pp. 165, 169.

company.[1] From such information it has not been easy to say precisely and authoritatively in what details and with what ideals the Company regulated the trade, and to what extent it left the individual enterprise of its members free scope. These ordinances show that in every respect the Staple Company was the archetype of regulated company and that the breadth of scope, combined with the minuteness of detail, of the regulations left the individual constantly restricted in the interests of the many. In 1565 there was not a process in the whole trade which was not subject to regulation by the Company.

The amount of wools and fells which each merchant might buy for export was strictly stinted,[2] no purchasing for sales within the realm was allowed,[3] the wools could only be shipped from certain ports,[4] they had to be viewed by the "Viewer" before they were shipped,[5] and they had to be shipped in vessels authorised and supervised by the officials of the Company.[6] They could only ship at the times appointed,[7] and to the town appointed. On the arrival of the wool fleet at the foreign port the wools and fells had to be inspected and passed by the officials,[8] and had to be entered up by the "Clerk of the collectrie". This official saw that the customs were paid and also kept a register of the wools which came to the Staple in any one year and of the rates at which they were sold. The wools then had to be inspected from time to time by the viewers and searchers,[9] until they were sold. They could only be exposed for sale on the appointed "shewe" days,[10] and could only be

---

[1] Heckscher, for example (*Mercantilism*, I, pp. 379 *et seq.*) has to use the ordinances of the Merchant Adventurers (codified 1608) and of the Levant Company (codified 1617) as the bases of his exposition of the essence of a regulated company. The Staple ordinances admirably illustrate the heritage of the regulated company from the gild; e.g. *infra*, pp. 147, 171 *et seq.*

[2] *Infra*, p. 149.   [3] Pp. 151, 162.   [4] P. 142.
[5] Pp. 143–4.   [6] Pp. 144–5.   [7] P. 143.
[8] Pp. 120, 126; cf. Power and Postan, pp. 59–60.
[9] Pp. 121, 130–1. For the payments of customs, cf. p. 174.
[10] Pp. 119, 124–5, 155.

sold through the offices of the broker of the company, who conducted the merchant stranger to the wools, recorded the bargain made, saw that the whole of the Company's officialdom had played its part in the sale,[1] that the wools were properly weighed by the Company's weigher and that the Treasurer of the Staple had issued an official receipt for the money paid by the purchaser, and kept a detailed account of all bargains in case disputes should arise.[2]

Even within these limits, the Stapler could not sell his wares as he chose. All sales had to be according to the system of "Free out". This system was no novelty in 1565. It had been complained of by the Staplers' customers in the fifteenth century;[3] it was again the subject of complaint at the Diet of Bruges, when the Staplers replied that it was in accordance with their former customs at Calais. Here, in re-enacting the "manner and fourme used at Callais", the ordinances allow us to see to what extent this system of selling "Free out" penetrated into every detail of the trade.

The wools of each year were to be a "rate" of their own, and those unsold in any one year were to have preference in the next year, when the merchant buyers were only allowed to buy new wools if they bought one sarplar of old with each two sarplars of new. This entailed an elaborate system of inspection of the wools in the mart awaiting sale, and the creation of the offices of viewers and searchers, who had to inspect the wools and to report thereon to the heads of the Staple. The "praiser of old fells" also played his part in this system, and the Clerk of the Collectrie kept the register of old wools and fells and finally enforced the system. A Stapler having new wools for sale, but lacking the old wools or fells necessary to utter them, was to buy the old at prices fixed by the Company, and the "transport" was to be duly recorded and to take place according to the rules of the Company. Likewise, there were strict rules against the purchase of new wools for the July

[1] *Infra*, p. 184.   [2] P. 125.
[3] *Cely Papers*, p. xxiv, and Power and Postan, p. 62.

shipment, and the attempt to prevent these new wools from being shipped and spoiling the market for the old entailed a system of inspection in the English ports.[1]

These are heavy interferences with the freedom of the individual merchant. Much of the interference is due to the old duty of the Company to collect the customs;[2] a great deal is simply the expression of the ideals of a regulated company. Both kinds of restriction carry us back to the Staple at Calais.

But the whole of the ordinances was not merely a recapitulation of former practices. Some items were expressly designed to overcome the difficulties which the trade was actually facing in 1565.

Chief of these ordinances which cast light on the trade in 1565 was that ordaining an "Extent" or "Stint" of shipping. From the wording of this ordinance it would appear to be an innovation, introduced because of the "Inordenate desire of certaine covetous personnes whereof summe have bought suche greate quantite of woulles and woulfelles as the young men could have none or very litle and summe other have charged themselves above their abilite withe excedinge nombre of woulles and woulfelles shipped to this estaple running thereby into the daunger of theire creditours and not able to satisfie them according to the faith of a good merchaunt but have ben forced of necessite to selle theire goodes under their value to theire utter undoenge and against the commune welthe of this estaple."[3] But even if the remedy was new in the Staplers' ordinances, the abuse was old, and the stint itself may possibly have been in force before this year. In 1560 the Staplers complained of their rivals, the Merchant Adventurers, that any Adventurer might ship as much as £5,000 worth of cloth in a year, whilst the Staplers might ship only thirty-five sarplers of wool.[4] It is improbable that the Staplers would have made such a statement in 1560 unless there were something to support

[1] For the system of selling "Free out" see *supra*, p. 61, and *infra*, pp. 120, 123, 129–30, 143, 148, 150, 153, 156, 164–9, 193.
[2] *Infra*, pp. 121, 174.   [3] Pp. 149 *et seq.*
[4] State Papers, 12, Vol. 15, No. 54.

it, and the amount of wool to which they then claimed they were restricted corresponds to the amount to which a householder was now limited. Moreover, the licence to ship granted at this time hints at some such arrangement, for the exports are "to be proporcioned and devided as to them and everie of them shall seme moste convenient".[1] Still, if this ordinance was already in existence in 1560 it must have been but little enforced, else there would have been no need for the preamble which was now thought necessary, nor, probably, would the penalties for infringement have been so heavy.

Along with this ordinance must be taken that forbidding Staplers to engage in brogging wools,[2] the "Stint" of apprentices,[3] and the rules for the employment of attornies or factors.[4] In all of these matters the Company was trying to prevent the wealthy merchant from dominating the trade to the exclusion of his less wealthy brother. The ordinance for attornies did indeed allow the development within the Company of a relationship of employer and employee, and clearly there were merchants who did not ship for themselves, but the system was none the less closely overlooked and measures were taken to ensure that no one became attorney to too many merchants, and that no merchant employed too many factors.

This care for the generality as against the few over-wealthy members did not imply an effective bias towards freedom in the Staple Company. There is a very great deal here which is sheer oligarchy and monopoly. As against the merchant buyers the Staplers were naturally bound into a solidarity by the strictest rules. Anyone divulging to a stranger the amount of old fells or wools remaining unsold (a Stapler had the right to know this) was liable to lose his membership,[5] and any member who married a foreign woman had to remove her from the Staple within a certain time, expressly from fear that information might leak out.[6] When a stranger refused to pay

---

[1] Staple Company, Register of Royal Grants, fo. 79 d.
[2] *Infra*, pp. 151, 162 et seq.; *supra*, pp. 69 et seq., 77 et seq.
[3] *Infra*, pp. 134, 138.   [4] Pp. 152 et seq.
[5] P. 167.   [6] Pp. 192–3.

the agreed price for his wools, alleging that they were defective, the Company sued him at the common cost.[1]

Further, within the Company itself there is clearly a strong feeling of privilege and oligarchy. From the ordinance for hances it is obvious that the freeman's son acquired membership of the Company much more easily than the apprentice,[2] whilst the redemptioner had to pay fifty ounces of gold if he were a "mere merchant" and a hundred ounces if he were an artificer or brogger. Moreover, during the stress which followed the loss of Calais the Staplers had taken the route so attractive to a declining company and had restricted their membership, refusing to admit any more redemptioners for the next seven years. This ordinance was now confirmed and extended for another seven years, until 1575.[3]

This exclusiveness of the Company may perhaps be excused to some extent if we bear in mind the circumstances of the time. Simple exclusiveness there undoubtedly was, but in addition the Staplers were trying to prevent grown men, who had already begun to make their money in other trades, from interloping in the staple trade. The wool-grower was excluded by the rule that no man over seventeen years old who owned land of the annual value of forty pounds should be admitted.[4] Similarly, an apprentice was not to be considered as an apprentice to the Staple unless the words "as merchant of the

[1] *Infra*, p. 159.

[2] Freedom by patrimony cost but forty pence, by apprenticeship fifty shillings—unless a double hance were incurred.

[3] Cf. the similar tendency in the Merchant Adventurers' Company (Heckscher, *Mercantilism*, I, p. 387). For the Staplers *vide infra*, pp. 139–40. The recent redemptioners were also excluded from the benefit of old wools (pp. 165–6), which robbed them of one of the chief safeguards which the ordinary merchant enjoyed, since he could be certain that his wools would be sold at a fair price. The dues payable to the Company on goods shipped were over twice as heavy for recent redemptioners as for older members: in this matter the Company showed a progressive exclusiveness in the years 1550–1565. Moreover the redemptioners' dues had to be paid on the arrival of their goods, not after their sale (pp. 182–3).

[4] *Infra*, pp. 134, 141.

Staple" were included in the indenture;[1] this was presumably
to deal with the situation which arose when Staplers conducted
many trades, and the principle here involved is further revealed
by the rule that no person free of both the Staplers and the
Merchant Adventurers should take an apprentice to both companies.[2] It is quite obvious from the wording of this ordinance
that the practice had become fairly common (we know from
other sources that many men were members of both companies),
and that the Staplers were anxious to preserve their identity
as a Company. The same feeling may be seen in the rule that
a freeman's son may not ship wools even as an attorney as
long as he is apprenticed to another trade.[3]

If these motives increased the natural tendency towards
oligarchy in 1565, it is noteworthy that as yet London does
not dominate the Company in theory, however much the
London merchants may in practice outweigh those of the outports. In the committee which drew up these ordinances the
"country" was represented by four members as against five
drawn from London.[4] But examination of the details of the
customs accounts reveals that although Edmond Hall, one of
the constables, was a shipper from Boston,[5] and William Darby

[1] *Infra*, p. 135.
[2] P. 192. For the general relations of the Staplers and the Adventurers *vide supra*, pp. 71 *et seq.* Cf. the will of Sir John Skevington,
merchant of the Staple, in 1524, in which he willed that his apprentice
Christofer Vavasour should be made free of the Adventurers at his charge
(*Letters and Papers, Henry VIII*, IV, i, p. 411). When the Staplers had
settled down as wool brokers (*supra*, pp. 77 *et seq.*) they became largely
indifferent on this question. In 1623 the Committee of the Council for
Trade asked which members of the Staple Company wished to be members
of the Merchant Adventurers also, and the Adventurers offered to admit
them at £5 each. The Staplers, unwilling to commit their Company in
writing, and unable to discover the size of the Adventurers' hances, left
the matter entirely to individual members to decide (Minutes Book,
8 Feb. 1622, and 14 March 1622). For a like offer from the Adventurers,
cf. *Acts of Privy Council, 1623–1625*, p. 260.
[3] *Infra*, p. 154.   [4] P. 105.
[5] E. 122/14/10, E. 122/170/4, E. 122/171/3, etc.

and Thomas Dalton shipped from Boston and Hull respectively, yet the fourth member for the "country", Mathew Cradock, was a London merchant and did none of his business from the outports.[1]

This is typical of the Staple Company at this period. The idea of a balance between London and the outports is there as a heritage from former times, but in actual practice the predominance of London is almost irresistible. Thus, for example, the emphasis is always on the staple port rather than on any one English town: in the staple port the meetings of the Company are to be held,[2] there the accounts of retiring officials are to be tendered, there the elections are to be held, and there alone can the oath of the apprentice be taken.[3] Similarly, the opinion of the shippers from all ports is considered as more important than the feeling of London. The assistants and constables are to be appointed "Indifferently from all the portes accustomed to ship to this estaple". All the ports are to signify their assent to the marriage of an apprentice, their assent is necessary for the alteration of the "rates" of wools, and any change in the ordinances can only be brought about by the Mayor and two of the three ports (London, Boston and Hull) signifying their assent under their staple seal.[4]

In similar vein, the ordinance for joint shipping was expressly designed in order that the provincial shipper should have the same advantages as the Londoner,[5] and London was expressly disavowed as the seat of the government of the Company.[6]

Despite all this, even in these ordinances London cannot be suppressed. It is the London fleet which marks the periods in the life of the Staple.[7] The constituent committee lapses unthinkingly into speaking only of the apprentice from London,

---

[1] E. 122/88/4, E. 122/171/3, E. 122/198/1.

[2] *Infra*, pp. 106, 108, etc.

[3] Pp. 106, 110, 115, 139, 188.

[4] Pp. 112, 134, 168, 197, 200. For this use of the staple seal, cf. p. 98.

[5] Pp. 142–7.   [6] P. 188.   [7] Pp. 139, 146.

and reveals that there is a "companies seele of London",[1] and the tendency towards concentration of the trade (and so, inevitably, of the organisation) of the Company cannot be mistaken. In the ordinance of the 17th of May for general shippings, the ports from which wools were to be shipped were enumerated as London, Boston, Hull, Ipswich and Sandwich.[2] At what date the power to ship staple wools was taken from the other English staple ports is not clear; probably this limitation is simply an acknowledgment of the fact that Southampton, Exeter, Chichester and Bristol could not profitably compete for the trade to Calais or Bruges, and that the trade of Canterbury, Melcombe, and other one-time staple ports had dwindled. The trade has quite clearly already been narrowed. And despite the feeling in 1565 against further concentration, even within these ordinances the facts lead the committee to narrow the field still further! For whilst five ports are enumerated on the 17th of May, by the beginning of June it is acknowledged that in actual practice only three ports (London, Boston, and Hull) deal with the trade.[3] The customs accounts fully endorse these conclusions. Sandwich and Ipswich are still shipping wools at the end of the fifteenth century,[4] but by Elizabeth's reign the occasional shipments which are made from those ports do not figure in the Staplers' accounts with the Exchequer any more than do the licensed shipments from Southampton, Chichester, or any other port.

Of the three English ports still left to the staple trade, London easily outdistanced the others. The simple fact that the "Assistance" travelling to Bruges from London only needed six shillings and eight pence for expenses, whilst from the other ports they needed ten shillings,[5] is here of significance. Her trade was immeasurably greater than that of the outports.[6]

In theory the bodies of Staplers in each of these three ports

[1] *Infra*, p. 137. [2] P. 142. [3] P. 197.
[4] Power and Postan, pp. 340, 356.
[5] *Infra*, p. 112. [6] *Vide supra*, pp. 31, 67.

were on an equal footing within the Company. But the exact
organisation of these local groups is not clear. The shippers
from London in the years around 1565 usually numbered about
ninety, whilst those from Boston were about thirty and those
from Hull about a dozen.

These ports were to signify their wills in matters affecting
the Staple under their staple seals, and there is almost certainly
here some connection between the local groups of members
of the Company of the Staple and those earlier civic groups
of Burgesses of the Staple in English ports which were by
now usually merely municipal oligarchies.[1] But the connection
is not a clear one, for it appears that the local Mayor of the
Staple of Boston was not necessarily a member of the Staple
Company:[2] he normally was, but it is plain that he might be
merely a civic official. Neither is it at all clear that the organisation of the Staple at Boston retained any vigour. There was
certainly a house and land belonging to the Staple there, and
it has been suggested that this might be held to imply that the
Staplers of Boston enjoyed some sort of social life together.[3]
But the Minutes Books of the Staple Company reveal that this
property of the Staple at Boston belonged to the Staple Company of England and not to the community (if any) at Boston.[4]
Moreover, by the time that the Minutes Books cover—from 1619
onwards—it is the practice that half the tenants of this property
shall be residents in London, and the other half residents of
Boston, if there are so many free of the Company.

If doubts as to the individuality of the organisation of the
Staple in Boston can be justified, Hull is in a far worse case.
Her shipments were more meagre, her Staplers less numerous,
and she did not even boast a Mayor of the Staple at this time.

Meanwhile London bulked ever larger in the shrinking trade.
The need to seek another staple port after the expulsion from

---

[1] *Staple Court Books of Bristol*, pp. 50–63.   [2] *Infra*, p. 144.
[3] Gross, *Gild Merchant*, I, p. 146, n. 2.
[4] Staple Company Minutes Book, 19 January 1619 (1620), 5 June
1662, etc.

Bruges, the necessity for "lobbying", the enhanced status which the Mayor of the Staple of Westminster enjoyed under the Statute of 1523 (by which he alone of the Mayors of the Staple might issue "recognisances in the form of a statute staple"), all increased the already heavy dominance. Members of the Company are still drawn from all over the country: they are so even after the establishment of the home staples in 1617,[1] but the London organisation is the only important organisation within the Company. We are not surprised that the Registry for Staplers' licences to broke wools is set up in London,[2] and we are prepared for the situation which meets us when the Minutes Books begin to give accurate and continuous information. Then the Company holds all its meetings at Leadenhall, and it decides that the "Mayor of the Staple hath ever byn an auncient knyght or Alderman of London". When no existing member is so qualified to be elected Mayor, Mr James Cambell, an Alderman, is elected gratis "for his own person" "to the Intente to be made Maior of the Staple".[3] The facts of concentration and oligarchy are triumphing over the tradition of diffusion and equality, and the attempt to ignore London's predominance which these ordinances reveal is most significant.

Apart from these main items, it is natural that such a document should contain many minor points of interest. We learn that Staplers were liable to swindle each other as well as their

---

[1] Minutes Book, 12 November 1619, *et passim*.　　[2] *Supra*, p. 70.

[3] Minutes Book, 30 May 1621. Further signs of the way in which by this time the London organisation is the only one which counts may be seen in the treatment of Lincoln. Here one of the home staples had been set up in 1617, and the local Staplers petitioned that they might be given some local organisation. Local enthusiasm was sufficient to pay the admission hances of enough Lincoln men to give that city a quorum to hold courts and assemblies. The chief backer of this venture at Lincoln, Mr Robert Moorecroft, was made Lieutenant of the Company for that city and immediately put out of trade some unlicensed wool-dealers, so perhaps there was something more in this curious transaction than local antiquarian enthusiasm (Minutes Book, 10–24 May 1620).

customers. Not only did they alter the wool-winders' vouchers as to the quality of the wools within the sarplars, but they also removed the labels bearing the owners' names and stole from each other.[1] The practice of eating meals "covered",[2] the selling of goods by stroke of mallet,[3] the rules for the apparel of apprentices,[4] the permits for widows to carry on their husbands' trade,[5] the question whether an apprentice were the son of a "bounde man",[6] the sidelight cast on the rising prices of sixteenth-century England,[7] the organisation of the Staple "House",[8] all add to the interest of this document.

The extent to which apprentices were allowed to ship either on their own account or for their masters is also worthy of remark.[9] This, with the way in which the generality of the Staplers at the mart is only permitted to play cards from Christmas until the 29th of January, whilst the officials are allowed to play whenever they like, and may call up to join them any other resident whom they choose,[10] leaves the impression that normally the permanent population of the Staple was predominantly composed of apprentices and young attorneys, who required severe discipline.

The enumeration of the frauds to which the trade was liable[11] again brings little that is fresh to light but provides a valuable and authoritative summary.

The ordinances "For frayes and bloudwipes" reveal this regulated company taking upon itself the mantle of the gilds of which it was in so many ways an expansion.

Most valuable for all who are interested in the jurisdiction exercised by the Staple Courts is the information here set down. The Staple Court of Calais had been similar to the other Staple Courts of England.[12] Its customs are now enumerated,

[1] *Infra*, p. 169. [2] P. 189.
[3] Pp. 162, 180. [4] P. 189.
[5] Pp. 136, 149. The customs accounts show that this was no dead letter.
[6] P. 141. [7] Pp. 163, 168 and n. 3.
[8] Pp. 185-193. [9] Pp. 150, 154.
[10] P. 191. [11] Pp. 129, 147, 156, 170, 194.
[12] *Staple Court Books of Bristol*, pp. 52 *et seq.*

with their processes of attachment, their moderate fees, their distrust of attorneys, their avoidance of vexatious suits and their speedy trial and execution[1] and are applied to the "Exchequer" of the Staple at Bruges.

More closely connected, possibly, with the actual trade are the ordinances dealing with the wool-winders.[2] Their frauds are once more denounced, and methods to combat them are promulgated. The wool-winders had been brought under the control of the Staple Company in 1550. They were controlled by their London Company, which could give testimonials of admittance only under the seal of the Mayor of the Staple, and the men were to take an oath before the Mayor of the Staple.[3] Here the Staplers may be seen administering the oath to the wool-winders and directing their business with some minuteness. It is not surprising that London and Leadenhall should bulk large in this part of the activities of the Company, although the Staple at Boston, with its Mayor, also finds its place.[4] The Mayor of the Staple of Boston had been entrusted with the duty of overseeing the wool-winders of his locality in 1562, and these ordinances also place him on an equal footing in this matter with the Mayor of the Staple of Westminster.[5]

This business of overseeing the wool-winders is probably the most durable part of all these ordinances relating to trade. The organisation of the Company did indeed persist into the twentieth century; but when the staple trade became an internal trade the ordinances here set down for trade lost their validity, with the exception of the ordinances relating to the wool-winders. By contrast, as long as the Staplers maintained any interest of any kind in the wool trade, they considered it their duty to ensure the fair sorting and packing of wools, and

[1] *Infra*, pp. 117, 119, 122, 172, 176.
[2] Pp. 129–30, 194.
[3] *Cal. S.P. Dom.* 1547–1563, p. 404.
[4] For Boston's Mayor of the Staple *vide supra*, p. 98.
[5] *Infra*, pp. 195 *et seq.*

throughout the period of unrestrained competition and absence of supervision in English industry this ancient Company continued to try to enforce its medieval standards of fairness in this matter.[1]

[1] Cf. Staple Company Minutes Books, minute of 12 May 1846, of 3 April 1806, and of 23 April 1852. The Company inserted notices on this subject in the *Farmers' Journal* and in many local papers and held itself ready to prosecute for offences, under the Statute of 23 Henry VIII. So close was its connection with wool-winding that the Staple Company found its name taken by a rival artisan association in the late eighteenth century. The artisan wool-sorters bound themselves into a national "Woolstaplers' Society" in 1785. Their object also was to regulate the sorting of wool, but in the interests of the workmen, whose wages and hours of work they tried to regulate (Hoskins, *Industry, Trade and People in Exeter*, 1688–1800, p. 60).

ORDINANCE BOOK
of
THE MERCHANTS *of* THE STAPLE

PREFACE

p. 1.

5 June 1565
see page 31.[1]

It is well known that in tymes past this estaple wheresoever the same hathe ben ordeyned and kepte hathe ben gouverned and rueled by lawes actes and orders especially for the maintenaunce therof devised as when the saied Estaple was kepte in Englond actes of parlement were manyfoldly established whereby the merchauntes of the staple had greate privileges and freedomes graunted unto them boethe for the decent disposition of theire persons as of their marchaundises by a lawe merchaunt to be demened whiche Estaple also afterwarde beinge to Calles diducted was not theire in respect and commoditie of that place withoute good lawes and ordenaunces to conserve the commune wealthe thereof contynued untill suche tyme that by warre the cheife ennemy of commune wealthes aswell the saiede Estaple as the saiede toune was subverted by occasion of whiche saiede subuersion the merchauntes of that Estaple being in great perille of dissolution were forced to make theire diligent sute to be succurred. Then followed that thoroughe the gracious clementie of our moost deare souveraigne princes and lady Quene Elizabethe (whome almighty god long preserve and prosper) the companie of this Estaple recovered newe letters patentes and privileges for the full redintegration and restitution of our auncient and wourshipfulle companie to our estate and trade of occupienge the same to be exercised here in Bruges orels where the saiede Estaple shalbe kepte and the staple

---

[1] This note is written in the margin in a much later hand.

merchaundise put to sale by the name of Maior Constables
and fellowship of merchauntes of the staple of Englonde
as by the saied lettres patentes more at length it may appere whereuppon the saiede companie findinge and under-
stondinge by reason and experience what commoditie and
benefite heretofore grewe to the hole companie by good
orders and lawes and by the contrarie no commune wealthe
or societe can stonde or endure did in the tyme of the right
wourshipfulle Walter Haddon doctor of the lawe civill
and one of the maisters of the requestes to the Quenes
Maiestie then being Lieutenaunt by the aide and helpe of
the same maister Haddon and of John Mershe Esquier then
commune sergeaunt of the citie of London Edmonde Hall
Esquier then beinge Constables of this Estaple Thomas
Wogan Adam Capcot and John Hampton then beinge
assistaunce and of suche other the wourshipfull companie
whiche then were in ample nombre assembled here in
Bruges aforesaiede labour and studie by alle the wayes and
meanes they coulde for to obviate and avoyde thincon-
veniences whiche for want of good orders mighte ensue
travailinge (by reason of our fourmer bookes lawes orders
and munimentes by longe course of tyme by the wis-
domes ⟨1ᵈ⟩ and prudenties of our grave auncestours made
collected and regestred were from us with the saiede toune
of Callais surpriused and witholden) first to serche oute
copies of our auncient lawes and orders aforesaiede suche
as coulde in any wise be obteyned and then therby as
otherwise by theire industries wittes and pollicies made of
newe and componed orders supplienge refresshinge or
alteringe our saiede orders and the same combininge and
regestringe in a booke therefore made and kept as by the
same booke remayning of recorde in this saied estaple att
large is apparaunt. And forasmuche as since that tyme
in usinge the saied ordonaunces (like as in all inventions
moost communly the beginninge cannot be parfaict in
every behalfe) many thinges have fallen into questions and
debate emongest the saied companie whereof none expresse

remedie hathe ben by the saied orders provided and therby
the companie hathe ben muche inquieted, the saied companie have therefore ben of very necessitie compelled to call
over hether the right wourshipfulle Sir Thomas Offley
knight Maior of this estaple and suche assistaunce as have
ben to hym appoincted that is to wit the right wourshipfull Sir William Chester knight, William Gyfforde Adam
Capcot, Blaise Saundres, and Robert Offley for London
Edmond Halle Esquier Thomas Dalton Mathewe Crad-
docke and William Darby for the countrey for to helpe to
amplifie and extende fourther the saiede ordenaunces who
accordingly endevoringe them selves have by good advice
mature deliberation and one mutuall assent and consent
in court for the commune wealthe of this estaple in the
name of our lorde God thautor and principle of all goodness, consequently to the profit of the realme of Englonde
and honour of the Quenes moost excellent maiestie have
devised constituted and established the lawes ordenaunces
and actes hereafter ensuenge inviolably to be observed
and kept according to the tenor thereof upon the forfaictures penalties and paynes in them and every of them
comprised not wishinge so muche the saied penalties to be
levied as the good lawes and orders aforesaied to be kept.

Ordenaunce for the Maior. p. 2

Forasmuche as this wourshipfulle companie alwayes hathe
and by vertue of the Quenes maiesties graunte presently
doethe consist of Maior Constables and fellowship of merchauntes of the staple of Englonde   It is therefore aswell
in continuaunce of our olde and auncient usage as in accom-
plishement of the Quenes maiesties letters patentes and
grauntes ordeigned concluded and agreed by generalle consent of court holden in this estaple the first daye of Maye
in the yeare of our lorde god xvclxv that from hence-
fourthe yearly the first daye of the monethe of Maye or
thearaboute the companie then present havinge voice in

court shalle procede to thelection of the saiede Maior for
the yeare next followinge *In* whiche election thre of the
moost wourshipfulle grave auncient and expert of the
companie being commune shippers and being free of this
estaple by patrimonie or apprentishode or suche as have
borne office in this estaple of Maior or lieutenaunt shalle
be nominated by suche of the companie as shalbe at the
place where the staple shall happen then to be kept and
the gooddes and merchaundise of the saiede estaple put to
sale. Of which thre parsons so nominated as is aforesaied
consequently one of them shalle fyrst be by commune assent
and voyce exempted and revoked in sorte as thelection of
the saied Maior shalbe driven holy to remayne upon two
of the saied right wourshipfull persons Incontinently this
done the names of the saiede two persons shalbe written
in two severalle peces of paper and affixed upon the boxe
ordeined aswell for thelection of the officers and admission
of redemptioners into the fredome as for other pourposes
therefore provided And then every brother of this saiede
estaple there present being shippers attorneis or havinge
staple merchaundise in the same estaple shalle arise from
his place and come to the compter or table whereon the
saiede box shalbe set in court and the treasourer of this
estaple for the tyme being shall deliver into the handes
of the saiede brother openly a button or ballet whiche
brother shall fourthwithe withoute covine fraude deceipt
or malingin put the same button or ballet into the saiede
boxe at that side of the saiede box whereon his name is
written to whome he geveth his suffrage and consent to
be Maior. *And* yf any fellowe of this estaple shalbe fownde
fraudulently to have proceded in the saiede election contrarie to the true intent of this ordonaunce shalbe holy
disfraunchised of his fredome of this estaple withoute favor.
And he of the saiede ii right wourshipfulle parsons that
shalbe chosen by the greatest nombre of buttons or bal-
lettes aforesaied shalbe Maior of this estaple to endure for
one yeare next ensueng (except for any sufficient matter

or cause he in the meane tyme be removed or discharged
of the saied romethe[1] in whiche caas there shalbe in like
manner and fourme an other chosen to supplie that romethe
for the residue of that yeare to wit untille the next daye
of election limited by ordenaunce *And* fourther for
avoyding of contention and incertaintie which may arise in
court in the saied election *It is fourther* agreed ⟨2^d⟩ concluded and enacted that yf it shalle chaunce the buttons to
fall in the saiede box even in nombre on either syde whereby
thelection is uncertaine or none election *Then it* shalbe
leifulle to thauncient Constable for the tyme being to gyve
his voice to one of those two (whiche shalbe in election)
for him to be Maior who being so chosen shall continue Maior of this estaple for the yeare next ensuenge
in as ample manner as he had ben by one mutuall
assent and consent of the hole companie chosen Maior
aforesaied. Every whiche Maior so chosen as is aforesaied shalle have for his yearly fee for exercisinge the saied
office accordingly xl^{li} st. by the yeare and no more. He
shalle well and truelydo his office according as shalbe unto
his /sic/ prescribed by this or any other ordenaunce or act
now made or hereafter to be made and according to his
oethe wherein his office and duetie more plainely ap-
pereth. *And* suche Maior aforesaied shalle make no manner
of costes or charges for the companie in any poursute in
Englonde at the parlement counselle or otherwise but by
thadvise of six or iiii of the moost auncientes of the companie commun shippers to this estaple *And* the saied
Maiour shalle once in the yeare to wit the last daye of June
next after his Maioraltie is expired exhibite and yelde up
his accomptes of alle his receiptes and payementes concerninge the affaires of this estaple to suche parsons of
the same and at suche place as by court of this estaple where
the same now is or shalbe kept and the staple merchaundise
put to sale shalbe for the vieuinge perusing and examination
thereof nominated assigned and appoincted upon payne the

costes &
charges

accompt of
Mr Mayor

----
[1] Office.

saiede Maiour offending in any article aforesaiede to forfaict for every suche offence C^{li} to the profit and use of the same estaple *And* it is fourther agreed concluded and enacted that at thelection of every Maiour aforesaiede the companie of this estaple shalle nominate and aucthorise in court x: viii or vi of the moost wourshipfulle of the same companie to take at or before the saied last daye of June the accomptes and rekenynges of the Maiour of this estaple for the yeare next before passed and the same accomptes to vieu peruse and examyne to the whiche after theire saied auditinge they shall subscribe theire names after the whiche accomptes so vieued and subscribed in manner and fourme abovesaied the same accomptant shall send or cause to be sent over hither to this saied estaple or elswhere the saied estaple shalbe kept and staple merchaundise put to sale the same his accomptes before the feast of saint Barthilmew the apostell next[1] after that ensueng for the same accomptes in court of this estaple to be abled according to thorder in such caas used *And* whosoever being chosen Maiour aforesaied shall refuse to exercise the saied office and to take thoeth and charge thereunto apperteyninge and hereafter ensuenge being ministered to him in Englond by such persons as shalbe by court assigned shalle forfaict to thuse of the generalitie C^{li} st. *And* further it is ordeyned that yf any person so hereafter chosen Maiour shalle come over not being sent for by generalle letters or not appoincted by the consent of alle the portes in Englonde for the generalle affaires of the companie and shalbe allowed ⟨3⟩ by waye of rewarde or otherwise accept or take any somme or sommes of money or other thinges of the generall tresour or charges of the companie for or towardes his paynes or charges or for any other respect, that then suche Maiour being so allowed and accepting by waye of rewarde or otherwise any somme or sommes of money or other thinges as is aforesaied shalle forfaict to thuse of the companie doble so muche as he shalle receave. Whiche

[1] August 24th.

forfaicture the next Maiour succeading shalle levie or do to be levied as muche as in hym is upon paine of forfaicture of so muche as the saied fourmer Maiour so offending as is aforesaied shulde or ought to have paied and nevertheles no childe or apprentice of the saied parson so acceptinge or receavinge by waye of rewarde or otherwise any somme or sommes of money as is aforesaied shalle enioye the fredome of this companie tille payement be made of such forfaicture as is aforesaiede   *And* it is fourther ordeyned that thattourney of him that shalbe chosen Maiour shalle presently after thelection put in surties accordyng to the auncient order that the saiede Maiour shalle welle and truely execute his office and thereupon authorite shalbe geven by lettres addressed from the court of this estaple yf the Maiour be not present in court to suche wourshipfulle parsonnes in Englonde as to them shalle seame good to minister thothe to that office apperteyninge to suche parsonne as shalbe chosen Maiour whiche othe so ministered by the parsonnes so to be appoincted shalbe of like force and effect as yf it were geven in court.

Thoethe of the Maior

Ye swere ye shalbe true to our liege lorde the kynge *and to his heires*[1] *kinges*   And well and truely yow shall do and execute your office of Maioraltie for the tyme that yow shalle occupie the same, and iustly tender thorders and establishementes, that are and shalbe made and ordeyned by commune consent for the commune proffit of the companie. Right and reason ye shalle do to eche one of the companie, and to all others, withoute any regarde havinge to your owne singuler profit, or any other mans profit, in decrease of the commune profit. The commune busines yow shalle well and truely poursue and the same to good ende and effect leade after your power. Thaccomptes of the commune silver and all other receiptes dispences and paye-

[1] "and successors" written above in a later hand: the words in italics are underlined.

mentes by yow and the receavers don in your tyme, afore
the Constables and other sufficient parsons of the companie
thereunto deputed and assigned ye shalle diligently heare
and all other poinctes to your saied office belonginge ye
shall kepte /sic/ and perfourme in that that in yow is so
helpe yow god etc. and by the contentes of that booke.

<⟨3ᵈ⟩>

Ordenaunce for thelection of the lieutenaunt.

Where in tyme past in the absence of the Maiour there
hathe ben for the moost parte a lieutenaunt who hathe
supplied his place when any urgent occasion hathe so
required for the weighty affaires of the companie *It is*
ordeyned at a court holden in this estaple the first daye of
Maye in the yeare of our lorde god xvclxv that whensoever it shalle seame necessarie for the setting fourthe of
the weighty affaires or commune causes of the companie
it shalbe leifulle within xiiii dayes at the furthest after
tharrivalle and howsing of the staple goodes and merchaundise from all the portes shipping that tyme for the companie resident where the staple shalbe kept to procede to
thelection of a lieutenaunt and to nominate thre wourshipfulle and grave personnes whiche ben fre of the companie
and whiche have borne office of Constables to be put in election and whiche at the tyme of suche nomination or within
that yere had or shalle have goodes theire of theire owne
adventure *In* whose election aforesaied shalbe proceded
by the box after the manner and fourme in every behalfe
as is prescribed for thelection of the Maiour by ordenaunce
therefore provided *And* the saied lieutenaunt so chosen
shalle continue in that office during the companies pleasure
but not above vi monethes *He shalle* have for his fee
xxˢ st every weke that he shalle so continue to be accompted
from the tyme of takinge his oethe untille the tyme of his
discharge *And* it is fourther ordeined that every parson
so elected to be lieutenaunt as is aforesaied being not
present at the tyme of his election shalle have warninge

iii monethes afore by the places letters at suche tyme as
the saied companie shalle appoinct him   *And* every parson
so elected and warned havinge no reasonable excuse vz.
sicknes or lacke of passage that shalle make default and
not come at the tyme appoincted or do refuse to take upon
him thexecution of the saied office or thoethe to that office
apperteyninge or do depart within vi monethes next after
that he hathe taken upon him the office withoute licence
of the companie shalle forfaicte to the court of this estaple
C markes   *And* it is fourther ordeined that every lieutenaunt hereafter to be chosen shalle once during the tyme
of exercising of his office at tyme moost convenient for
that pourpose cause alle thordenaunces then stonding in
force to be openly red at one or more court or courtes
generalle upon paine of forfaicture to the court of this
estaple x^{li}.

Thoethe of the lieutenaunt

Ye swere ye shalbe true to our liege lorde the kinge and
to his heires kinges   And welle and truely yow shalle do
and execute your office of lieutenaunt for the tyme that
yow shalle occupie the same and iustly tender the orders
and establishementes that are or shalle be made and
ordeyned by commune consent for the commune profit
of the companie. Right and reason yow shalle do to eche
one of the companie and to alle others withoute regard
having to your owne singuler proffit or any other mans
proffitt in decrease of the commune proffit   The commune busines yow shalle welle and truely poursue and
the same to good ende and effect leade to your power
Thaccomptes of the commune silver and alle other receiptes
dispences and payementes by yow and the receavers done
in your tyme afore the Constables and other sufficient ⟨4⟩
parsons of the companie thereunto deputed and assigned ye
shalle diligently heare and alle other poinctes to your saied
office belonginge ye shall kepe and perfourme in that that
in yow is so helpe yow god etc.

Ordinaunce for assistaunce and Constables

Also it is ordeined and enacted that yearly the daye of election of the Maior there shalbe ten grave and discreat parsons free of this companie and having gooddes here at that present or which have shipped to this estaple within thre yeres before the same daye and which then shalbe under thage of lx yeres nominated and appoincted for assistaunce indifferently from alle the portes accustomed to ship to this estaple to be elected whereof iii shalbe for the quarter from the feast of saint Michaelle tharchaungelle untill the feast of Nativitie of our lord god then next after that ensuenge, other iii from the same feast untill the feast of Annunntiation of our lady sainct Marie then next after that ensuenge and two from the saied feast of Annuntiation of our lady sainct Marie untill the feast of Nativitie of sainct John Baptist next after that ensueng and other two from the same feast untill the feast of sainct Michaelle tharchaungelle then next after that ensuenge and so consequently that order to be kept for thassistaunce aforesaied from tyme to tyme and yere to yere untill otherwise shalbe by court of this estaple decreed and established *And* it is fourther concluded and enacted that two of those whiche shalbe appoincted assistaunce for the wynter quarters shalbe suche as shalbe thought moost able men of the companie and whiche have not ben tresourers of this estaple before that tyme so long as there be any fownde for that place or calling mete to serve and the thirde to be chosen that hathe ben assistaunce before   *To* every of whiche saide assistaunce repairinge to this estaple out of the countrethe shalbe allowed by this place for theire passage to and fro x^s st. and to every of those whiche shalle come to this saied estaple from the port of London vi s viii d And every Constable whiche shalbe elected of the saied assistaunce after he is entred unto commons within the staple In or howse here in Bruges shalle have allowaunce of this place of vii^s st. every weke for his commons and

every assistaunce aforesaied of v⁸ st every weke for his
like commons as long as he or they continue or serve in
this estaple as assistaunce aforesaide dureinge theire saied
quarter *With* this it is fourther enacted that the treasourer
of this estaple for the tyme being shalle make payement
of the premisses from tyme to tyme as the same shalbe due
and thereof shalbe discharged in his accomptes by vertue of
this present ordenaunce in suche manner and fourme as he
is shalle or ought to be ⟨4ᵈ⟩ of all other officiers fees and
deuties belonginge to this saied estaple withoute further
warrant in that behalfe by him therefore to be demaunded
And the saied assistaunce so chosen shalbe warned by letters
sent from this court iii monethes at least before his daye
of apparaunce or his quarter to give his attendaunce at the
place where the staple shalbe kept of which assistaunce at
the tyme of theire apparaunce shalbe chosen in fulle court
of suche as have voice in court of the moost wourshipfulle
and grave persons one or two Constables as shalle seme to
the companie then present to be necessarie and requisite
for theire commune affaires and that every parson so being
chosen assistaunce and warned as is aforesaied making
defaulte not comynge at the day prescribed and having no
iuste excuse of unfayned sicknes and lacke of passage or
do departe within thre monethes ʷᵗʰoute licens shalle forfaicte and lose to the court of this estaple xl marks st.
It is further ordeined that no parson shalle fro' hensfourth
be elected and chosen Constable but suche of the companie
as hathe ben Constable or at the tyme of thelection hath
ben fre by the space of xii yeares at the least   *And it is*
further ordeigned that the Constables for the tyme being
and every of them shalle assist the Maior or lieutenaunt
geving theire best advise in alle matters concerninge this
estaple and good gouverment of the same and shalle ons
in the tyme of his or theire office in thabsence of the Maiour
or his lieutenaunt cause thordenaunces to be red at one or
more courtes and shall cause the state of the companie to
be vieued and thaccomptes of every treasourer to be vieued

noo parson
elected Con-
stable un-
lease fre xii
yeres

and abled and shalle also within the same tyme cause the
beame and waightes to be vieued serched tried and refourmed yf occasion require *It is further* ordeined and
enacted that no parson shalbe called over as assistaunce
but once after thende of every thre yeres after he hathe
ben called over to be assistaunce *Provided* alwayes that
suche assistaunce as shalle serve in the winter quarter shalle
when they be next elected assistaunce be called over in the
sommer quarter.

Thoeth of the Constables

Ye swere etc. /sic/ Justiciable and obeisaunt to the
Maior or his lieutenaunt and companie of merchauntes of
the staple in alle matters apperteyninge to the saiede estaple
and welle and truely yow shalle do your office of Constable
for the tyme that ye shalle occupie the same and iustly
tender thordenaunces and establishementes that are and
shalbe made & ordeigned by commune assent for the commune profit of the companie Right and reason ye shalle
do to eche one of the companie and to alle others withoute
any regarde having to your owne singulier profit or to any
other mans profit in decrease of the commune profit The
commune busines well and truely you shalle poursue and
the same to good ende and effect lead to your power
Thaccomptes of the commune silver and alle other receiptes
dispences and payementes done in your ⟨5⟩ tyme before
sufficient parsons thereunto deputed and assigned ye shalle
diligently here And alle other poinctes to your office of
Constable apperteining yow shalle kepe and perfourme in
alle that in yow is so helpe yow god etc.

Ordenaunce for the tresourer.

In thelection of the treasourer of this estaple there shalbe
alwaye two named by the heades whereof thone shalbe
elected treasourer by the court. And yf he be absent oute

of this estaple at the tyme of his election and that therupon lettres be sent to him from the court to repaire to this estaple to exercise the same romethe at the daye by the same letters to be prefixed and shalle make default of his apparaunce at the saied daie or yf he be present in the saied court at the tyme of his saied election and shalle refuse to take upon him the same romethe and charge or do breake his daye of apparaunce shalbe forfaicte to the court of this estaple xx^li   *And* every treasourer so elected shalle put in two sufficient sureties to the court for him and his office and either of them to be bound for alle and in the hole to save the courte harmeles according as hathe ben accustomed   *And* every suche treasourer aforesaied shalbe allowed wekely for his fee v^s st. And shalle continue in that office untille the ende of the quarter the quarters endes of every yere ben these vz. the viii of the feast of Annuntiation of Sainct Mary the virgin, The viii of Nativitie of saint John Baptist, The viii of St. Michelle tharchaungelle, and the viii of Nativitie of our lorde god so that the daye next following after any of the saiede o^vllis [1] (which is one of the feastes aforesaied) the treasourer succeading shall enter into his charge in sort as thaccomptes of his predecessour be not in any manner of wise entermedled or mixed withe thaccomptes of the successours   *He* shalle charge himselfe in his accomptes withe his receipts of the commune silver aswelle proceding of hances impositions forfaictures to the court as of alle other incidentes and droictes to the treasourie of this estaple belonginge and wth thencrease and profit growing of the commune money by & duringe alle his tyme   *And* also shalle discharge himselfe with his dispences and payementes made for the place by commune consent of the companie   *He* shall make none apprest to any parsonne of any of the places money or goodes withoute an especialle act of court for his warraunt and discharge in that behalfe   *After* he is elected treasourer and hath entreed into his quarter he shalle not

[1] Octaves.

departe oute of this estaple before his accomptes ben vieued by the companie as hath ben accustomed and abled in court except he have licens by court to departe before that tyme putting in a sufficient deputie suche as ⟨5ᵈ⟩ hathe ben tresourer on paine of forfaicture to the saiede court xxˡˡ for suche default besides this he shalle surrendre up into the court of this estaple his accomptes ᵂᵗʰoute rasure blemishe or blott in the sommes of the pagine or totalle summes within one monethe next after thende of his quarter upon the penaltie he to forfaict to the court of this saied estaple xxˡˡ st. *Also* the treasourer shalle not seele or deliver any billes of sales for or to any man that is indebted to the place for impositions forfaictures or for other matter whatsoever untille suche tyme as the same tresourer be satisfied or agreed for that duetie upon paine the charge and ieopardie therof to stand to the same tresourer and his sureties   *It is* further concluded and enacted that the tresourer aforesaied for the tyme being shalle deliver unto his next successour tresourer of the same estaple at the first daye of the saied successour quarter a bille of the names and summes of alle suche parsons as remayne indebted to this place by his accomptes   *And* in caas his saied successour be not at the same daye present in the saied estaple to receave the saied bille then he shalle deliver the saied bille to the husbande of this estaple for the tyme beinge which bille the said husbande shalle deliver further over to the saied treasourer successour aforesaied at his cummyinge or to his deputie   *And* in caas the goodes of any debtour shalle happen to passe and that debt not clered by bille oute of the tresourie by meannes that the fourmer tresourer hathe not delivered suche a bille of the names and sommes in manner and fourme aforesaied   *Then* it is further agreed concluded and enacted that the same debt shalle be to the charge and ieopardie of the saied fourmer tresourer to be aunswered to this place by him and his sureties.

Thoethe of the tresourer

Ye swere etc /sic/ and iusticiable and obeisaunt unto the
Maiour his lieutenaunt Constables and companie of merchauntes of the staple in alle matters concerninge the saied
estaple well and truely yow shalle do your office of tresourer
for the tyme ye shalle occupie the same iust and true
accompt ye shalle yeld of alle your receiptes dispences and
payementes done in your tyme before suche parsons of
the companie as shalbe thereunto assigned withe the due
encrease of alle suche money and coyne as shalle come to
your handes by reason of your office of tresourer aforesaied   And alle other thinges to your saied office apperteininge well and truely yow shalle do and perfourme to
your power so helpe yow god and by the contentes of that
booke

Ordenaunce for the upperclarke

It is agreed concluded and ordeigned that thupperclarke
of this estaple for the tyme being shalle have for his fee
and salaire xl^{li} st. by the yere and shalle geve his attendaunce
in thexchequier of this estaple at all tymes convenient and
requisite to enter plainctes betwene partie and partie in
the registres ⟨6⟩ of this estaple and to enter other matters
of recorde at the request of the parties   *He* shalle have
for entre of every plainct iiii^d Item he shalle have and
perceave for extending of every single obligation vi^d st.
Item for every single recognoisaunce xii^d Item for every
lettre of warninge sent under the staple seele upon matters
of variaunce depending in court xvi^d st.   Item for every
lettre at the request of the partie xvi^d st.   Item for serchinge
of the recordes and bookes of this estaple as the partie and
he can agree   Item for registringe of every fremans testa-
ment whiche shalle have goodes here at the houre of his
deceasse according to thuse and custume in suche caas heretofore used that is to saie according to the testatours

substaunce and as the partie and he can agree   Item for entring of every transport betwene fellowe and fellowe vi^d Item for registring of every lettre of atturney in the recordes of this estaple xvi^d st. Item he shalle geve no copies of any plainct entred into the registres withoute consent of the partie or consent of court   Also he shalle not be favorable to any accomptant of this estaple   Alle ordenaunces made and to be made in this estaple for the commune wealthe of the same he shalle cause to be observed and kept to the best of his power   He shalle saufly kepe alle the recordes and munimentes of the saied estaple belonging to his charge and shalle not deliver any copie of them or any of them to any parson nor shalle suffer any suche copie to be taken by any parson to his know-ledge withoute the consent of the companie at a court or assemble.

Thoethe of thupperclarke

Ye swere etc.   *Justiciable* and obeisaunt unto the Maior his lieutenaunt Constables and companie of merchauntes of the staple in alle matters concerninge the saied estaple Ready & attendaunt at alle tymes requisitie in the place where your office is to enter plainctes and other recordes to your office apperteininge   Alle ordenaunces being in strengcth you shalle do to be kepte to the best of your power you shalle geve no copie of any manner of orde-naunces act of court or processe except by consent of parties or by consent of court   Alle other thinges to your saied office of upperclarke apperteininge yow shalle well and truely kepe and perfourme to your power so helpe yow god etc.

Ordenaunce for the underclarke

It is agreed and concluded that thunderclarke of this estaple shalle have for his fee xl. merkes st. by the yeare and shalle geve his personalle attendaunce in thexchequier of this estaple at all tymes convenient etc.

Thoethe of the underclarke [6d]

Ye swere etc. Also true and attendaunt unto thupperclarke of this estaple in alle thinges touchinge his office alle counsailes and privities of the staple suche as shalle come to your knowledge yow shalle kepe secret and to none them publishe etc.

Ordenaunce for the wayer

It is ordeyned that the wayer of this estaple shalle have for his fee and stipende l marks by the yere He shalle geve his attendaunce at the wayhowse at alle tymes convenient and requisitie to serve the merchaunt he shalle se the beame and scales of the wayhowse from tyme to tyme to be kept in an indifferent estat yf any faulte shalle chaunce to be in the same beame he shalle cause the same to be refourmed wth alle speade by thoversight of suche of the companie of this estaple as shalbe therunto deputed he shalle geve to every one his weight truely withoute favour to be shewed to any personne he shalle lende no weightes belonginge to his office to any of the fellowship or to any other parson withoute especialle licence of the gouvernours for the tyme beinge he shalle suffer no woulles to remayne in the wayehowse but as sone as they be wayed shalle be rolled fourthe into the streate He shalle suffer no woulles to pas the beame to any merchaunt buyer tille he se he bille past the treasourie The woulles which shalbe brought to the beame shalle come in at the east dore and ✗¹ after the same be wayed shalbe fourthe whith rolled out at the west dore. And suche parsonnes as first take shewe shalle first be served at the beame yf his woulle be brought ✗ to it. And yf he be remis or negligent and cause not his

¹ The crosses are inserted in the margin to call attention to important practical points.

✕ woulles to be brought to the beame then he that taketh the
next shew shalbe served and so consequently one after
another[:] yf any of the companie of this estaple do move
or stirre hym to attent any thinge contrarie to his charge
and office aforesaied shalle forfaict to the court of this
estaple xl^s for the first tyme and v^l for every tyme after.

Thoethe of the wayer

Ye swere etc. Justiciable and obeisaunt unto the Maior
his lieutenaunt Constables and companie of merchauntes
of the staple in alle matters apperteyninge to the same
estaple Ready and attendaunt at all tymes requisite in the
wayehowse to serve the merchaunt and to geve true and
iuste weight according to thorders of the staple in sort that
neither the merchaunt seller nor buyer maye be indam-
maged thoroughe your default And alle other thinges to
your saied office of wayer belonginge welle and truely yow
shalle do and perfourme to your power not letting for love
or hatered winninge or losing or any other thinge that may
be with yow or against yow so helpe you god and by the
contentes of that booke.

Ordenaunce for the clarke of the collectrie.

The clerke of the collectrie of this estaple shalle geve his
attendaunce upon his office at alle tymes requisite and convenient not onely at tharrivalle of every flete or fletes but
also at alle other tymes convenient (except he have licence)
leavinge a sufficient deputie in his place to ingrose the
✕ cocketts of all portes into a boke that done to draue^1 and
gather every mans parcelle particulerly of suche woulles
and felles as ben shipped into a booke and to make thargent
of the custume of the same and then to enter every mans
parcelle of the saied woulles and felles so shipped into a
booke of sales called the booke of rates and every rate to
issue oute by itselfe and theldest rate issued then to enter

^{1} I.e. draw.

into the next rate   And the saied clerke of the collectrie
shalle make fourthe his billes of olde and newe woulles
and felles accordinge as alle the sortes shalle be remayning
in every rate   Also that he deliver oute no billes for
issuenge oute of any goodes untille thowner or his attorney
have made reaport what sortes of woulles he shipped.
Also that he suffer but two partes of the goodes to issue
out tille order be taken for payement of the custume
according to thordenaunce   And that he be also certified
from the clerke wither the merchaunt have deposed for his
goodes ye or no   And also he shalle not make any parson
or parsonnes prive or certaine what nombre sort or
quantite of olde woulles or olde felles do remayne in the
bookes or toune unsolde except it be to the head for the
tyme beinge.

Thoethe of the clerke of the collectrie

Ye swere etc. Justiciable and obeisaunt unto the Maior
his lieutenaunt Constables and companie of merchauntes of
the staple etc. Ready and attendaunt at all tymes requisitie
in your office of collectrie to geve oute billes for issuing
oute of woulles and woullfelles acccordinge to the rates of
olde and newe and that yow shalle se the same rates from
tyme to tyme duely observed and kept and alle other
thinges to your office of collectrie apparteininge well and
truely yow shalle kepe and observe to your power so helpe
yow god etc.

Ordenaunce for the sergeant.

The sergeant of this estaple shalle have for his fee
xx merkes st. by the yere and his commons he shalle set
iiii sufficient and able parsons to be sureties to the court
to save the companie of this estaple harmeles and un-
damaged of and for alle thinges concerninge himselfe and
his office and shalle geve his attendaunce upon the Maior

his lieutenaunt or Constables of this estaple for the tyme
being at alle tyme requisite none arrest shalle he make
of any parsonne or his goodes withoute the plainct be
first entred in the recordes in thexchequier of this estaple
except the partie defendaunt ⟨7ᵈ⟩ be suddainly fownde in
this estaple or be fugitive and that the clerke cannot so
readely be fownde in whiche caas it shalbe leifulle to him
to arrest suche deffendaunt so that the plainct be afterwarde
entred into the saiede recordes before the sonne be set or
else suche arrest to stande as voyde and of none effect
upon thexecution of his warraunt that is to saie after that
he hathe arrested the partie yf the same partie cannot finde
sufficient suerties for his fourthe comminge to aunswer unto
the lawe he shalle bring the same partie deffendaunt to
prison whereoute the saiede partie deffendaunt shalle not
be enlarged but by consent and order of court be it upon
sureties or otherwise to thintent that the cause of thinlarge-
ment may be recorded by the saied clerke yf the saied
partie deffendaunt do finde sureties the same sureties shalbe
presented by the saied sergeant in thexchequier aforesaied
to be entred and recorded for sureties for the commynge
fourthe of the saied partie defendaunt and to aunswer unto
the lawe   Also he shalle not arrest any goodes of any
parson in any parsonalle action where the parson himselfe
may conveniently be arrested   He shalle have for his
arrest the iiiᵈᵉ parte of the plainctes silver   And yf the
saied partie defendaunt be a prisonner and shalle happen
by force or violence commynge to the court to be taken
awaye from the saied sergeant the same sergeant and his
sureties shalbe quit of any damage or hinderaunce thereby
except he were fownde in negligence

Theoethe of the sergeant

Ye swere etc. Justiciable and obeisaunt unto the Maior
his lieutenaunt Constables and companie of merchauntes
of the staple etc. Redy and attendaunt to serve arrestes

and sommonces and that yow shalle make none arrest
upon any parson or theire goodes except yow have first
a bille from thupperclarke unles the partie be fugitive
or the saied clerke cannot be fownde. All theise thinges
and other to your saied office apperteyninge yow shalle
well and truely do and perfourme to your power so helpe
yow god etc.

Ordenaunce for the husbande

The husbande of the companie is bownde to geve attendaunce at all courtes and assembles to vieue and se quarterly
alle woulles and felles shipped to the staple by any of the
companie remayninge then unsolde and to vieue and se
quarterly every accompt of the treasourer and other parsonne accomptable and to se that thordinaire fees be paiede
by the tresourer and to controlle thaccomptes yf any
allowaunce be demaunded whiche ought not to be   Likewise to charge the tresourer withe all money groenge by
hanses impositions, forfaictures, plainctes or by any other
meannes whatsoever due to the howse and to kepe a iust
note what money is yearly sent to the sollicitor of the
staple or any other in Englonde or delivered to any other
personne on this side the sees or where the staple shalle
be kept to thintent that every of them may be there with
charged upon theire accomptes   He shalle suffer no specialte
or other writing sealed withe the companies seele to passe
⟨8⟩ before he have entred it into his booke therefore
provided   And also to comptrolle wekely quarterly
monethely as shalle seme to him best alle oulde woulles
and felles wither they be issued oute according to thordenaunce or not as is geven unto the tresourer by the brokers
when they do entre   Item to comptrolle and overse yerly
thexpences and allowaunces demaunded and made from tyme
to tyme by the Maiour and the totalle summes thereof to
engrosse in his booke and to infourme the court from tyme
to tyme as occasion shalle serve of alle and every suche as

offende any penalle ordenaunce or be indebted to the howse   He shalle make and yearely revue a perfect inventorie of alle suche stuffe and implementes as do belonge from tyme to tyme to the companie and then deliver to every officer to whome it apperteineth one parte of an Indenture made tripartie of alle suche stuffe and implementes as shalbe wthin his charge and deliver one other parte to the lieutenaunt or Constable for the tyme beinge and the thirde he shalle reserve to hym selfe   And shalle also vieue and survey alle reparations wherewithe the companie shalbe charged   He shalle deliver from tyme to tyme to the tresourer for the tyme beinge the names of alle suche parsonnes as havinge goodes in this estaple do or owe to paie any extraordinaire impositions or be indebted to the howse as principalle or suretie   Moreover he shalle kepe a registre of the cocketts custume and subsidie of every flete   And finallie he shalle as muche as in him is from tyme to tyme infourme the heades for the tyme being of alle suche thinges as by any meannes may redounde to the profit or losse of the companie

Thoethe of the husbande

Ye swere etc   Justiciable by the Maiour his lieutenaunt Constables and fellowship of merchauntes of the staple in alle matters apperteinge to the saiede estaple well and truely you shalle exercise and occupie thoffice and charge that yow be admitted unto of husbandrie.

Ordenaunce for the woulbrokers and felbrokers

It is ordeigned that there shalbe but thre woulbrokers in this estaple whiche shalle at every shewe daye geve theire attendaunce upon the englishe bourse to bring and direct the marchaunt straunger aswelle to those of the companie
x   whiche have wolles suche as they do desire as also to the

shewe. He that shalbe assigned broker to the merchaunt
at the shewe shalle well and truely enter into his booke the
bargaine betwixt the merchaunt seller and the merchaunt
buyer to that intent that yf any variaunce shalle happen
to arise betwene the parties merchauntes aforesaied in anything touching theire bargaine the variaunce may be determined by his recorde and further upon his receipt of the
tresourers bille he shalle enter the same bille into his bookes
and se the woulles to be wayed oute to the merchaunt
straunger in ordre apperinge in thordenaunce of wayer
And shalle se that the saied merchaunt have his ⟨8ᵈ⟩ waight
staienge and holding at the waieng thereof the scales from
swaienge or tottering for indifference and equallitie of
boethe parties   He shalle truely enter into his bookes the
name countrethe & weight of the woulles so passing the
beame and write upon the clothe[1] the true weight thereof
He shalle not suffer the merchaunt buyer to departe the
toune before he have paied the tresourer and other officers
theire dueties but shalle bringe them to the saied tresourer
and se the dueties paiede upon paine the same broker to
paie it himselfe yf thoroughe his negligence the saied
duetie shalle happen to be unpaied[:] the saied brokers
shalle have and perceave to their uses xviᵈ st. for every
sarpler of woulles solde and wayed oute at the staple
beame whiche shalbe to them paiede by the marchaunt
seller   Every of them shalle make iust and true accompt
to thother of that thone shalle receave for his fellowes he
shalle not blame dispraise or commende any of the companies goodes to the merchaunt straunger whereby the
merchaunt straunger may be incoraged rather to buye of
thone then of thother

Thoethe of the woulbrokers and felbrokers.

Ye swere etc. Justiciable and obeisaunt unto the Maiour
his lieutenant Constables and companie of merchauntes of

[1] I.e. the canvas packing.

the staple Ready and attendaunt at alle tymes requisite
to enter and recorde the bargaines made betwene merchaunt
✗ and merchaunt. And also geve your attendaunce on the
court dayes before the court halle to declare and witnes
thinges whiche shalbe in doubte concerninge matters in question betwixt parties wherin your testimonie shalbe required
No manner of merchaundise you shalle blame or impaire
to the hurt or losse of the merchaunt seller or to thadvantage
of the merchaunt buyer   No covyne or collusion ye shalle
knowe to be pourposed contrarie to thordenaunce of this
estaple but anone yow shalle it shewe to the heades of the
same estaple in secret or in openwise   Theise and alle
other thinges to your office of broker apperteininge yow
shalle welle and truely do and perfourme to your power
so helpe you god etc.

Ordenaunce for the felbinders.

The felbinders of this estaple shalle howse and cause
to be howsed alle and singuler the companies felles of the
saied estaple welle and saufly at tharrivalle of every flete
And serche every mans marke and telle oute to the merchaunt straunger according to the brokers bille. They shalle
have and perceave to theire uses for theire labours as here-
✗ after ensueth[1] Imprimis for sorting of every thowsand
felles in the ship iii^ds Item for telling of every m^l felles
oute of the ship iii^ds Item for howsing of every m^l felles
ii^s i^d and so after thafferaunt Item for sorting of every
m^l felles in the howse iii^ds Item for setting of ⟨9⟩ every
thousand felles iiii^d Item for castinge over of every thousande
felles ii^d Item for pilinge of every m^l felles iii^d Item
for making of one hundrethe burnt felles iiii^s ii^d Item for
serving of C rent felles ii^s ii^d Item for tellinge of every
m^l felles to the hollendars or other merchauntes straungers
ii^d Also the saied felbinders or any of them shalle not

[1] It is fairly easy to guess at the meanings of the terms here used,
but difficult to be certain of their exact technical significance.
Perhaps they are best left to the reader to interpret.

remove any felles from one howse to an other w^{th}oute especialle licence of the heades of this estaple for the tyme being in that behalfe had

Thoethe of the felbinders

Ye swere etc. Justiciable by the Maior his lieutenaunt Constables and fellowship of merchauntes of the staple etc. welle and truely you shalle se that the merchauntes goodes aswelle denisins as straungers shalbe welle and saufely kepte and not impaired thorough your default and you shalle take no more for your paines then by ordenaunce to you is or shalbe appoynted. And what soever thone of you shalle receave for thother by reason of your office due and true accompt you shalle make thereof to thintent equalle distributions betwene you may be had   Nothing you shalle heare or knowe to be spoken or pourposed to the preiudice or diswourship of the staple but yow shalle immediatly disclose the same openly or secretly to the heades of this estaple for the tyme being   Alle theise thinges and others to your office apperteyninge you shalle well and truely do and perfourme to your power so helpe you god etc.

Thoethe of the woulporters.

Ye swere etc. Justiciable by the Maior his lieutenaunt Constables and fellowship of merchauntes of the staple And that you shalle se the merchauntes goodes from tyme to tyme welle and saufly charged and discharged for savegarde of the saiede goodes you shalle take no more for your labour and travaile then is or shalbe by the companie to you appoincted. Of alle the receiptes whiche thone of you do receave for thother due and true accompt you shalle make to your fellowes yow shalle not knowe or understonde any thinge dishonorable or preiudicialle spoken or pourposed against the companie of this estaple   But that incontinently and withe alle spede you shalle it declare to the heades of this estaple for the tyme being in open or in secret wise   Alle theise poinctes and other to your saied office apperteining you shalle welle and truely kepe and perfourme to your power so helpe yow god etc.

⟨9ᵈ⟩ ## *Thoethe of* the sollicitour of this estaple

Ye swere that you shalbe true to our liege lorde the kinge and to his heires kinges of Englonde. Justiciable by the Maior or his lieutenaunt Constables and fellowship of merchauntes of the staple of Englond in alle matters apperteyninge to the same   Juste and true accompt ye shalle yelde unto the saiede Maior his lieutenaunt Constables and fellowship of merchauntes or to any other person or personnes by them deputed of alle suche billes obligations specialties ready money and bullion and of alle other manner of thinges whatsoever that shalle come to your charge concerninge the hole body of the saiede estaple. And yf you shalle make any payementes to the kinges m'tie or to any other parsonne or parsonnes to his use on the behalfe of the saiede Maior and fellowship (their consentes therein had) ye shalle take a sufficient discharge for the same   welle and truely ye shalle poursue the causes of the generalitie of the saied estaple which apperteineth to your office as long as you do occupie the same. Theise wᵗʰ alle other poinctes to thoffice of our sollicitour in anywise apperteininge welle and truely ye shalle perfourme withe alle your dexterite so helpe you god etc.

Thoethe of thattourney in lawe

Ye swere etc.   well and truely yow shalbe healping and counsailing to the commune profit of the generalitie of the staple of Englonde. The commune counsailes of them you shalle kepe secret   ye shalle nothinge poursue that maybe derogation hurt or harme to the generalitie of the saied estaple. The foresaied estaple & alle franchises privelegies and liberties of the same graunted and confirmed by our liege lorde the kinge or any of his progenitours you shalle truely supporte and mayntayne to your power and learninge and diligently yow shalle sollicite alle sutes actions and causes as concerne the generalle weale of the saied estaple at alle tymes requisite so helpe yow god and by the contentes of that book

Thoethe of the woulpackers.

Ye swere etc.   ye shalbe obedient to the Maior and Constables of the staple of Englonde and to theire successours and be ready to perfourme theire lawfulle commaundementes in alle things concerninge your occupation and truely and indifferently serve the merchauntes aswelle denisens as straungers in alle thynges touchinge your saiede occupation yow shalle w^{th}oute fraude collusion or deceipt make your packinge of woulles truely indifferently and sufficiently so that yow shalle not packe or wrappe or cause to be packed or wrapped in the fleces of the woulle, earthe, stones, dunge, or sande   And ye shalle truely name alle manner of woulles by yow packed of the countrethe were they were groen after the nature of the saied woulles and not of any other countrethe in any manner of wise and that yow shalle write or cause to be written wth open greate lettres upon every sarpler ⟨10⟩ poke or pockett of good marche woulles (theise wordes) good marche   And upon the sarplers of midle marche woulles shalle write or cause to be written midle marche and upon alle sarplers of good woulles of cottiswolde good cottiswolde and the same order you shalle kepe and observe of alle woulles that you shalle packe or do to be packed of the growinge of alle countries within the realme of Englonde   And also ye shalle write or cause to be written upon alle and singuler sarplers aforesaied your owne surname in suche wise that the name of the woulles nor your surname may not be put oute withoute breaking of the saied sarplers pokes or pocketts   And yf you knowe any that doethe contrarie to theise ordenaunces ye shalle shewe it prively or openly to the Maior or Constables of the saied estaple as sone as you may conveniently come to them or any of them so helpe you god etc.

Thoethe of praisers of olde felles.

Yow swere yow shalle vieue and consider alle suche felles as yow have in charge to praise and truely and indifferently yow shalle praise the same havinge respect to the tyme of the provision thereof and as the like felles were solde for after tharrivalle of that flete except synce the saied arrivalle they be decaied by burnynge rot or worme eten whiche you shalle consider and therefore to abate according to your good discretions. This yow shalle not let to do for gift promes love hatred or any thynge that may be withe you or againest yow so helpe yow god and holidome and by the contentes of that booke.

Thoethe for the vieuers and serchers of woulles and felles.

Ye swere etc. alle woulles and felles within this toune yow shalle truely and faithfully vieue and serche every man in the quarter where yow are or shalbe assigned and thereof w^thin /Blank/ dayes next ensueng yow shalle bring true reaport to the heades of this estaple for the tyme being to wit of alle the woulles and the true nombre of alle the felles w^thin this toune remayninge as far as your discretion may serve not letting this to do for gift promes love hatred or amitie or any thing that may be wth you or againest you so helpe you god and holidome and by that book.

Thoethe of the vieuars and awarders of woulles

Ye swere that alle suche woulles as ye be appointed and assigned to vieue and awarde you shalle welle and truely vieue awarde and adiuge the same for the countrethe and nature that they be of according to your discretion of the whiche your saied awarde and adiugement you shalle make ⟨10ᵈ⟩ relation to the heades for the tyme being not letting so to do for favour frendship love enemitie or hatred or any thing that may be wᵗʰ you or againest you etc.

Thoethe of hances to be taken knelinge

Ye swere ye shalbe true to our Soveraigne ^{Lord the} *lady the* _{king and his heires} *Quenes majestie and to her heires and successours,* and Justiciable by the Maior or his lieutenaunt Constables and companie of merchauntes of the staple of Englonde, in alle matters apperteining to the same estaple welle and truely ye shalbe healping and counseilling to the commune proffit of the saied companie: The commune counsailles of them alle you shalle kepe secret, ye shalle no thing poursue ne do that may be derogation harme or hurt to the generalitie of the saied estaple. The foresaied estaple and alle franchises of the same graunted and confirmed by our souveraigne ⁄ladye the Quene¹⁄ or any of ⁄her¹⁄ progenitours ye shalle truely support & maintayne to your power   Alle ordenaunces that be or hereafter shalbe made by commune consent of this saied companie that owe to be used and exercised for the commune wealth of the same welle and truely ye shalle kepe and observe   And yf ye know any parsonne or parsonnes that shalle do againest the saied ordenaunces or any of them ye shalle open it to the Maior his lieutenaunt or to the Constables of the saied estaple in secret or in open wise or els obeye the levie of suche sommes of money and paines as shalbe put to you for the

¹ Deleted in the MS.

breache of the same   Alle theise poynctes yow shalle welle and truely kepe and perfourme to your power so healpe yow god and by the contentes of that booke.

Ordenaunce of hances.

It is to be remembred that the wayes and meannes to attaine to the fredome of this estaple are and tyme oute mynde of man have ben divers that is to saie by patrimonie redemption by fre gifte commonly called gratis and by apprentishode. To claim by patrimonie is when the sonne being of thage of xvi yeres at least of any parsonne who enioyeth the fredome of this companie by patrimonie or

1. apprentishode doethe demaunde or challenge the same fredome as sonne to his father being fre wether he be borne before his father be admitted to the fredome or after. And whosoever is or shalbe borne afore his father be admitted and sworne he shall pay Ls for his hance at the tyme of his admission   And borne after thadmission of his

2. father shall paie at his admission xl^d. Likewise the sonne

3. of any redemptioner being of like age of xvi yeres at the tyme of his demaunde of the fredome and borne after

4. thadmission of his father shalbe admitted unto the fredome paieng only xl^d And he that is or shalbe borne afore thadmission of <11> his father unto the fredome of this estaple by redempcion shalle not at any tyme claime the fredome aforesaied by patrimonie. And that no man nor childe be admitted to the fredome aforesaied by reason of claime of patrimonie by his graundfather but onely by his father. *To clayme* by redemption is when any personne who hathe no right to the fredome of this companie by patrimonie or apprentishode desirethe to be fre by composition or aggrement that is payenge suche hans and contributinge to suche charge and payement as in suche cases shalbe taxed by the companie of whiche parsonnes commynge in by redemption aforesaied there are divers sortes to wit the mere merchaunt, thartificer, and the

brogger. The mere merchaunt whiche in this caas is to be understonded he that neither is free or exercisethe any manuel occupation nor is or hathe ben any brogger of woulles or woullfelles desiring to be fre of this companie by redemption shalle paie for his hans at his admission to the fredome yf his request be graunted l ounces of fine golde or the valewe thereof in redy money wthoute any respect or daye of payement *And* he that is fre or bearethe the name of an artificer[1] or usethe or hathe used brogging that is to saie buyenge or selling of woulles or woullfelles wthin the realme of Englonde desiring to be fre of this companie by redemption shalle paie at his admission yf his request be graunted one hundrethe ounces of fine golde or the valewe therof in redy money wthoute any respect or daye of payement[2] *And* he that hereafter shalbe admitted frely called gratis shall enjoie the fredome but for his owne parson and his children nor apprentices to claime the fredome aforesaied by suche parsonne admitted gratis The children of thupperclarke of this estaple being borne after theire fathers admission onely excepted who shalle enioye the fredome as the sonnes of other redemptioners and shalle at the tyme of his or theire admission paie

5.

6.

---

[1] "or handycraftsman by occupation or usethe or exercisethe an handycraft or manuel occupation" is written in the margin.

[2] The heavy discrimination here shewn in favour of patrimony and apprenticehood was probably a fairly recent innovation. In 1510 it was alleged that all Staplers paid a hundred marks for their hance (Schanz, II, p. 560). At the current price of gold in 1565 the redemptioner's hance of fifty ounces of gold would work out at £150: the brogger's hance of a hundred ounces would equal £300! (Feavayear, *The Pound Sterling*, pp. 62–3 and 347). By 1619 redemptioners are paying £10 each to the "undertakers" for the new charter, are paying Lord Fenton (the chief "undertaker", *vide* p. 81) in addition, and promise to pay the Company twenty shillings a year (Minutes Book, *passim*). The hances for apprentices and sons of members were made six shillings and eight pence in 1623, and so they remained for many years. Levies were from time to time made upon members and entrance fines were also exacted. In 1835 the hance for admission by patrimony was fixed at £8, by apprenticehood at £10, and by redemption at £20 (Minute of 10 March 1835). These were the hances which the wooldealers of the North objected to paying (*supra*, p. 2).

fredome by Apprentishodde

Apprentice not to exceade xxiiii yeares nor under xvi & to be bounde for ix yeres at lest.

The prentice to continue unmaryed except licensed

7.

8. A Inheritor of xl^{li} land not to be bounde after xvii years of adge

9.

10. To ship 4 several yeres

11.

duble hans

12. extent for taking apprentices to the staple

xl d—*Apprentishode* is when any serveth for his fredome for suche nombre of yeres and wth suche conditions as are hereafter expressed that is to saie he that shalbe bounde to any of this saied companie and mindeth therby to enioye the fredome as apprentice must be bound by Indenture in due fourme to be made when he shalle not exceade the nombre of xxiiii yeres nor shalbe under thage of xvi yeres he must be mulier borne and no bastarde borne of father and mother Englishe and bounden after his M^{r} to whome he is bounde is admitted and taken his oethe *He* must be unmaried at the tyme of his bounde of apprentishod (whiche bounde must be for ix yeres at least) and so continue for terme of his yeres (except he be at his M^{r}s request licensed to marry by the court of this estaple wth thassent of all the portes accustomed to ship (under the staple seele) havinge also at that tyme of the licens graunted at the moost but two yeres to serve *He that* is inheritour or possessioner of xl^{li} lande by the yere or above in possession or reversion shalle not be taken apprentice after he be past thage of xvii yeres *None* shalbe bounde as apprentice withe his father or father in lawe The M^{r} of every apprentice withe whome he is bounde or servethe oute his yeares shalle ship iiii severalle yeres in the tyme of his apprentishode *And* every apprentice being bownde in manner and fourme aforesaied and having served withe one or more being mere merchauntes of the staple and no redemptioners which shalbe made fre ⟨11^{d}⟩ before thexpiration of his terme shalle paie for his hans L^{s} and made fre after thexpiration of his terme shalle paie v^{l} whiche L^{s} and v^{l} shalbe paied by his Mr *And* every apprentice whiche is or shalbe bownde withe any redemptioners wether he serve oute his yeres withe his first M^{r} or withe any other fre of this companie or wether he be made fre within the terme of his apprentishode or after thexpiration of his terme shalle paie for his hans at the tyme of his admission a forthe part of suche hans as his master to whome he was first bounde paied. *And* it is ordeined that no parsonne fre of this companie shalle have above two apprentices at one

tyme bound to the feate of this estaple except suche as
have ben Maiors and lieutenauntes to either of whiche it
shalbe leifulle to have thre apprentices at one tyme and
no more *It is* further ordeyned that yf any M^r or meistres
do refuse or denie to paie ye hans of his or theire apprentices
at the tyme of his admission Then every suche M^r or
meistres so refusing and denieng and not paieng the hans
of suche apprentice shalle forfaicte and paie to the court
of this estaple double so muche as the hans of suche
apprentice ought to paie whereof thone moitie shalbe
counted to be the hans of the same apprentice yf the forfaicture be paied in court or the treasourer for the tyme
being contented *And* yf the penaltie be not paied or the
tresourer for the tyme being not contented then shalle
thapprentice paie his hans him selfe and the saied forfaicture
shalbe levied upon the gooddes of the saied M^r at his
next shipping and in defaulte of his shipping then to be
paied to the court by his childeren whiche then shalle next
come to claime the fredome of this estaple and the saied
forfaicture so levied shalbe restored and paiede to the saied
apprentice *And* whosoever takethe more apprentices then
by this present ordenaunce is permitted shalle forfaicte to
thuse of the generalite for every such offence L^{li} st. and
besides that suche apprentice or apprentices as are taken
above the saied nombre shalle never enioye the fredome
of this companie. *And further* it is ordeined that in every
Indenture of apprentishode wherein is not conteyned that
suche one hathe bounde himselfe apprentice to his M^r as
merchaunt of the staple shalbe taken as voyde and of none
effect and no fredome in this estaple therby to be claimed//
And it is further ordeigned that every parsonne whiche
taketh apprentices shalle make report of the same in
thexchequier of the same estaple exhibitting the indenture
to be enroled by the underclarke of the same estaple in a
booke^1 therfore by the saied underclarke to be provided

the M^r denieng to pay the hance of his appren-tice

l^{li} is the penaltie of suche as have at one tyme more apprentices then by this ordinance is limited

the Inden-ture voyded yf merchaunt of ye staple be not in ye same 13.

Inrowlment wthin one yeare uppon payne

---

^{1} No trace of such a book for this period has yet come to light.
But apprenticeships are recorded in the Minutes Books of the
Company from 1619 onwards.

according to thuse and custome in that behalfe heretofore used wthin one yere next following after the commencement of the terme of his apprentishode upon paine not onely to forfaicte to the court of this estaple xl^s for the first yere in the whiche the saied apprentice shalle not be reaported but also v^{ll} for every other yere after succeadinge as long as suche apprentice shalle so remayne unreaported as is aforesaied *The saied* underclarke taking for his

inrolment

enrollement vi^dst and no more *It is* further ordeined that every apprentice after the deathe of his M^r shalle serve and continue the residue of his yeres of apprentishode to come wth his meistres as long as she is widowe except he shalle have somme reasonable cause to depart from her to serve any other of this companie *And* yf any apprentice shalle by the deathe of his M^r or upon any other occasion departe from his M^r withe whome he was first bounde

14
Setting over
of apprentices

and serve withe any other fre of this companie Then suche apprentice so departing and serving with any ⟨12⟩ other shalbe set over in court of this estaple by the consent of the executours of his M^r deceassed or by consent of his M^r lyvinge by lettres sent from them *And* where above in this ordenaunce is ordeyned that no man shalle have mo apprentices at one tyme than by the same is limited *It is further* ordeined that yf it shalle happen any parsonne of this companie to have by occasion of mariage or executourship any mo apprentices then is above permitted That then the saied parsonne having suche apprentices shalle wthin iii moneths after suche apprentice shalle come to his service either by mariage or executourship prouide to suche apprentice or apprentices so exceeding his nombre or extent a M^r or mistres fre of this estaple at Bruges or els where the same estaple shalbe kepte wthin the saied iii monethes to thintent that the saied apprentice maybe set over in court accordingly *And* in caas suche parsonnes aforesaied cannot provide to the saied apprentice or apprentices M^{rs} fre of this companie wthin the saied thre monethes then the same parsonnes shalle signifie to the court of this

estaple w^{th}in the saied thre monethes by their lettres the
names of suche apprentices whiche they shalle have above
theire nombre & therby shalle require the companie here
to appoinct unto the same apprentice a M^r or meistres as
to the same court shalle seme convenient   *And* yf neither
the same M^r neither the court can appoinct unto suche
apprentice M^r or meistres according as is abovesaied that
then it shalle not be preiudicialle to suche parsonne havinge
suche apprentices above his nombre to kepe the saied
apprentice neither to any of the saied apprentices an impediment or barre of the fredome of this estaple so alwaye he
do his duetie any thing to forerehersed to the contrarie
notw^{th}standing   *It is further* ordeined that when any
apprentice shalbe destitute of a M^r or shalle have any
iuste cause to seke him another Mr That then upon the
request made by him to the Maior of this estaple for the
tyme being to be set over in court of this estaple to serve
any other of this companie during the residue of his yeares
and the same request afterwarde being certified by lettres
under the companies seele of London to the court of this
estaple thereunto adioyned and had the consentes aswelle
of his fourmer M^r as the consent of thother to whome
he requirethe to be set over shalbe set over in court of this
saied estaple accordingly and in due manner and fourme
althoughe suche apprentice be not personally present in
court as hathe ben accustomed whiche setting over aforesaied shalbe as good and valueable as thoughe the parties
had ben here personally present *It is further* ordeined concluded and enacted that every apprentice whiche shalbe
made fre of this estaple according to thordenaunce shalle
bring lettres from his M^r with whome he servethe whereby
his M^r or maistres requireth that he may be made fre in
like manner yf an apprentice be made fre w^{th}in his terme
he shalle w^{th}in one yere after thexpiration of his terme
bring or send a lettre from his M^r or his meistres ⟨12^d⟩
with whome he served testifienge that he hathe welle and
truely served him as an apprentice ought to do   *And* yf

15.
apprentice
destitute of a
M^r, & to be
set over to
another,

16.
to certefie
good service

his M.^r or meistres shalle certifie that he hathe faithfully served by alle his terme and yet in dede he hathe not so done   Then shalle the master & meistres so untruely certifieng forfaict and paie to the court of this estaple one hundrethe poundes st. *Provided* alwayes that yf an apprentice do at any tyme departe from his maister or meistres or be put awaye from his maistre or maistres for any his offence or lewde demeanours yf suche apprentice do reconcile him selfe to his maister or meistres wthin one monethe next after and do serve so muche more tyme above his terme of his apprenticehod as he was awaye from his maister or meistres that then suche absence shalle not be imputed to him as a breache of his apprentishode nor the maister shalle incurre any dammage for certifieng his good service in that caas   *And* yf the maister or meistres do refuse or wille not certifie the court of the good service of his apprentice in manner and fourme aforesaied being therunto required by thapprentice then suche maister or mistres so refusing and not certifieng shalle forfaict to thuse of the companie x^{li} and the parsonne made fre by apprentishode shalle nevertheles enioye the fredome the lacke of suche certificat not wthstanding yf by his true and faithfulle service he hath deserved it and that it be so tried by court   *And it is further* ordeined that no parsonne made fre by apprentishode shalle wthin two yeres next after thexpiration of his terme take any apprentice except he be maried and in that caas shalle take but one and no more in iiii yeres after the taking of his first apprentice withoute his first apprentice die or so misdemeane him as he be therby disfranchised and in that caas he may take another so as in six yeres after thexpiration of his terme he have but one apprentice at one tyme   Item no parsonne fre by patrimonie shalle take any apprentice untille he be of the age of xxii yeres except he do marry and then after he be xxi yeres olde to take and have but one apprentice tille he have ben maried fowre yeres or els shalbe fulle xxviii yeres of age   *It is further* ordeigned and enacted that no parsonne whatsoever shalle from hensfourthe be admitted

untrue certificat

reconciliation for want of service

17 extent for taking of apprentices & allso the tymes lymited

unto the fredome of this companie or take thoethe appoincted for the same in any other place than where the
staple shalbe kept and the staple merchaundise put to sale
and that in open & full court to be holden wthin vi wekes
at the furthest after tharrivalle of London flete   *And it is
further* ordeined aswelle in avoyding of displeasure as for
other causes that from hensfourþh no parsonne what soever
be admitted to the fredome of this companie by redemption
or gratis except the consent of the court be therin first had
wthin the tyme of vi wekes before limited and tried by
balleting like as at Callais was at the surprise thereof used
And it is further ordeyned that no personne for any respect
whiche shalbe infamous or knowen to be an unquiet parsonne or a commune disturber shalle at any tyme be admitted
unto the fredome of this ⟨13⟩ wourshipfulle companie by
redemption or gratis   *And* yf ignorantly or negligently
any suche infamous or unquiet parsonne shalbe admitted
than upon notice and proufe therof had suche admission
shalbe voide and suche personne so admitted shalbe
fourthwithe disfraunchised   *And* it is further ordeined
that yf any parsonne bounden as an apprentice do use
himselfe obstinatly or sturdely or do not serve his maister
or meistres as an apprentice ought to do during the
tyme of his service that then upon certificate of his
maister or mistres he shalbe disfraunchised yf the court
wille therunto agree and consent   *And forasmuche* as it
hath pleased the Quenes maiestie of her gratious goodnes
to confirme alle the auncient privileges and usages which
were used by the companie of merchauntes of the staple
of Callais at the tyme of surpriuse thereof or wthin one
yeare before the surpriuse thereof and also to commaunde
us by her hightness especialle lettres to reduce ourselves to
our auncient gouverment and execution of our olde orders
and also to forbeare for certaine yeres ensueng to receave
any into our companie and fellowship other than suche
as have right unto it   *It is* therefore aswelle in accom-
plishement of the Quenes maiesties lettre as for the commune welthe and benefite of the companie decreed and

18
time ap-
pointed for
admission &
also ye place

19.

20. Appren-
tice of mis-
demenor

the q maies-
ties lettres.

21.

ordeined that the abovesaied articles ordenaunces and clauses and every of them be from hensefourthe inviolably kept and holden as an ordenaunce *And* where by the ordenaunce made the xxiii daye of August xv^c lxi it was concluded by court then holden that no personne after the same daye shulde be admitted to the fredome of this companie by redemption or gratis within the space of vii yeres then next ensueng as more plainely apperethe by

date of making this ordenaunce

the saiede ordenaunce[1] *It is* now at this present court holden the xvii daye of maye xv^c lxv decred and ordeined that the article aforesaied for none admission into the fredome shalbe holly observed and kepte and that no personne after thexpiration of the saied vii yeres shalbe in any manner of wyse admitted into the fredome of

a time to kepe out re-demptioners expired in anno 1575 fforfaict for speaking or writing in any parsonne apprentice behoofe con-trary to this ordenaunce.

this companie by redemption or gratis wth in the space of vii yeres next after that ensueng And whosoever shall directly or indirectly write speake or consent wittingly or willingly to the making fre or admitting into the fredome any parsonne or parsonnes other then suche as ben or then shalbe of the kinges moost honorable privye counsaile or of the moost noble order of the garter whereby any par-sonne or apprentice may or shalle attaine or enioye the fredome of this companie contrarie to the true meannyng of this ordenaunce or any braunche or article therein conteined shall forfaict and paye to thuse of the generalitie of this estaple yf he be maior or lieutenaunt C^{li} yf he be Constable C merks and every other brother xl^{li} and the saied parsonne so admitted shalle nevertheles be dis-fraunchised *And* it is further ordeined that all other ordenaunces touching hances of fremen shalbe clerly voyde and of none effect and this present ordenaunce to stand in strenght with the proviso concerning fremen ⟨13^d⟩ mencioned in the late ordenaunces of this estaple made the xxiii day of August aforesaied whiche then and before that tyme were admitted *And it is further* ordeined that

---

[1] There is no record of this ordinance in the Register of Royal Grants.

none apprentice shall be admitted to the fredome of this
estaple as apprentice untille he have aunswered upon his
oethe to the articles hereunder written

Articles for every apprentice to be examined of before
he be admitted to the fredome of this estaple

1. ffirst wether thindenture made betwene yow and your
maister is made betwene you and him withoute cowler
fraude or deceipt
2. *Item* wether you have served your maister according
to your Indenture
3. *Also* yf you have done him good service heretofore so
you shalle continue the same the residue of your yeres
to come and better yf you can as nigh as god will geve
you grace or with summe other of the companie unto
whome by consent of court you shalbe appoincted.
4. Item wether your father or you or any of your affinites
or alliaunces have geven any gift or rewarde or made
promes of any gift or rewarde to your saiede maister
whereby yow shulde be retained in name & not in
dede as apprentice
5. Item wether you be mulier borne that is to saie of father
and mother certaine in matrimonie
6. Item wether you be mere englishe borne boethe of
father and mother certaine
7. Item wether ye be the sonne of any bounde man or no
8. Ye swere by god and by the holie contentes of that
book that ye have truely aunswered to every of the
saied articles & questions to your knowledge and
understanding, so helpe you god etc.

Admonitions to be geven to every apprentice
at his admission to the fredome.

Item to examine every apprentice what lande he might
dispende or was inheritable to when he was bounde apprentice

enquirye for
lande

Althoughe ye be presently admitted into the fredome of this companie upon good hope that ye wille welle and truely serve your maister as an apprentice and faithfulle servant ought to do yet I do admonishe yow that if hereafter by certificat from your maister or otherwise it be proved and considered by the court here that ye do departe from your maister unlawfully not serving oute ⟨14⟩ your yeres of apprentishode as by ordenaunce therefore provided ye ought to do or that you marrye within your terme withoute consent of this howse, your maister and the portes by writing according to thordenaunce, or that you do obstinatly or sturdely use your selfe, or do not serve your maister or maistres as an apprentice ought to do, y^t then notwthstandinge your admission nowe, ye shalbe clerly disfraunchised from the liberties and fredome of this wourshipfulle companie, as though ye had never ben admitted to it

Ordenaunce for generalle shippinges

fforasmuche as the companie of the staple ben disparsed and inhabitinge in many places of the realme of Englonde it is to be foresene that no brother of the same be preiudiced in his trade and occupienge by distaunce of place and therefore and to the intent that every one may have knowledge howe to provide and furnishe himselfe in his occupieng and trade in one unifourme order and at tyme convenient *It is* agreed and ordeined that there shalbe but two generalle shippinges in one yeare to be kept at dayes and places and in manner and fourme hereunder written that is to saie that no brother of this companie shalle ship or cause to be shipped any woulle or woullfelles but onely at the port of London, Boston, Hull, ipswiche and Saundwhiche or at any of them the same woulles and woulfelles onely to be transported to the toune of Bruges in flaunders or to suche other place whereas the staple shalbe kepte and the staple merchaundise by the saied

portes to ship at

merchauntes of the staple put to sale and to none other
place upon paine that every parson that shalle ship from
any other porte or to any other place then is above recited
or at any other time then is hereafter expressed shalbe
clerely disfraunchised from the liberties and fredome of disfranchised
this companie *And* it is further ordeined that the first ffirst ship-
shipping shalle beginne yerely by the xx daye of Marche ping at 20th
and not before or as sone after as conveniently may be m'che or so
And the second shipping shalle beginne yerely the xv daye sone after as
of July and not before but as sone after as conveniently maybe con-
may be *Provided* alwayes that yf upon any respect it shalle venient
seme good to the companie here in fulle court to be as- ii^de shipping
sembled within one moneth next after tharrivalle of the at 15 Julii or
last flete of the latter shippinges not to make two shippinges sone after as
in the yere next following or other wise to alter the tymes is con-
of shippinges aforesaied or any of them that then it shalbe venient.
leifull to the court aforesaied to appoinct by theire com- for alteration
mune consentes one or more shippinge for the yere next of number
following at suche tyme and in suche order then to be & tymes of
devised as to them shalbe thought necessarie and ⟨14^d⟩ shippinges.
convenient whereof the portes shalbe certified by the places
lettres wth the daye certaine of shippinge in alle spede duely
to be observed upon the paines aforesaied *And* to thintent
that no newe woulles be shipped by occasion of which no newe
newe woulles many inconveniences have and may ensue wolles to be
as experience hathe taught *It is* ordeyned that no parson shipped
shalle at the seconde shippinge shippe any woulles but Woll to be
olde woulles whiche shalbe at the porte at or before the at the port
xx daye of June upon paine of forfaicture of xl^s for every at ye 20 of
sarpler so shipped and so after the afferaunt and the same June
woulles nevertheles not to issue oute by the space of one forfaict
hole yeare and never to take preferment of olde woulles vieuars for
And it is further ordeined that certayne parsonnes shalle new shorne
yearly be appoincted and assigned at every porte aforesaied wolle
where any staple merchaundise shalbe shipped before the
first daye of June wch shalle before the xx daye of June
vieue what woulles every brother of this companie hathe

redy at the porte where the same shalbe shipped *And*
suche parsonnes so to be appoincted for the port of London
shall take a corporalle oethe before the Maior of the staple
for the tyme being yf he be there resident or else afore
the auncient of the companie that hathe ben Maior or
lieutenaunt that they shalle truely and faithfully vieue what
quantite of woulles is in every mans howse woulhowse
and lofte or of any of them and the same vieue shalle
reaport and deliver in writing to the Maior for the tyme
being upon the xxi or xxii daye of June aforesaied upon
paine that every parson so appoincted whiche shalle refuse
or neglect to vieue and make reaport as is aforesaiede shalle
forfaict every of them to thuse of the generalitie v^{ll} *And*
it is further ordeyned that the Maior of the staple of Boston
for the tyme being yf he be fre of the companie of the
staple of Englonde and be resident at or nere the port of
Boston or els the auncient shipper at that porte which
hath borne office of Lieutenaunt or Constable in this
estaple shalle appoinct vieuers in manner and fourme aforesaied whiche vieuers shalle vieue and reaport the quantite
of woulles to be shipped at that port in manner and effect
aforesaied upon paine aforesaiede *Like* order shalbe taken
in alle thinges by the companie and auncient shipper whiche
hathe borne office of Constable in this estaple whiche shalle
shippe at any of the portes of Hull Saundwiche or Ipswiche
and shalbe executed as is aforesaied in all thinges upon like
paine *It is further* ordeined that yerely the first daye of

pointers for shippings

March or the first day of June or at suche tyme as the
shipping shalle beginne shalbe assigned by the saied companie at every port where the staple merchaundise shalbe
shipped iiii iii or ii parsons fre of the companie whiche shall
provide and appoinct sufficient nombre of shippes and
bottoms mete for the sure and saufe convey of the woulles
and woulles /sic/ felles to be shipped at the shipping following from every the saied portes and shalle by alle menes
serche and trie wether the same shippes and bottoms be
thight or no and well ballested and shalle take order for

shippinge the gooddes of every brother withoute the shippes to be peasired[1] above the hatches or any goodes laden before the maste excepte it shalle seame otherwise good to the poincters to be otherwise ordered to theire discretions *And in* case ⟨15⟩ any shippes of the woull- flete laden withe woulles or felles shalle happen to sale in leake the saied poincters shalle endevore themselves to se and cause the same gooddes to be saufly shipped yf nede be in summe other ship that is thight to the moost profit of the ownars and shalle in alle other thinges do as at shipping tymes hathe ben accustomed and shalle levie by impositions upon every sarpler of woulles and woulfelles equally taxed alle suche charges as shalbe expended during the shipping tyme and thereof shalle make a perfect and true accompt at the port where the same shalbe shipped to the companie there shippinge or to suche as thauncient of the port shalle appoinct *And yf* any money shalle remayne in theire handes the same shalbe paiede to the next poincters towardes the charges of the next shipping *And* yf any money shalbe due to the poincters upon the fote of theire accomptes the same shalbe paied to them by the next poincters and levied by impositions as other charges be *And it is* further ordeined that yf any parsonne fre of this companie shalle do carrie or conveye or cause to be carried or conveied any woulle or woulfelles into any ship or bottom withoute thassent or privite of the customer and comptroller of the port where the goddes shalbe shipped or shalle wittingly or willingly by any indirect meannes defraude the Quenes maiestie her heires or successours of any custume or subsidie due for any his woulles or felles to be transported shalle forfaict and paie to thuse of the generalite xl^{li} for every suche offence whereof the presenter shalle have the thirde parte *And* for avoiding of coulorable shipping wherby boethe the Quenes maiestie may be deceaved in her custume and also the good orders of the companie made for extent of shipping defrauded and

ffor shippes in leake

accompt of pointers

for defraud- ing of cus- tom to forfaict xl^{li}

---

[1] I.e. poisired, weighted or loaded.

broken *It is* therefore ordeined that every brother of this companie whiche shalle ship any woulles or woullfelles in manner and fourme aforesaied shalle before the same goodes be put to sale or suffered to issue oute take a corporallè oethe upon the holy evangiles either in the court of this estaple or before the Maior of this estaple for the tyme being or summe other brother that hathe borne office of Maior lieutenaunt or Constable that the goodes shipped by him and in his name either ioinctly or severally are his owne goodes in parte or in alle and shipped at his owne adventure withoute any fourmer bargaine or promes of bargaine made to any parsonne whiche oethe so taken oute of the court by any the parsonnes aforesaied shalbe certified under the handes of him that takethe it to the court of this estaple w^{t}in vi wekes after tharrivalle of the London flete *It is further* ordeined that yf it shallè at any tyme be tried that any brother of this companie taking suche oethe do commit periurie in shipping any goods in his owne name or ioinctly wth any other whereof contrarie to his foresaied oethe he hathe made any fourmer bargaine or promis of bargaine shalbe disfraunchised from ye fredome and liberties of this estaple as a coulourable ⟨15^d⟩ shipper and a parsonne periured *It is* further ordeined that every brother of this companie whiche shalle from hensfourthe ship any woulles oute of any parte of Englonde being not packed to rightes that is to saie by a sworne packer shalle forfaict for every pocket so shipped v^{ll} *And* it is further ordeyned that no po^{tt}[1] whiche hereafter shalbe shipped oute of any porte of Englond shall at the weight thereof waye at the Quenes beame in Englonde above xii todde at the moost upon paine of forfaicture to this estaple for every po^{tt} that shalle so waye above xii todde v^l. *And it* is further ordeined that no parson from hensfourth shalle ship any lokes marche lokes onely excepted upon paine of forfaicture of v^{ll} for every po^{tt} and so after the afferaunt *And* it is further ordeined that no parsonne fre of this

othe to be had & taken for propertie of goodes beforesaied

former bargaine or promesse of bargaine

packed to rights

xii tod in a po^{tt} at ye most

---

[1] I.e. pocket. *Vide supra*, pp. 20, 30. A todd was 28 lb. or 4 cloves of 7 lb.

companie shalle from hensfourthe gelde or augmente any
po^{tt} by putting in or taking out any woulles either in the
wayhowse or in any other place after the same shalbe
shipped upon paine of forfaicture of xx^d for every po^{tt} so
augmented gelded or diminished *And* it is further ordeined that yf any po^{tt} to be wayed at the beame where the
staple is or shalbe kept shalle excede the waight of one
sacc iiii naile that then the Ownars of every suche po^{tt}
shalle forfaict the vth cl.[1] of that over waight of that woulles
of what nature or countrethe soever the same be or the
valewe thereof the same to be rated at the fulle price and
of every other naile above the said v cl. shalle forfaict
xii^d alle the same to be applied to the boxe of the poore
the officers dueties deducted oute of the said forfaictures
Provided allwayes that theise penalties for hevy po^{tts}
brought to the beame shalle not extend to suche pockettes
as shalbe upon licens of the heades of this estaple for the
tyme being be reported here in this estaple by reason
of any iuste cause any thinge before rehersed to the
contrarie in any wise notwthstanding *And* it is further
aggreed that no brother of this companie shalle paie any
freight here tille the shipper have delivered his cocket to
the clerke of the collectrie for the tyme being and that the
saied clerke have set his hande to his bille of lading upon
paine that every parsonne that shalle do contrarie shalle
forfaict xx^s for every suche offence to be put into the boxe
of the poore *It is further* agreed that none of the companie
of this estaple shalle either selle bargaine or make promis
of bargaine of any woulles or woulfelles shipped or whiche
shalbe shipped to this estaple before the same woulles or
woulfelles shalle arrive to the port of the Sluise here in
flaunders upon paine the offender to forfaict xl^s for every
sarpler and so after the afferaunt.

Thoethe of particuler shippers to be sent to the portes

Ye swere etc that alle suche gooddes as ye have shipped
or have caused to be shipped in your name from the port

[1] I.e. clove of 7 lb.

of London or any other port within the realme of Englonde
to this estaple since the xxv daye of marche last past ben
your owne proper goodds and shipped to your owne
proper use and adventure wthout any fourmer bargaine or
promes of bargaine thereof made to any parson or parsonnes and the same be not shipped to any other ⟨16⟩
parson or personnes use or proffit or any parte or parcelle
thereof nor y^t you have your gooddes shipped or caused
to be shipped in any other mannes name but onely in your
owne withoute coulour fraude or deceipt so helpe you
god etc.

Theothe of ioincte shippers

Ye swere that ye shalle truely declare how muche is
apperteining to you of suche goodes as ben ioinctly shipped
by you or your copartenar or copartenars from the port of
London or any other port within the realme of Englonde
to this estaple since the xxv daye of marche last past and
that the same ben your owne proper goodes and shipped
to your owne proper use and adventure withoute any
fourmer bargaine or promes of bargaine thereof made
to any other parsonne or parsonnes use or profit or any
parte or parcelle thereof withoute coulour fraude or deceipt
etc.

The addition hereunder written to be red at the latter shippinge.

ffurther ye swere that alle suche your woulles as you
have shipped or caused to be shipped at this generalle
shipping from the porte of London or any other porte
within the realme of Englonde to this estaple at Bruges are
olde woulles and no parte or parcelle thereof newe woulles
of the groethe and shere of this present yere to your
knowledge and that the same were at the porte where you
shipped the same at the xx daye of June so helpe you god etc.

Ordenaunce for extent of shippinge.

fforasmuche as in alle bodies polliticke and corporations of felloweshippes the membres and partes of the same be not of equalle aucthorite and reputation but there is a greater respect to be had to the superiours then to the inferiours in that most communely those ben at greater charge in keping theire estate and familie then thother for maintenaunce whereof and for due proportion of shipping to be had according to every personnes degre of this estaple especially exchueng and suppressing the inordenate desire of certaine covetous personnes whereof summe have bought suche greate quantite of woulles and woulfelles as the younge men coulde have none or very litle and summe other have charged themselves above theire abilite withe exceding nombre of woulles and woulfelles shipped to this estaple runninge thereby into the daunger of theire creditours and not able to satisfie them according to the faithe of a good merchaunt but have ben forced of necessite to selle theire gooddes under the value to theire utter undoenge and againest the commune welthe of this estaple *It is therefore* agreed concluded and enacted at this present court holden in this estaple the xvii daye of Maye xv⁰ lxv that it shalbe leifulle to him that hathe ben is or shalbe Maior of this estaple to ship to the same estaple lx sarplers of woulles or woulfelles in a yere and not above (v⁰ felles smalle tale rekened for a sarpler) *Item* to every one that hathe ben is or shalbe lieutenaunt l sarplers of woulles and woulfelles in a yere and not above *Item* to every one that hath ben is or shalle ⟨16ᵈ⟩ be Constable xl sarplers of woulles or woulfelles in a yere and not above *Item* to every other parsonne of this companie whiche hathe ben is or shalle be maried xxxv sarplers in a yeare and not above *Item* to every widoe bearing charge of housholde xxx sarplers in a yere and not above *Item* to every brother not maried bearing charge of housholde to wit two parsonnes besides him selfe whiche hathe continued or shalle

mr Maior
lx sarpler

lieutenaunt
l sarplers

the constable
& every
maryed man
& wydow &
bachelor
howseholder

continue the saied charge by the space of xiii monethes before his shipping xx sarplers in a yeare and not above

Item two parsonnes fre of this companie being ioinct shippers or severalle shippers inhabiting boethe togither in one howse and keping iii parsonnes at their equalle charges by the like space of xiii monethes may shipp xx sarplers of woulles or woullfelles in a yeare every of them and not above   *Item* to every other fellowe of this

estaple being not apprentice and above thage of xxi yeares x sarplers in a yeare & not above   *Item* it shalbe leifulle to every fre mans sonne not being apprentice to any

forener[1] after he be of thage of xviii yeares to ship to this estaple iiii sarplers of woulles or woullfelles in a yeare and not above untille he be of thage of xxi yeres   *Item* it

shalbe leifulle to every apprentice fre of this estaple to ship to the same by consent of his maister after he have served fulle vi yeares iiii sarplers of woulles and woullfelles in a yere and not above   The same to be accompted as parcelle of his maisters extent in that yeare *provided* that his Mrs suche consent be had and certified to the companie resiaunt where the staple merchaundise is solde by lettres directed from his Mr in that behalfe at the shipping of the saied

woulles or woullfelles   *And it is* further ordeyned and enacted that yf any parsonne shalle ship to this estaple any greater quantite of woulles or woullfelles then is above limited and appoincted that then every suche parsonne so offending shalle forfaict to the court of this estaple for every sarpler of woulles or felles exceading his extent and proportion aforesaied v[ll] st and so after thafferaunt and the same woulles or woullfelles nevertheles shalbe staied from sale by the space of one hole yeare next ensuenge and never to be issued oute to take the benefite of olde wolle

or olde felles[2]   *It is further* ordeined and established that yf any parsonne shalle seke coulourably to defraude this

---

[1] I.e. to a member of any other company; cf. the restraints against such a one acting as attorney, *infra*, p. 154.
[2] *Vide infra*, p. 164.

acte or to ship in any other mans name his woulles or felles
or do procure any other parsonne to ship any woulles
or felles to this estaple whereby he shalle by any slight
device or malingine receave any manner of commoditie or
benefite what soever that then suche parsonne so offending
or doenge and also the parsonne so shipping goods coulorably or contrarie to the true intent and meannynge of this
acte shalbe clerely disfraunchised from the fredome and
liberties of this companie *And* aswell for the better
inforcing of the premisses as for avoyding of the daunger
and perille of the lawes and statutes of the realme of
Englonde and for avoyding of greate slaunder whiche the
companie hathe sustained by buyeng engrossing and brogging of woulles *It is further* ordeined that if any parsonne
fre of this companie doo from hensfourthe bargaine or selle
to any manner of parson what soever within the realme
of Englonde any kinde of woulles or woullfelles whiche
may be shipped to this estaple (midle Linsey midle Keston
and refuse woulles and woulles of his owne groethe onely
excepted) suche parsonne so offending shalle ⟨17⟩ forfaicte
to the court of this estaple for his first defaulte duely proved
v^{li} on every sarpler by him solde and so after the afferaunt
And for his seconde offence duely proved after his first
conviction shalle forfaicte x^{li} on every sarpler and so after
the afferaunt *And for* his thirde defaulte and offence duely
proved after the like conviction shalbe disfraunchised of
the fredome of this estaple The moitie of which forfaictures of v^{li} and x^{li} aforesaied shalle be to the presenter
of the faulte and thother moitie shalle remayne to the court
Provided alwayes that it shalle not be hurtfulle to any
brother of this companie in respect of this ordenaunce to
selle in Englonde as muche of his woulles or woullfelles
as shalle amount to halfe his extent so the sale be made to
any brother of this companie and that it exceade not halfe
his extent aforesaied Certifieng the maior of this estaple
for the tyme being thereof either by his lettres or els by
woorde of mouthe within two monethes next after suche

for sale of staple wolle not to be sold in Englonde

sale upon paine of forfaicture to the court of this estaple
xl^s on every sarpler toties quoties and the same woulles
and felles solde to be accompted parcelle of the sellers
extent *And* yf any brother aforesaied shalle happen to
selle within Englonde any woulles or woullfelles to any
brother aforesaied above halfe his extent in that yeare
contrarie to the fourme and effect of this order shalle
forfaict of every sarpler so solde above halfe his extent
v^{ll}.

Ordenaunce for attorneis made the xixth daye of Maye xvc lxv

The companie of this estaple of Englonde animad-
vertinge what trouble and disquietnes may rise to the court
of the same estaple by attorneis usurping farther aucthorite
then by theire constituantes is to them prescribed and what
preiudice may growe to divers merchauntes of the same
havinge goodes there for lacke of attorneis have for quietnes
of the same especially that the requisite power of every
attorney in this estaple may be knowen ordeined and
enacted that no parsonne or parsonnes of the staple shalle
make sale and delivery of any woulles or woullfelles here
in the staple at Bruges except he be the proprietaire thereof
or his lawfulle and sufficient attorney of thage of xxi yeares
at least aucthorised by lettre of attorney under autenticque
seale of summe toune or the sele of suche right wourshipfulle person as is Maior or for the tyme being shalbe Maior
or hathe ben Maior of the same estaple or having aucthorite
by acte of entre of constitution in the regestres of this
estaple upon thoffender in that behalfe to forfaicte to the
court of this estaple x^{ll} st. upon every sarpler and so after
the afferaunt solde and delivered toties quoties *And that*
every attorney shalle have power to receave his constituants
goodes and make sale thereof to the merchaunt straunger
Likewise to demaunde and receave the debtes or billes due
to his saied master *Item to* paie suche impositions as ben

due by his ⟨17ᵈ⟩ constituant and alle other sommes of money as his constituant is or shalbe cessed by court to paie concerninge the commune welthe & charges of this estaple *Also* yf nede be to sue poursue and impleade alle and every personne obstrict[1] to his constituant either in action of debt or trespas done in the goods of his constituant being in his charge and to recover   *Also* upon any action of pl/ain/t moved or commenced in this estaple againest his saied constituaunt the saied attorney to aunswer and defende for and in the name of his constituaunt   *Of* his receiptes and recouveries it shalbe leifulle to him to give acquittaunces and other lawfulle discharges also may bind his constituant for the custume and subsidie due by the same his constituant and for payement to be made for suche olde wolles as he shalle buie for issueng oute of his constituantes newe woulles[2] but otherwise not nor shalle make transport of any goodes withoute expresse aucthorite in the lettre of atturney or acte of entre of constitution in the regestres of this estaple to make transporte   *Also* it shalbe leifulle to every atturney being thereunto aucthorised to make a substitute and to geve him suche power and aucthorite as he himselfe hathe aswelle in transportinge as otherwise whiche substitute may continue substitute unto tharrivalle of the next flete following after the tyme of entre of his aucthorite except suche substituaunt him selfe do come or retourne to this estaple at any time before the saiede arrivalle and then the power of suche substitute shalle from thensfourthe cease and be utterly voyde   *Provided* that if the maister of suche substituaunte do retourne to this estaple at any tyme within thabsence of his atturney it shalbe at his pleasure to revoke or continue the aucthorite of suche substitute   *And* every lettre of atturney shalbe entred into the bookes of this estaple there to remayne of recorde as hathe ben accustomed and none to be admitted attorney by any lettre missive nor shalle take upon him to be atturney by pretext of any lettre of atturney before he be thereunto

---

[1] Indebted.   [2] Cf. *infra*, pp. 164 *et seq.*

admitted in court or assemble   *Provided* alwayes and it is
further agreed concluded and enacted as followithe to wit
y^t whosoever of this estaple shippethe to the same estaple
xx sarplers or above of woulles or woullfelles in a yere that
is to saie from the xxv daye of marche unto the 25 daye
of marche shalle not be atturney at any tyme within the
same yeare either by constitution or substitution *Also* whosoever shippethe x sarplers and not above xv sarplers of
woulles or woullfelles in a yeare may be atturney by constitution and substitution for iiii^xx sarplers[1] more in that
yeare and not above   *Likewise* he that shippethe v sarplers
and not above x sarplers in a yeare may be atturney by
constitution and substitution for C sarplers more in that
yere and not above   *Item* whosoever being none apprentice shippethe not above v sarplers in a yere may be atturney
by constitution and substitution for ii^c sarplers in that
yeare and not above   *Also* it shalbe leifulle to every
apprentice being admitted to the fredome of this estaple
whose master shippethe xl sarplers or under in a yeare to
be atturney by constitution and substitution for xxxv
sarplers more besides his M^rs in a yeare and not above   *And*
it shalbe leifulle to every apprentice aforesaied whose
maister shippethe L sarplers to be atturney by constitution
and substitution for x sarplers more in a yeare and not
above *And it* shalbe leifulle to every apprentice (bounde to
any brother of this companie) ⟨18⟩ being a fremans sonne
to be atturney by constitution and substitution to his maister
and others besides for L sarplers in a yeare and not above
And whosoever of the companie is no shipper may be
atturney by constitution and substitution for ii^c L sarplers
in that yeare wherein he doethe not ship   *It is also* agreed
that the Mr & apprentice shalle not be atturney boethe
at one tyme   *It is further* agreed that a fremans sonne
being apprentice to any not fre of this companie shalle
not be atturney here in this estaple nor shalle ship any
staple merchaundise during the tyme of his apprentishode

[1] I.e. eighty sarplers.

It is further ordeined that ioinct shippers shalle ioinctly in alle theire names make theire lettres of atturney. Except any of them do parsonally repaire to this estaple to whome it shalbe then leifulle and to every of the saied ioinct shippers being in the saied estaple withoute any lettre of attorney to him from the reste to be made aswelle to make sale of the hole goodes as parcelle thereof also to constitute his attorney by acte of entre in the regestres of this estaple to make sale thereof in as large manner and fourme as he the saied constituant might do or shulde do in his proper person yf he were thereat present *And* whatsoever parsonne or parsonnes of this estaple shalle offende in any articles abovesaied shalle forfaict to the court of this estaple for the offence of every suche article x^l st toties quoties *Alle* and every suche forfaictures yf the offender be an apprentice and offende therein withoute his M^{rs} commaundement to be levied upon him and his goodes at his first shipping and that suche apprentice shalle not be atturney or substitute untille suche tyme as he hathe satisfied the court of his forfaicture *And yf* suche apprentice do offende by his maisters commaundement then the saied penaltie to be levied upon his saied maister and his goodes *And* yf the offender be a fre man of this estaple to be levied upon him and his goodes withoute grace favor or pardon *Provided* alwayes that the atturney or substitute be not charged w^{te} any more woulles or felles touchyng the feate of his atturneship then shalbe remayninge in this estaple at the tyme of his admission

Ordenaunce for shewes

In avoyding of divers inconveniences whiche might ensue to this companie yf the mechauntes buyers shulde linger upon theire markettes *It is* convenient and necessarie that the olde order for dayes of shewes and tymes and places of sales be observed *And* it is therefore ordeined concluded & enacted that no personne fre of this companie

shalle shewe any woulles or felles to any merchaunt
straunger or other minding to buye, before shewe be geven
to them by the heades of the companie for the tyme being
resident where the staple shalbe kepte upon paine of forfaicture of xl^s for every tyme so offendinge   *And* it is
further ordeined that the shewe to be geven to the straunger
requiring to buie shalbe in manner and fourme followinge
vz. that he shalle buie his olde woll and olde felles first
and withe one olde he shalle take two newe he shalle do
his feate wthin ⟨18^d⟩ two shewe dayes and one daye next
after which shewe dayes are to be accompted Mondaye,
Wensdaye and fridaye yf it be for felles from the annuntiation of our lady tille Michelmas wthin iii shewe dayes and
one daye after and from Michelmas tille annuntiation of
our ladye within fowre shewe dayes and one daye after
and the daye wherein he takethe shewe yf it be a shewe
daye to be accompted one   He shalle paie his money
according to the table except he can otherwise agree withe
the merchaunt and shalbe assigned his broker   *And* it is
further ordeined that the last night of the tyme of buieng
prescribed the broker so assigned to him shalle bring reaport
to the hedds of the companie for the tyme beinge resident
at the place of the staple what feate he hathe done and what
goodes his merchaunt or merchauntes have bought   *And*
it is further ordeined that yf any merchaunt taking shewe
clere not his shewe bill but departe withoute doeng any
feate that tyme or raise shalbe exempted from buyeng any
merchaundise within this estaple by the space of one yeare
next ensuenge   *And it is* further ordeined that no personne
fre of this companie shalle from hensfourthe shewe any
woulles or woullfelles to any merchaunt straunger after his
tyme of shewe expired tille a newe shewe be geven by the
heades of this estaple for the tyme being upon paine of
forfaicture of xx^s for every sarpler of woulles and felles

no wolls to yssue but in the name of the very buyer

and so after the afferaunt   *And it is further* ordeigned that
no billes shalbe taken oute for issuinge of any goodes upon
the shewe of any other than the very buyer upon paine

the taker oute of suche bille to forfaict for every sarpler
of woulles or woulle felles so taken out xx^s and so after
thafferaunt   *And it is* further ordeined that no merchaunt
straunger having taken shewe for woulles and woullfelles
shalle take any new shewe for any woulles w^{t}in vi dayes
after thexpiration of his first shewe upon paine of forfaicture
of x^s to be paied by suche broker as shalle present or
demaunde the shewe   *And it is* further ordeined that every
merchaunt straunger buyeng felles wch hath ben accustomed
to buye woulles shalle buye withe every xvc felles and so
after the afferaunt one sarpler of woulles fit for theire
draperie yf there be sufficient in the toune of suche sortes
to furnishe him[1]   *And it is* further ordeyned that it shalle
not be leifulle to any of the companie to bargaine or selle
to or withe any manner merchaunt straunger whatsoever
or make promes of bargaine or set any price upon liking
or otherwise or procure or cause any woulles or felles to
be solde or deliver any woulles upon any bargaine made
by any other parsonne to or withe any suche marchaunt
straunger aforesaiede of or for any woulles or felles shipped
or to be shipped to the staple but onely in that place where
the staple is or shalbe kepte upon paine the offendor to
forfaict for every sarpler of woulle and woullfelles so
bargained or solde or whereof any promes of bargaine
shalbe made or any promes of bargaine or price set as is
aforesaied or y^t shalle do or consent to do any thinge in
defraude of the true meannyng of this article shalle forfaicte v^{ll} for every sarpler and so after thafferaunt whereof
thone halfe shalbe to the presenter making due proufe of
thoffence and thother halfe to the court.

Ordenaunce for bringing againe of woulles defective[2]

The companie of this estaple have hetherto by alle meanes
and wayes sought to mayntaine truethe and abandone

[1] *Vide supra*, pp. 61–2.
[2] On this subject, *vide* Power and Postan, p. 60, and *supra*, p. 62.

falshode for continuanuce whereof and maintenaunce of theire auncient wourship and estimation it is ordeined at this present court holden the xix daye of Maye anno xvᶜlxv that yf paradventure the merchaunt straunger at his retourne home into his countrethe do finde the woulles by him bought in this estaple defective and not good for the countrethe and nature they ought to be of and were solde for and do cause the same woulles so suspected defective to be brought againe to the staple and do depose the same to be the selfe same woulles withoute diminishing augmenting or altering the same Then the woulles so retourned after the partie buyer have deposed in that behalfe as hereunder shalbe specified shalbe repoised at the beame for the iust trialle of the weight as it issued oute and shalle then be viued awarded and adiudged by certaine discrete personnes of the companie of this saied estaple thereunto by court of the same to be appoincted and sworne wᵗʰ a sworne packer adioyned to them. That is to saie woulles retournable oute of flaundres shalbe brought hither againe wᵗʰin thre monethes next after the sale thereof and woulles retournable out of Hollande or the frenche Kinges dominions shalbe retourned hither againe wᵗʰin iiii monethes next after the sale thereof. This done yf the saied woulles shalle happen to be founde defective as not good or not perfect for the countrethe or nature yᵗ the same is intituled for Then the merchaunt shalle satisfie content and paie to the straunger alle suche costes as he hathe susteyned by cariage and recariage of the saied wolles and also to paie to the court of this estaple for a fine xlˢ for every sarpler and so after the afferaunt *And* in caas the merchaunt buyer and the merchaunt seller cannot agree upon the costes then the court of the saied estaple shalle determine the variaunce in that behalfe *And yf* the saied woulles be founde good and perfect according as they ought to be then the saiede merchaunt straunger shalle receave the saied woulles againe and stonde to his bargaine withoute refusing to make payement of his debte for the same at the tyme or tymes

of payement limited by his bille obligatorie in sorte that yf
he woulde protract the solution thereof any longer by
occasion of the premisses or of any other cavillation he
shalbe compelled to make due satisfaction to his creditour
withe alle costes dammages and interest rising or groeng
thoroughe suche protraction or dilaye after the awarde of
the court *And it is* further ordeined that of suche woulles
as be retourned defective the wayer of this estaple after
his repoisinge therof shalle certifie the heades of this estaple
declaring in writing the sortes and nombres of the pocketts
the whiche the sergeant of this estaple shalle receave into
his custodie untille the merchaunt straunger come and make
his deposition for the same in manner as is and hathe ben
accustomed and used. *And it is* further ordeined that the
waier for his repoise and presentement aforesaied shalle
receave iii^s iii^d on every sarpler and so after the afferaunt
whereof ii^s shalle be to the saied wayer xii^d to the brokers
and iiii^d to the wayers man And the sergeant likewise
shalle have for his labour for kepinge the saied woulles
of every sarpler ii^s and so after the ⟨19^d⟩ afferaunt, alle the
same to be to them paied by the treasourer of this estaple
for the tyme being oute of the forfaictures aforesaied *And*
it is further ordeined that it shalle not be lawfulle to any
merchaunt seller to agree withe the merchaunt straunger
buyer or make any amendes or geve any betteringes for
any defective or faulty woulles being not retourned as is
aforesaied upon paine of forfaicture for every sarpler so
agreed for x^{li} and so after the rate *And it is further* ordeined
that yf any merchaunt straunger do detayne any parte of
his debte (due to any brother of this companie) clayminge
bettering of woulles by the saied straunger supposed to
be defective so that the saied brother shalle be forced to
sue him for his debte *Then* the saied sute for the recouverie
of the same debte shalbe poursued at the costes and charges
of the generalitie as far fourthe as suche brother having
his debte detayned from him do make the court first prive
to his saied sute before he shalle commence the same

Ordenaunce againest bartering of woulles

In exchewing of many inconveniences whiche may ensue to the hole generalitie of this companie by bartering of woulles or woullfelles for other wares or merchaundises *It is* ordeined concluded and enacted firmely hereafter to be observed and kepte that every fellowe and member of this estaple of what soever degre estate or condition he be of that makethe any bartering of woulles or woullfelles by himselfe or by any other parsonne for him or in his name or to his use & profit for any wares or merchaundise by wayes of commutation changinge and dealing of the said woulles or woullfelles for any wares or merchaundise or coulourably by any newe invention of fraude crafte and subteltie makethe any sale or alienation of his saied woulles or woullfelles then onely for sterling table money or after xxviii$^{\text{S. fl.}}$[1] for the pounde or for bullion shalle forfaict v^{ll} st of every sarpler of woulles or woullfelles and so after the afferaunt so bartered withoute favor or pardonne thone halfe to be paied to this estaple and thother halfe to the finder

Ordenaunce for transportes.

fforasmuche as alienations of woulles and woulfelles and transportes have ben heretofore used and yet ben used in the staple the benefit whereof thorow ignoraunce of suche order as hathe ben observed and ought to be observed in and concerninge the same alienations might perchaunce be misused yf an expresse acte in fulle declaration of the true order thereof were not made *It is therefore* agreed concluded and ordeigned that alle and every alienation of woulles or woulfelles made from any straunger to a brother of this companie and from one of the companie shalbe had and made in open court or assemble of the staple yf he wille receave the benefit of transporte *And in caas* it shalle happen hereafter any of the fellowship of the same

[1] Flemish.

estaple to set over his or theire goodes in the clerke of the
collectries bookes by ignoraunce or in contempt of this
present acte withoute makyng transport in court then the
proprietie of ⟨20⟩ the same goods shalle not be altered
but it shalbe leifulle to every other personne to commence
his action upon the same goods to poursue the same by
proces and due cause of lawe according to thuse and
custume of the court in suche cases used and to have thereof
condemnation to him the setting over of the saied goods
in the clarke of the collectries bookes in any wise not-
w^{th}standinge   *And* it is agreed ordeined and enacted that
none attorney or personne being apprentice or any other personne of the saied fellowship shalle from hensfourthe make
any transport or alienation of the gooddes of his or theire
maister or constituauntes without sufficient power and
aucthorite to the saied atturney or apprentice by theire
constituauntes and M^{rs} committed and geven either by
expresse woordes of transporting in writing or by cognoisaunce of entre of atturney in the recordes of the saied
estaple withe like woordes of aucthorite for transportinge
Also it is agreed concluded and enacted that every parsonne
of the saied fellowship whiche from hensfourthe shalle
make or receave any alienations of woulles or woulfelles
by transport to be made in open court or assemble shalle
then and there knowledge and confesse the saied alienation
by his oethe to be taken in open court or assemble to be
upon plaine bargaine and firme sale made by contract and
agrement aswelle of the alienatour as of the recever withoute fraude or covin to his knowledge withe the whiche
bargaine and sale the saied parties and either of them holden
them contented satisfied and pleased   *And* the partie
recever of suche alienations to have recevid the saied goods
aliened yf the same be woulles by pois or weight delivered
unto him at the staple beame and yf the gooddes be felles
to have received them by nombre & tale nombred and tolde
by a sworne felbinder or els that the saied recever of suche
alienations hath the keye or keyes of the howse or howses

where the woulles or woulfelles so aliened lye delivered
unto him by the alienatour or his sufficient atturney for
defaulte and lacke of cognoisaunce of theise saied thre
poinctes or articles or any of them the aforesaied alienation
by transport to be had insufficient of no force strengethe
or effect   *Also* it is agreed ordeined and enacted that after
cognoisaunce and knowledge taken of the saied alienatours
in manner and fourme abovesaied and the same alienations
past by court and stroke of mallet the parties unto whome
any suche alienation shalle be made by transport shalle
have holde enioye and peasible possesse the same woulles
or woullfelles to his or theire proper use and behoufe
withoute any claime or chalenge thereunto to be made
by any personne or personnes whiche then after that wille
pretende or make title unto the same goods so aliened by
waye of action or otherwise   The Quenes duetie for her
custume and subsidie and the courtes right alwayes reserved
of whiche transport the saied partie shalle have a bille to
be certified to the clerke of the collectrie there to be
entred accordingly yf he require the same

‹20ᵈ›   Ordenaunce against brogging of woulles

Where in tymes past by reason of sundry and divers
regratours and forstalers of woulles within the realme of
Englonde not being fre of this estaple woulles have growen
to suche highe and excessive prices that none coulde be
bought in Englonde to be brought or shipped hither to
this estaple here to be afforded to be solde at any reasonable
price whereupon of late at the great sute made by the
fellowship of this estaple unto our late souverayne lorde
king Edwarde the sixt it hathe ben by acte of parlement
provided and established that no manner of parsons other
then the merchauntes of the saied estaple there servauntes
and factours & other then suche shulde convert woulles
into clothe or yaren by them bought within the realme of
Englonde shulde buye any woulles as by the same acte
more at lengethe apperethe thintent whereof was and is that

the saied merchauntes and clothiers theire servauntes or
factours shulde or ought to set no parsonne or parsonnes
aworke to buie woulles but suche as woulde as muche as
in them laie rather go aboute to pulle downe the price of
woulles then to enhaunce the same *And now* it is manifest
that divers and sundry parsonnes of this companie tendering
more theire private wealthe and lucre then the commune
welthe and continuaunce of the saied estaple or thobser-
vation of the acte aforesaied and thintent of the same have
made divers and sundry personnes suche as were nether fre
of this estaple nor theire apprentices or theire housholde
servauntes theire attorney to buie woulles for them lending
and advancinge to them muche money aforehand by whiche
meanes woulles have growen to a more excessive price to
the utter dissolution of the saiede estaple yf spedy and
opportune remedy be not therefore provided *It is* therefore enacted at a court holden the xxii daye of Maye
xv^clxv that no manner of parsonne or parsonnes of this
companie shalle set a worke any parsonne or parsonnes
other then his apprentice bounde for the fredome of this
estaple or one being fre of the companie of the same estaple
to buie or bargaine any woulles for him or in his name nor
that any suche of the saiede companie shalle lende or
advaunce any summe or summes of money to any parson
not being fre as is aforesaied (other then to those whiche
ben before excepted)[1] to buie any woulles for him or them
upon paine the offendor or offendours to forfaicte to the
court of this estaple for every personne that he shalle so
set a worke contrarie to the true and intier meanynge of
this acte the same meanynge to be taken scanded inter-
pretated and declared by the court or courtes of this estaple
at alle tymes requisite for the first offence duely proved
xl^{li} st for the seconde offence after his first conviction
duely proved iiii^{xx} li. and for his thirde offence after the
like conviction shalbe crossed this place and shalle not be
readmitted to the fredome aforesaiede under the hans *And*

who may
be set on
work to bye
wolles

the forfaict

---

[1] This second bracket is omitted in the MS.

to thintent that due execution of this acte may be had for asmuche as it makethe gretly for the continuaunce of this estaple *It is* further condescended and agreed that what soever personne shalle accuse or detect any parson or parsonnes to have offended this present acte or any article thereof shalle have for his suche doenges the moitie of the forfaictures aforesaiede

loke more in thordi- naunce of extent of shipping

⟨21⟩

Ordenaunce for rates of woulles & woulfelles

Considering that alle and singuler woulles and woulfelles shipt hether to this estaple do attende a sale and utteraunce and that it chauncethe in some yere a greter quantite to be shipped then in y^t yere can welle and profitably be solde whereby of necessite the remaynder ought to have a preferment to be solde before any other woulles or woull- felles consequently shipped and the rather by cause tholde woulles and olde felles hath ben the grownde and upholding of this place and supporting the prices and hathe heretofore brought the commoditie of the realme of Englonde in estimation like as by the recordes of the staple at Calleis was clerely apparaunt *It is* therefore agreed concluded and enacted that every yeares shipping shalbe a rate by it selfe and the remaynner of that yeres shipping shalbe olde in the next yeres rate and have preferment to be uttered and solde withe one olde ii newe after the manner and fourme used at Callais [1] *It is* further ordeyned that no brother of this companie shalle selle to the merchaunt straunger otherwise then fre oute and that no merchaunt or brother of this companie shalbe forced to take any higher sortes of woll to fre oute his newe woulles as he shalle selle then suche sortes as his newe woulles are *Item it is* ordeyned that every fellowe of this estaple lacking olde woulles to fre oute his newe of what nature soever it be

every yeers shipping to be a rate by it selff

every man shall make his sale fre oute to ye straunger None shalbe forced to take any higher sorte of old woll then his new woll is

[1] Compare with this definition of new and old wools that by which "old" wools are held to be the spring shipment only, wools which must have been shorn in the previous summer (Malden, *Cely Papers*, p. xii).

maye resorte to the heades for the tyme being yf he cannot
agree withe the parties that hathe tholde woulles who shalle
appoinct him suche woulles as he lackethe to paie for it at
the fulle price of this estaple at suche tyme as the head
aforesaied and thre more of the companie assigned and
sworne by court for the same pourpose shalle determine to
be reasonable according to the sorte and tyme so that the
hole companie may knowe what tyme of payement the
saied heades withe iii persons more to him assigned doethe
appoinct   *And for by cause* it is necessaire that every man
delivering olde woulles in manner aforesaied be assured
of his money at the dayes appoincted   *It* is ordeyned that
every man that shalle receave any olde wolles in manner
aforesaiede shalle for the same yf he paie not reddy money
set sufficient suerties for that he takethe wch shalbe suche
as the saied head and iii of the saied companie wille allowe
in theire consciences to be sufficient   *And yf* the buyer
can set no sufficient suertie than he to deliver to the seller
of the olde woulles either a sufficient pawnde or redy money
Provided that yf any of the thre persons have any olde
woulles in any rate that then they shalle not be iudges in
that behalfe   *And* further It is ordeyned that yf any of
the companie shalle refuse to take the fulle price of any
sortes of olde woulles wch he shalle have for thissueng oute
of the newe supposing to have more benefite to kepe
them as newe then to sell as olde shalle never after receave
for the saied woulles so refused the benefite of olde woulles
Also it is ordeyned according to an ordenaunce made the
xxvii daye of Septembre xv^cliiii that no woulles of any
redemptioners or other personne admitted gratis whiche
since the yeare of our lorde god xv^clv hathe ben admitted
or that hereafter shalbe admitted to the fredome of this
wourshipfulle companie shalle in any manner of wise have
or enioye the benefit of olde woulles or be entred in the
rate of olde except onely so muche of the same theire owne
proper gooddes as they wille have or kepe for olde to issue
oute theire newe woulles of theire owne ⟨21^d⟩ proper ship-

Uppon
Refusall
of the full
price y^e
benefitt of
of olde
woolles loste

Redemp-
cioners

ping but shalle alwayes (yf they have none olde woulles of theire owne proper shippinge for freinge oute of theire newe) take olde woulles of other of the companie whiche have tholde according to the order and fourme of rates of olde and newe used & exercised any acte lawe or ordenaunce in this estaple to the contrarie in any wise not withstanding *Also* yf any suche redemptioner or parsonne admitted gratis shalle happen at any tyme to buie woulles in this estaple either by coulour transport or otherwise of any of the companie or any other personne whatsoever or shalle selle of his owne proper gooddes to any of the companie It is then further concluded and enacted that all and every suche woulles so bought or solde in this saied estaple as is aforesaied shalle not have or enioye the benefite or preferment of olde woulles but shalbe solde uttered and issued oute as newe woulles to alle intentes and pourposes in whose handes soever it shalle come from him or them *And it is* further ordeyned that yf any fellowe of this companie ship ionctly withe any suche personne so admitted or hereafter to be admitted since anno xv^{c}lv by redemption or gratis y^t then theire woulles so shipped ionctly shalbe taken reputed and ordered as touching the rates of woulles as woulles shipped wholy and onely by suche redemptioner or redemptioners or personnes admitted gratis *And* whosoever of the companie of this estaple shalle do commit or attent any thinge or thinges directly or indirectly or coulorably by any manner of wayes to the breache of this act or any parte or article thereof shall forfaicte to the court of this estaple x^{ll} on every sarpler solde or issued oute for olde and so after the afferaunt toties quoties *And it is* further ordeined that no felles shalbe solde but fre oute that is to saye that every merchaunt straunger shalle buye withe every two newe felles one olde yf there be any olde *And yf* any of the companie have olde felles withe whome the merchaunt straunger cannot agre of price then the head of the companie for the tyme being withe thre or iiii of the discretest of the companie having none olde felles of their owne

being sworne shalle make suche reasonable price of them
as to theire conscience shalle seame good observing theire
oethe *Provided* alwayes that no merchaunt straunger shalbe
forced to take any olde felles wch be not fit for his or theire
draperie *Item* it is ordeined that the clerke of the collectrie shalle at thende of every quarter of the yere declare
in writing unto the heades for the tyme beinge what sortes
quantite or kinde of woulles remaynethe at that tyme and
the rates thereof *And* yf any of the companie shalle
require at the same tyme of the saied clerke of the collectrie
a like declaration it shalbe leyfulle to the saied clerke to
gyve the saied information *And it is* ordeyned that yf
any of the companie or officier of this estaple shalle in any
manner of wyse declare unto the straunger the sortes
quantite kinde or rate aforesaied yf he be a brother to be
disfraunchised and yf he be an officier shalle lose his office
for theire suche offence

The Rate of prices of olde woulles

The companie of this estaple considering that it is right
necessarie for thaccomplishement of thordenaunce of rates
to have the prices of olde woulles established. Therefore
have at a court holden the xxiiii daye of Maye xv^clxv
agreed concluded and enacted that none of the companie
of this estaple shalle in any manner of wise be compelled
to ⟨22⟩ buye take or receave in this estaple any olde woulles
to issue oute his newe woulle above the prices hereunder
limited *Also* that none of the saiede companie shalbe in
any manner of wise compelled to selle or deliver his olde
woulles at the saied prices hereunder especified but it
shalbe at the pleasure of him whiche hathe the saied wolle
either to receave the saiede price or to lose the preferment
of his olde woulles *And* yf the preferment thereof be
once refused then the same his olde woulles shalle never
there after have or enjoye the benefite or preferment of
olde woulles in any manner of wise

Imprimis A	Lymster	iiii^{xx} li
m[1]	Lymster	lxi li
A	Marche	lviii li
m	Marche	xlv
A	Cottes	xliii li
M	Cottes	xxxii li
A	Barkes	xxxviii li
M	Barkes	xxx li
A	Younge Cottes	xxxiiii li
A	Lynsey	xxxii li
A	Lescon[2]	xxx li
M	Lescon	xxiiii li
	Refus marche	xxx li[3]

And it is further agreed concluded and enacted that the prices aforesaiede shalle continue from tharrivalle of the next flete and the same not to be altered except it be by Mr. Maior or his lieutenaunt and a sufficient nombre of his assistaunce from alle the portes to be called over and to be

[1] I.e. middle. [2] ? Leicester.
[3] A comparison of some of the more important of these prices with those obtaining in the fifteenth and early sixteenth centuries shows the extent to which increased demand for wool and debasement of the coinage had raised wool-prices. These prices are selling-prices at Bruges for a sarplar (about three sacks) and are part of an effort to keep up prices. Column I in the following small table shows a suggested *minimum buying-price* in England and does not necessarily represent the actual prices paid. Columns II and III purport to give the actual selling-prices in the trade. On fifteenth-century wool-prices, *vide* Power and Postan, pp. 12, 71, 367–8.

	I	II Late 15th cent. (Nombre of Weights: MS. Cott. Vesp. E. IX, fol. 106^d)	III	IV
A sack of	1454 (Rot. P.v, p. 275)		1527 (Schanz, II, p. 571)	Minimum *selling-price* 1565
Lemster	14 marks (£9 6 8)		£21 6 8	1st quality £26 13 4 middle ,, £20 6 8
March	14 marks (£9 6 8)	20 marks (£13 6 8)	£15 0 0	1st ,, £19 6 8 middle ,, £15 0 0
Cotswold	12½ marks (£8 6 8)	*Fine* 18 marks (£12 0 0)	£12 0 0	1st ,, £14 6 8 middle ,, £10 13 4

present in court of this estaple or by the court of this estaple
and consent of alle the portes of Englonde accustomed
to ship first had in writinge in whiche caas of alteration
of the rates and prices aforesaied the saied Maior or his
lieutenaunt and assistaunce shalle provide that it be upon
one yeares warnynge at the lest to be signified in writinge
to alle the saied poortes that every of the companie of the
saied estaple may dispose himselfe accordingly *Provided*
always that alle suche woulles as shalle be in the staple
at the alteration of the rates and prices aforesaiede shalle
receave the benefite of the rates and prices of olde woulles
before mencioned in as ample manner & fourme as none
alteration had ben made any acte or lawe hereafter to be
made to the contrarie in any wise notwithstandynge
Provided also that thimpositions shalbe paiede to the
tresourer of this estaple for the tyme being according to
the prices of olde tymes used and now paied

Ordenaunce for woulles and felles lost
by casualtie of seas

Where there was an ordenaunce in the staple at Calles
concerninge woulles and woullfelles lost by casualtie of
seas the same ordenaunce now being lacking is very necessarie to be revived and established to be hereafter observed
and kept *It is* therefore agreed ordeyned concluded and
enacted that whensoever and as often as by reason of
tempest or other misfortune upon the seas any woulles or
woullfelles shalle happen to be caste over borde for thalleva-
tion of the ship in saufgarde of the ship and gooddes
therein being or that any ship wth woulles shalle happen
to fall in daunger ⟨22^d⟩ of the gittes[1] or other perille the Juties[1]
whereby in recoveringe or savinge thereof any pocket or
pockettes of woulles or woulfelles shalbe used torne or
lost That then alle the goodes in suche ship remayninge
shalbe had in average and contribution pounde and pounde

---

[1] The exact meaning of these words is obscure, but it is probable
from what follows that "jettison" is meant.

like and so after the rate towardes the losse of the saiede
woulles and woullfelles and every of the same so cast
over borde used torne or lost   *Also for* wolle scatered
oute of the canvas in the ship by reason of rupture of
canvas   It is agreed that suche woulles yf any question shalle
happen to arise amongest the companie for the propriete
thereof shalbe vieued by certaine of the companie thereunto
by court to be appoincted who shalle serche and examine
by the best meannes they can to whome the saied woulles
do apperteine and thereof make report unto the court of
this estaple that the same may determine the question either
by due proufe of the proprietie either by the report of the
personnes deputed as is abovesaied or otherwise by theire
discretions. *But* suche woullfelles as shalbe fownde un-
merked and the proper owner or owners of them not
knowen by due circumstaunce and good proufe to be
allowed by the hole court then suche felles shalbe brought
to the halle in the staple howse and solde by the sergeant
as was used at Calles and the money commynge of the sale
thereof shalbe employed and put in the boxe of the poore
reserving to the sergeant his accustomed duetie   *And* for
avoydinge of many inconveniences whiche may chaunce
by reason that summe of the companie of this estaple may
alter the markes of woulles and felles whereby the very
owners especially of felles cannot come by theire proper
goodes   *It is* condiscended and agreed at this present court
holden the xxvi daye of Maie anno xvᶜlxv that what
brother of this companie soever he be shalle alter or
chaunge or cause to be altered and chaunged from hensfourthe in this estaple at Bruges or els where the staple
shalbe kept the marke or markes of any pocket or pockets
of woulles into any other marke or markes then the same
was marked withe at the shipping thereof shalle be clerely
disfraunchised from the fredome and liberties of this estaple
Also whosoever shalle alter or chaunge or cause to be
altered or chaunged in this saiede estaple or els where the
same estaple shalbe kepte the marke or markes of any felle

the sergeants fee

or felles into any other marke or markes then the same were marked withe at the shipping thereof shall forfaicte to the court of this estaple for every felle so altered xx^s

Ordenaunce againest unfitting langage
and contemptuous behavior towardes
the heades of this estaple

fforasmuche as in every administration and gouvernaunce of the commune wealthe due estimation wourship and reverence is to be exhibited to suche personnes as ben constituted in dignitie and gouvernaunce whome always for thoffice sake every inferiour person ought to use modestlie reverently and wth alle comely woordes absteyninge from alle those thinges whiche in any wise might iustly offende the magistrate secretly or openly by worde or behavior to the lesion of his estate   It is therefore and also for condigne punishement and correction of suche offendour whiche hereafter shalle misuse himselfe to or against the head or heades of this estaple for the tyme being gevinge them or any of them unfittinge langage ⟨23⟩ opprobrious slanderous or contumelious langage or shewing towardes them indecent or contemptuous behavior openly or secretly ordeyned and enacted at this present court holden the xxvi daye of Maie anno xv^{c}lxv that every suche offendour shalle for his suche offence be committed to prison there to remayne untille suche tyme he do in open court acknowledge his offence requiringe pardon and remission thereof in alle humble manner The note whereof to remayne of recorde as for his first offence   *And* yf he shalle happen afterwarde to commit the like and thereof duely be convicted he shalbe imprisoned by the space of xv dayes and further be restrayned from shipping to this estaple of any staple merchaundise or being atturney for any man within the terme of two yeares then next after ensuenge withe like note as is abovesaied for his seconde offence   *And* for his thirde suche offence he shalbe crossed this place for ever

It is also enacted that none of the companie of this sayed estaple be so hardy or presume to repaire to suche offendour in prison making him any bancket or compotation whereby thoffendour is rather animated and supported in his evill doings then reduced to repentaunce or exhorted to reconciliation upon paine that whosoever of the saied fellowship shalle trespas contrarie to this clawse shalle forfaicte for every suche offence x^s whiche penaltie is not ment to extende upon any well disposed parson or frinde of thoffendour havinge licens of the heades and is desirous to give suche offendour good advice in prison to the furtheraunce of iustice and execution of this acte

Ordenaunce for frayes and bloudwipes

Item it is ordeyned that no parsonne of the fellowship of this estaple or belonginge to the same of what state or condition soever he or they be of shalle make any manner of trespas in fightinge withe any of the saied fellowship or other personne by malicious violence or crualtie smitinge withe his hande or fist gevinge a stroke or a buffet violently pluckinge wrasteling hurlinge tearinge scratchinge castinge or by any other violent or malicious wise be it by foote or hande ponchinge or by any other parte of the bodie by the whiche to any membre or outwarde parte of the bodie harme hurt or blemishe might ensue upon paine that he that shalle do the contrarie to the tenor and effecte of this lawe and ordenaunce yf he beginne to give the first stroke of violence and hurt shalle for his suche offence and trespas be committed unto prison by the hed or heades for the tyme being and to make amendes unto the partie dammaged as he shalbe appoincted by court yf he do not agre withe the partie over and above that to paie unto the court of this estaple x^s st *Item* that no manner of personne above saied drawe or bringe fourthe any weapon in malice to avenge any occasion or cause had to any of the saied felloweship or other be it swerd knife dagger bille bowe

stafe stone or any other weapon whatsoever it be upon
payne of imprisoment at the discretion of the saied heades
and fellowship and also to paie to the court of this estaple
xiii^s iiii^d to be levied upon him that is the beginner thoughe
no stroke be stricken   *And* yf any stroke withe any kinde
of weapon be geven That then he that stroke the first
stroke shalbe imprisoned ⟨23^d⟩ by the head or heades of
this estaple for the tyme being there to remayne accordinge
to the discretion of the saied heades and fellowship and
to paie to the saied court xl^s *And* he that upon other
drawethe blud withe any weapon shalle forfaicte to the
saied court iii^{ll} withe imprisoment as is abovesaied and
to make satisfaction to the partie so dammaged after the
quantite of thoffence and hurt   *And* it is further ordeyned
and enacted that suche manner of personne once fownde
culpable and eftsones commitinge the like offence shalle at
the seconde tyme paie iiii^{ll} and for the thirde tyme x^{ll} and
after that to be punnished at the discretion of the heade or
heades for the tyme beinge by thadvice of the companie
And for the due execution of the premisses it is ordeyned
for a generalle rule and lawe firmely to be observed and
kepte that in alle manner of trespasses of frayes makyng
the parties of the fraye shalbe fourthwithe and immediatly
committed to warde or prison and at convenient leysure
the heades for the tyme beinge shalle sende for the parties
and of them take suerties to be bounde by recognoisaunce
to kepte /sic/ peas and after that taken then alle suche as
were present at the fraie shalbe examined by vertue of
theire oethes to saie the truethe in whose defaulte the same
fraie was made and who stroke first and yf any bloud be
drawen who drewe it the punnishement whereof shalbe
made as is aforesaiede yf none were present at the fraye
then the parties fighters to be examined aparte in the best
manner whereby the truethe in that behalfe may be knowen
or els boethe the parties to be condemned in the fraie and
equally punnished after the fourme abovesaiede

Ordenaunce againest rehersalle of olde grudges

None of the saied fellowship shalle make rehersalle of any olde grudges faultes or offences committed by any personne of the saiede fellowship or of any hereafter to growe or to be done or made except suche rehersalle as shalbe had in charitable wise in manner and fourme of accusation before the head or heades of the same estaple for thinges that shalbe committed contrarie to the lawes and ordenaunces now established or hereafter to be established or any of them   *And* in likewise no personne shalle take grudge or displeasure withe or towardes his accusatour *And* whatsoever person of the fellowship that shalle do contrarie to the mynde tenor or effect of this lawe statute or ordenaunce so often as the offence shalbe fownde and proved shalbe committed to his chaumbre solitarely there to abide unto suche tyme as he duely be reconciled and over that to paie v⁸ flemmishe for his suche offence the same to be employed to the boxe of the poore

Ordenaunce for aunsweringe the custome

Since it hathe pleased the Quenes maiestie by her lettres patentes to appoinct the companie to paie the custume and subsidie due for woulles and woullfelles to be shipped to the staple in her graces Exchequier within thre monethes after the departure of the flete¹ It is very convenient and necessarie to take suche order for the sure payement thereof as the saied companie do incurre no daunger of losse of their liberties and privileges for none payement of it *It is* therefore ordeyned that every personne fre of this companie of the staple of Englonde whiche ⟨24⟩ shalle at any tyme hereafter ship any woulles or felles oute of the accustomed poortes to the staple shalle enter into bonndes withe one other able brother of the companie inabled at an assemble in London or Bruges whiche two shalbe bownde

¹ This was in accordance with the terms of the Charter of 1561.

ioinctly and severally to the Maior of the staple of Englonde for the tyme being in a greater summe (that is to saie a thirde parte more then the custume and subsidie of the principalle partie bownden doethe amounte unto) upon condition that they and either of them shalle within aleven wekes at the furthest after the departure of the flete paie to the handes of the saied Maior for the tyme beinge suche custume and subsidie as shalle be due by him or them for his or theire saied custume and subsidie *All* whiche bondes that is to saie the names of the personnes bounde and theire suerties shalbe certified over by the saied Maior afore any more then two partes of the goodes be put to sale *And* yf it fortune that any brother of the companie shipping to this estaple do not put in bonndes as is aforesaied and paie not his custume and subsidie by the daye prescribed in manner and fourme aforesaied that then every suche brother making default of payement shalle forfaict for every pownde that he shulde have paied iii⁸ iiii^d and so after the rate *And further* it shalbe leifulle to the companie resident at the staple to put to sale by praisement in court as was accustomed at Callais as muche of the goodes of the partie so making defaulte as shalle amounte to the custume and subsidie due by him withe the penaltie aforesaied *And* yf any parson bounde for the custume and subsidie as is aforesaiede do make defaulte of payement thereof at the daye in the saied obligation prescribed and do not within thre monethes then next after ensueng at the furthest welle and truely satisfie content and paie the same custume and subsidie togither withe the over plus mencioned in the obligation that then suche personne making defaulte to paie the hole summe in the saied obligation especified and being the principalle partie shalbe disfraunchised from the fredome of this estaple *And* yf thother partie or parties beinge bounde in the saiede obligations withe the saied principalle shalle happen not to paie the summe conteyned in the saied obligation within six monethes next after the daye of payement in the saied

penaltie of iii⁸ iiii^d uppon ye pownde for not paying cust. at ye daye or put not in bond

obligation especified and that within the saied six monethes
lettres of warnynge be to him or them directed and delivered
from the court of this estaple admonishing him or them
of the saied debt that then in suche caas suche partie or
parties aforesaied shalbe also disfraunchised of the fredome
of this saied estaple *It is further* agreed concluded and
enacted that thupper clerke of this estaple for the tyme
beinge shalle have for makinge of every suche lettre of
warninge xii^d to be to him paid by the treasourer of this
estaple for the tyme beinge

xii^d to the
clark for a
lettre

Ordenaunce for plainctes

It is ordeyned condiscended and agreed by commune
assent that yf any merchauntes fre of this companie or
other wille complaine of any personne beying fre of this
companie for any debt or duetie he shalle first entre his
plaincte in the bookes of this estaple withe two sufficient
pledges to poursue his plaincte and thereupon shalle have
oute his warraunt to the sergeant whiche done the defendaunt shalbe attached by his bodye and finde sufficient
suerties to the court to aunswer ⟨24^d⟩ redely to the plainctyfe at the daye assigned by court   *And* yf he finde no
sufficient pledges he then shalbe committed to prison as
accordeth   *And* yf the plainctife have right in his poursute
and so fownde by iudgement he shalle recouver his demaunde withe his costes and dammages after the awarde
of court   *And* yf the playntife make not poursute or be
nonsute he and his pledges shalle paie unto the court
xii^d and over that aunswer to the defendaunt for dammage
after the awarde of the court   *And* yf the defendaunt knowledge the debte or demaunde of the plainctife he shalle
have respit of viii dayes to be at large under sufficient
suerties to the intent to selle his gooddes or other wise
helpe himselfe so that the playnctife shalbe satisfied by
thende of viii dayes as is abovesaied   *And* yf the defendaunt may not deliver him selfe and be not fourthe com-

mynge for execution of the iudgement within viii dayes
then his pledges shalle satisfie the plainctife for him withoute
further iudgement *And* yf the defendaunt be not fownde
or present at the tyme of the plaincte entred then shalle
his gooddes be arrested to aunswer to the plainctife at
the daye assigned by court *At* the whiche daie yf the
plainctyfe or his attorney be present and the defendaunt or
his atturney absent and in Englonde he shalle have respit
of six wekes And yf he be in flaunders or other parties on
this side the seas he shall have respit of one monethe and
a lettre of warninge to him there upon from the court shalbe
directed *And* in the meanne tyme tharrest made upon the
gooddes shalle stonde in strength And yf the defendaunt
or any other for him come not to aunswer in the meanne
tyme the saied respit so expired and the continuaunce of
the plainct after the auncient rules & laudable customes of
the court elapsed and past then as muche of the goodes
arrested as will satisfie and agre the plainctife by iudgement
of the court shalbe awarded to be delivered unto thatturney
or frende of the defendaunt yf any suche be present And
yf none be there that wille take upon him the charge then
asmuche of the saied gooddes as will suffice to agre the
plainctife as above shalbe praised by good personnes thereunto by court deputed and sworne truely and iustely to
praise the saied gooddes or els solde in plaine court to
hym or them that will geve moost And he that moost
offerethe shalbe bownde to take to him the same gooddes
for the price that he hathe offered in plaine court to be
paied without delaye the saied plainctife setting sufficient
suerties withe hym in the court to aunswer to the defendaunt of asmuche as he hathe so recouvered in thabsence
of the defendaunt withe the dammage in caas the defendaunt
or any atturney for him sufficiently fownded do come into
the court within one yere and a daye and prove evidently
that the plainctyfe wroungfully hathe recouvered *Moreover* yf the partie plaintife and defendaunt be present
in court and in defaulte of proufe of the plainctyf the

defendaunt be put to his oethe for knowledge and declaration of the truethe to be had for determination of the plainct and the defendaunt by waye of deposition wille not confesse the truethe of that that he is surmised upon by the plainctyfe and afterwarde be fownde culpable and so adiudged by them shalbe committed to prison withoute delaye and there abide as belongethe   *Also* it is ordeyned that yf any merchaunt of the staple take plainct of trespas or breache of peas in the court of the staple upon any merchaunt ⟨25⟩ of the same and fynde pledges as apperteynethe the defendaunt shalle be arrested by his bodie and in defaulte of sufficient suerties shalle be committed to prison and being fownde culpable shalle agree withe the parties and court for his contempt   *Also* it is ordeyned by commune assent that at the entre of every plainct taken in the court of this estaple betwixt fellowe and fellowe of the companie the plainctyfe shalle paie xii^d to be devided into thre partes that is to wit thone halfe to the commune boxe and thother halfe to be devided betwixt the clerke and the sergeant for entre of the plaincte and execution of the warraunt   *And* yf any personne of the companie be arrested by his body or goodes and breake or disobeye the arrest he shalle have imprisoment by the space of xl dayes at least and after that be punished after the direction of the court   *Also* it is ordeigned that none arrest or proces shalbe made agaynest any personne before the plainctife have entred his plainct and pledges fownde to poursue the plainct and to aunswer to the defendaunt and to the court yf his demaunde be wronge unles the defendaunt be then sodenly fownde within the iurisdiction of the staple and the plainctife doubte that he be fugitive and will escape that then in such cases he shalbe arrested and afterwarde the plainct to be entred and pledges fownde as abovesaied *Also* the plainctife shalbe sworne to saye the truethe in his demaunde and the defendaunt in his defence and so shalle other be sworne that have knowledge of the truethe to declare the same at the demaunde of the iudges as often

and in suche manner as to them shalle seame moost expedient for trialle of the variaunce whereby they maye
procede to geve true and righteous iudgement *And yf*
any in that caas be `fownde disobedient he shalle forfaict
to the court x⁸ and over that be punished by his bodie and
goods after thawarde of the court *And yf* the truethe
cannot be tried oute by this manner wherby the court
cannot plainely be infourmed to procede to the plaine
iudgement Then the defendaunt shalbe quit by his oethe
in case the plainctyfe prove not his demaunde of recorde
and of the tyme done within the iurisdiction of the staple
after the awarde of the court *And forasmuche* as the lawes
of the staple ben ordeyned and grounded upon reason good
faithe and equite withoute long ple or dilaye therefore it
is ordeyned that the plainctife in his proper personne shalle
declare his owne demaunde and not to be rebuked or
abashed for telling of his tale but theffect of his right to
be taken withoute coulour of termes or subteltie of ple
and after right and good conscience it to be adiudged *And*
in likewise the defendaunt to aunswer in his proper personne in his defence and that no man pleade for thother
except he be partie in the plaincte nor speke in the matter
unles he be willed or required by the iudge wherein he
shalle make no crafte or subteltie but shew the plaine
truethe and thereto shalbe sworne and what personne that
so impleadethe for other or speakethe before he be demaunded the plainctife or defendaunt or theire attorneis
being present shalle forfaicte to the court for his first
offence xii^{ds} for the ii^{de} ii^s and the thirde tyme to be committed to prison there to abide and to be punnished after
the awarde of the court *And* it is ordeyned that no manner
of plainct of what nature condition or manner it be shalle
depend in court withoute it be called and poursued within
⟨25^d⟩ thre court dayes next holden after thentre of the same
by the plainctife or his atturney for suche plaincte shalbe
called openly at the next court holden after the saied entre
yf by the plaintyfe or his atturney it be followed and desired

and in likewise at the seconde court and yf the saied plaintyfe appere not at the thirde court that is to wit at thende of thre wekes next after thentre of his saied plaincte nor any atturney for him sufficiently fownded before the Maior or his lieutenaunt or Constables or otherwise and so entred of recorde then he shalbe nonsuted and lose his plainct withoute grace or more respit and his pledges to be amerced to the court at xii^d and that the parties plaintyfe and defendaunt shalle not accorde betwixt them selves withoute licens asked of the court or els that they certifie the clarke of theire suche accorde to the intent it may be entred of recorde upon the plaint the parties doeng contrarie shall forfaicte to the court aswelle the plaintyf as the defendaunt xii^{ds} upon the pounde wthoute pardon   *And* yf the parties accorde not within them selves but abide the sentence and iudgement of the court that then the plainctife shalle recover alle that he can prove to him due of his demaunde wth alle his costes and dammages runnynge upon the same and the defendaunt to be adiudged by court to content and aunswer the saied costes and dammages suche as shalbe awarded by court as also the principalle duetie   *And* yf the plainctife in his demaunde aske or clayme by accompt more then can be proved to him due be it by waye of action trespas claime of debte or otherwise shalle forfaicte to the court upon every pownde xii^{ds} that he so takethe more then his duetie yf it exceade x^{li} withoute favour or pardon and so after the afferaunt of every summe   *Also it* is ordeyned that no plaintife or defendaunt whatsoever he be shalbe suffered to impleade or aunswer in court of this estaple by any attorney but onely in proper person withoute cause reasonable approved by court   *And to* thintent that due execution and satisfaction shalbe had upon condemnations according to the iudgement and awarde of the court It is ordeined that yf the partie condemned agre not wth the plainctife by the ende of viii dayes next after the iudgement the goods arrested shalbe praised either by the mallet in plaine court and so execution to be had as afore is

ordeyned or els by sufficient persons thereunto by court
deputed and upon the holy evangiles sworne truely and
iustly to praise the same goods and thereof to make due
reaport *And* when the saied praisement and reaport is
made yf he wille not take the same then shalle the praisers
be bounde to take the same at theire suche praisement
and reaport and make satisfaction unto the plainctife wthin
viii dayes next after that ensueng that is to wit as muche
money as theire saied praisement shalle amount unto *Also*
it is ordeyned in exchewing long dilayes and continuaunce
of plees summe tymes commenced more of malice then
for the prosecution of iustice that yf the plainctife prosecute
not his action duely and diligently withe effect so that the
same action take not a lawfulle ende by iudgement or
otherwise with in one yere and a daye next after the daye
of entre of the saied action that then the saied action shalbe
discharged by aucthorite of court as at a nonsute *Provided*
alwayes that suche manner of discharge be not preiudicialle
to the plaintif but that he may beginne his saied action in
the saied court or ⟨26⟩ eles where as to the plainctife shalle
seme best *And* it is further ordeyned that yf any brother
of this companie do upon any suggestion remove any
matter or plainct depending in court of this estaple into
any court of recorde or other place whatsoever within the
realme of Englonde or els where and after the same matter
be remitted to the iudgement and order of this court for
lacke of due proufe of suggestion that then every parson
so removing any suche matter whiche shalle so be remitted
againe shalle forfaict and paie to the use of the generalitie C^{li}
And it is further ordeyned that yf any brother of this
companie shalle by any indirect extraordinaire or sinister
meannes seke or attempt to staie the court from proceading
to any matter depending there to a finalle sentence or
determination of the cause according to iustice and equitie
that then every parson so offending upon due proufe
thereof shalbe disfraunchised from the liberties and fredome
of this wourshipfulle companie

Ordenaunce for true aunswering the revenewes of the howse

Long experience hathe taught this wourshipfulle companie that for maintenaunce of the good governement thereof there are many officiers requisite to whome divers fees are to be paiede and also that divers extraordinare charges do dayly growe the payement and maintenaunce whereof tyme oute of mynde of man hathe ben levied by thre especialle and ordinaire wayes viz. by impositions, hanses and forfaictures arising and groenge by breache of any of the ordinaunces *It is* therefore and to thintent that the state of the howse and companie may the better be continued withoute afterdeale ordeyned concluded and enacted at a court holden the xxvi daye of Maye anno xv^{c}lxv that every person shipping woulles to this estaple shalle paie after the rate of ii^d on the pounde of the value of the goodes by him shipped the same goods to be rated after the full price of the staple for every sorte of woulles of olde tyme set *And* every person shipping woullfelles to this estaple shalle paie for impositions after the rate of ii^d on the pounde of the value of the felles solde the same to be rated as the felles shalbe solde and faithfully reaported by the seller of them to the clarke of the collectrie by thoethe that he hathe taken to the howse *And* it is further ordeyned concluded and enacted that every person whiche hathe attained the fredome of this wourshipfulle companie by redemption or gratis shalle paie suche imposition upon every sarpler of woulles and woullfelles by them to be shipped accompting every v^c felles for a sarpler of woulles over and above thimpositions aforesaied and in suche manner and fourme and for so many yeres as was taxed at the tyme of his admission into the fredome viz. suche as were admitted afore the yere of our lorde god xv^{c}l shalle paie vi^s viii^d upon every sarpler for vii yeres shipping *And* suche as were admitted and made fre after the yere of our lorde god xv^{c}l ⟨26^d⟩ and afore the yere of our lorde god xv^{c}liiii vi^s viii^d upon every sarpler

by the space of tenne yeres shipping and after the yeare
of our lorde god xv^cliiii tille this present daye and from
hensfourthe tille newe order be taken xiii^s iiii^d for every
sarpler for twelve yeares shippinge   *All* wch impositions
aforesaied of vi^s viii^d and xiii^s iiii^d shalbe paied to the
treasourer of this estaple for the tyme being wthin the same
quarter that the goodes shalle arrive in and the ii^d upon
the pounde in that quarter that the woulles or woullfelles
shalbe solde in   *Provided* alwayes it shalbe leifulle for the
companie to diminishe or inlarge thimpositions of ii^d upon
the pounde of woulles or woullfelles as to them from tyme
to tyme shalle seme expedient and necessarie   *And* it is
further ordeined concluded and enacted that every person
whiche hereafter shalbe admitted into the companie by
redemption or gratis shalle paie such hanse and impositions
as at the tyme of his admission shalbe cessed and appoincted
And it is further ordeyned that every person whiche hereafter shalle attaine the fredome of this companie wether
it be by patrimonie apprentishode or redemption shalle at
his admission paie in redy money to the tresourer of this
estaple wthoute dilaie or respit to be geven suche somme or
summes of money for his hans as by thordenaunce of
hanses is for suche personnes expressed and appoincted
And where it was ordeined at Calles that every personne
whiche shulde claime his fredome by patrimonie whose
father by whome he claimethe had not done his duetie
that is to saie had not thoroughly paied and borne his parte
of the greate charges whiche the companie sustained shalle
for his admission be ceassed to paie suche summe as *[to]*
the companie then present in court shulde seme good   *It is
ordeyned* that every persoun whiche shalle hereafter clame
his fredome by patrimonie whose father hathe not paiede
and borne his parte towardes the charges and burthens
as is aforesaied shalle at his admission fourthwithe paie in
redy money suche summe of money as shalbe ceassed by
the court whiche so to be ceassed shalle not at any tyme
be under v^{li}   *And also* where there are divers and many

goodly ordenaunces and actes made for the good gouverne-
ment and order of the companie and the keping of the
staple merchaundise in estimation to be observed and kept
upon paine of forfaicture of divers penalties and summes
of money by suche as do transgresse or offende the same
whiche ordenaunces and actes were better not made then
not executed *It is* therefore ordeined concluded and
enacted that whosoever shalle hereafter be convicted of
the breeche or not observinge of any ordenaunce or acte
made or hereafter to be made shalle fourthewithe paie
suche fine, summe of money penaltie or forfaicture as by
suche ordenaunce or act standing in force whiche he hathe
transgressed is or shalle be appoincted for such offence
And it is expounded and declared by theise presentes that
payement made within the tyme of suche tresourers charge
as the duetie shalle rise, is and shalbe accompted in the
premisses redy money *And it* is further ordeined that
whosoever shalle willingly or obstinatly refuse or denie

for paiment
of duties

to paye suche impositions as by this ordenaunce is due,
or by any acte hereafter shalbe due or shalle speke write
or do any acte in the favour of any personne whereby
any imposition hans money or any suche forfaicture or
penaltie for breche of any ordenaunce or acte shalle not
be paied according ⟨27⟩ to this ordenaunce or thordenaunce
of hanses or els that any summe due for impositions hanse
money or breche violation or not observing of any ordenaunce or acte shulde be mitigated or restored suche person

forfaict

so offending shalle forfaict and paie asmuche as the person
(in whose favour he shalle speke write or do any acte as is
aforesaied) shulde or ought to have paiede and shalle also
forfaicte and paie to thuse of the generalitie xl^{li} *And it is*
further agreed concluded and enacted that no staple merchaundise shalle issue oute of this saied estaple before the
merchaunt seller or his sufficient atturney do take oute a
bille from the clarke of the collectrie for the tyme being
for issueng oute of suche gooddes according to the auncient
orders aforesaied the whiche bille the same merchaunt or

his atturney shalle deliver to the tresourer of the saied estaple also for the tyme being to be sealed withe thaccustomed seale of the tresourie and the same so sealed shalle further deliver or cause to be delivered to the brokar for thexploit thereof whiche brokar therupon shalle diligently se that the goods do passe and issue fourthe according to the same bill   *And* shalle cause the merchaunt buyer duely to paie alle impositions and droictes to the tresourie competing and apperteyninge by reason of suche sale wherein yf the saiede brokar shalle happen not to adhibite so diligent care & attendaunce as he ought to do shalle paie double so muche as the straunger departing w^{th}oute payement of his duetie or droictes shulde have paiede *Besides that* it is agreed concluded and enacted that no brokar of this estaple shalle receave any impositions growing of sale for the tresourer but shalle bring and accompanie the merchaunt straunger buyer to the tresourie and se the same merchaunt paie his dueties   *And that* the brokar shalle deliver in court at thende of every quarter of the yere the billes whiche they recevid from the collectrie and tresourie for issueing oute of woulles and felles that quarter to thintent that at the auditing of the tresourers accomptes the same accomptes may be conferred and tried by the saied billes to knowe what quantite of woulles and woulfelles ben issued oute that quarter and what impositions is recevid for the same according to thauncient custume of the staple

brokers bills.

Ordenaunce for keping of courtes

Evin as no societie or companie can continue and stande w^{th}oute order, but in short tyme must for want thereof come to distruction and confusion even so is there in alle societies and companies certaine limites and meannes how to devise them as occasion and alteration of tyme shalle require and being devised to put them in execution. And emongest other the wayes and meannes how to devise good orders and meannes for the generalle benefite and

preservation of this wourshipfulle companie of the staple
and theire merchaundise and to put the same into execution
hathe ben tyme oute of mynde by commune consultation
of suche wourshipfulle and other personnes fre of the saiede
companie as have assembled in one place at certaine dayes
communly called the court howse ⟨27ᵈ⟩ *It is therefore*
according to thauncient order and usage ordeyned at a
court here holden the xxvi daye of Maye anno domini
xvᶜlxv that from hensfourthe it shalbe leifulle to the Maior
lieutenaunt or Constables or any of them to assemble the
saied companie being xii in nombre at least that have voice
in court upon any tuwesdaie Thursdaie and Satterdaie
being no festivalle dayes in summe convenient howse to
be appoincted in suche place where the staple shalbe kept
and there betwene the houres of seven & eleven to treate,
consulte, heare, determine, ordeine and enacte according
to thordenaunces any matter touching the hole companie
or any membre of the same or theire merchaundise or any
thing apperteyninge to theire trafficke and also any matter
or question arising or groing touching or concernynge the
violation or breache of any ordenaunces *And it is* further
ordeined that at the first entre into the court the Maior
lieutenaunt or Constables whiche for the tyme beinge shalle
then be head shalle after he is set in court strike a stroke
wᵗʰ the mallet commaunding alle the brethren there present
to sit downe and take theire places and cause the dore to
be shut. And this done shalle geve a second stroke withe
the mallet and then the clarke shalle rede the doinges of
the court precedent whiche being allowed and confirmed
the thirde stroke of the mallet shalle also be geven by the
head and he that commethe after the thirde stroke to paie
iiiiᵈˢ *And* he that shalle come into the court the halfe
houre expired after the thirde stroke the same halfe houre
to be runne up by the glas shalle paie vˢ st. *And* he that
commeth not into the court sitting the court shalle lose
tenne shillings licens by the heades alwayes forprised and
excepted *And yf* any shalle make sale by himselfe or by

any other personne or personnes whatsoever the court
sitting or shalle talke withe any merchaunt for sales shalle
forfaicte to the court xx^s st. on every sarpler aswelle of
woulles as felles and so after the afferaunt   And that none
depart oute of the court the court sitting wthoute licence
of the head upon paine to be punnished at the discretion
of the court   *And whosoever* being demaunded by the
tresourer for the tyme being to make payement of suche
forfaicture shalle refuse or denie and do not make present
payement of it shalle forfaicte the double or be committed
to warde by the head for the tyme being there to remayne
at his discretion   *And it* is further ordeyned that suche
as shalle have ben Maior of the staple Lieutenaunt Constable
Maior or alderman of any citie or toune or iustice of peace
shalle sit upon the highest benche next unto the Maior
Lieutenaunt or Constables for the tyme being as they shalbe
in auncient by bearing of office in this companie. *And*
every other brother shalle take his place in degre as he
hathe borne office in the same   *And* whosoever shalle
refuse to sit downe and take his place accordingly and as
he shalbe by the sergeant commaunded shalle forfaict to
thuse aforesaied iiii^{ds} *And* whosoever shalle in any commune matter speke in the court he shalle rise up and
reverently in quiet manner and decent termes declare his
mynde   *And he* that wille speke in any private matter shalle
rise oute of his place and stand before the heades for the
tyme being and shalle declare his mynde in honest and
decent wise wether it be ⟨28⟩ in any request touchinge
himselfe or in speaking of any matter touchinge any par-
ticular brother of the companie   *And* it is further ordeyned
that no personne shalle speake in court in any matter or
controversie touching any brother of the companie so
long as the person whome the matter touchethe or his
attorney be present in court upon paine of imprisonement
at the discretion of the heades or head   *Also* it is further
ordeyned that no person shalle have voice in court but
the Maior Lieutenaunt Constables assistaunce and suche

other of the companie as shalbe shippers or atturnes   *And*
for avoydinge of confusion of voices in decyding of causes
and controversies it is further ordeyned that suche personnes as have no voice in court shalle sit in the court
howse upon a fourme or benche fourmes or benches therefore appoincted from the rest of the court severally, *It is*
also concluded & ordeyned that none office of this estaple
whatsoever highe or lowe or any fee for terme of lyfe or
for terme of yeares to be percevid of the revenewes of this
estaple in any manner of wise shalbe graunted or geven
at London or els where oute of this estaple at Bruges or
els where the staple shalbe kept and the merchaundise of
the same estaple put to sale but onely here in the court
of this estaple and that within six wekes after tharrivalle
of either of the fletes   *Also* that no reversion of any suche
romethe or office shalbe graunted or geven to any person
or personnes before the office or romethe be voyde and
in the courtes disposition by reason of deathe surrendre
or otherwise upon paine suche grauntes and gyftes to be
to alle intentes and pourposes utterly voide and of none
effect, *Also* he that disclosethe any secret matter shewed
or moved in Court whiche ought to be kept secret or that
may tourne to any mans displeasure and be thereof convicted yf he be apprentice shalle be crossed this place
except he wille serve his M^r for his first offence one yeare
above the expiration of his terme & for his second offence
serve his M^r two yeres above thexpiration of his fulle
terme and for his thirde offence to be disfraunchised   *And*
every other brother offending in this article and being
thereof duely convicted shalle forfaicte to the court of this
estaple for his first offence x^{li} for his second offence xx^{li}
and for his thirde offence to be disfraunchised clerely for
ever.

Ordenaunce for apparelle of apprentices

It is ordeyned at this present court holden the xxvi daye of Maye xv^clxv for the better order of apprentices that none apprentice shalbe suffered to weare in this estaple or els where out of his M^rs sight in his shirt hose doblet coate, Jerkin, Jacket, cloke or gowne any manner of silke unles it be one stitche of silke in his dublet coate or cloke or smalle buttons of silke to the same. And that none apprentice shalle in his doblet weare any other thing then fustian canvas or worstead in his Jacket any other thing then clothe nor in the lyninge of his coate or gowne any other thing then cotton or worstead at the best ⟨28^d⟩ *Nor* shalle weare any shirt but wth a single ruffe nor shalle weare any spanishe lether or cut shone upon paine he that offendethe in any the premisses shalle forfaicte to the court of this estaple for his first offence xii^ds *And* for his second offence ii^s And at the thirde tyme that any suche apprentice shalle so offend shalbe sent over into Englonde to his M^r withe a lettar declaring his demeanour and breache of the ordenaunces and the saied offendour therafter not to be admitted to be atturney here in this estaple for his M^r or for any other during the tyme of his apprentishode *It is* further agreed that none apprentice shalle sit at any other table or tables at meales in the staple than suche as shalbe appoincted unto them by heades of this estaple for the tyme being except it be to furnishe suche table there as lackethe companie in whiche case he sittyng at the table withe other the companie shalle sit bareheaded for the reverence of his superiours unto suche tyme as he shalbe commaunded by the head for the tyme being there present to be couvered *And* yf he shalle presume otherwise to do shalle forfaicte for every suche offence iiii^ds And alle & singuler suche forfaictures abovesaied to be paied to the tresourer of this estaple for the tyme being to be therewithe accomptable boethe withe name and summe. *And for* that this ordenaunce shalbe the better had in remem-

beraunce and to be executed by the head aforesaied It is
agreed that /the/ clerke of this estaple for the tyme being
shalle rede this present ordenaunce or cause the same to
be red to the head of this estaple at his oethe taking   *With*
this also it is agreed that immediatly thereafter the sergeant
shalle deliver unto the saied heades in writing the names
of alle and singulier those apprentices whiche shalbe at
that tyme resident and at table within the saied In   *And* it
is further ordeyned that every fremans sonne being apprentice shalle be taken in respect of this ordenaunce as other
apprentices abovesaied be   *Provided* always that this ordenaunce shalle not extend to those apprentices whiche
have or shalle have but two yeres to serve so farfourthe
the master be content therewithe

Ordenaunce againest keaping of concubins
the xxvi daye of Maye anno xvC lxv.

In asmuche as by goddes lawes every christian man ought
to live in decent and lawdable order exchewing the companie of eville women   *It is* therefore agreed concluded
and enacted for avoiding of thindignation of almighty god
and slaunder to the companie of this estaple that no fellowe
of this saied estaple shalle privatly or appertly keape any
concubin or woman for misrule or shalle haunt any infamed
place of misrule upon paine thoffence proved thoffendour
to paie for the first tyme of his offence xl^s and for the
second tyme iiii^{li} And the thirde tyme x^{li} and not to be
accompted one of this estaple untille he be newe hansed
Also yf any apprentice of ⟨29⟩ this estaple shalle happen
to offende the lawe abovesaied he shalle for his first offence
abide suche correction as by the court of this estaple shalbe
awarded in that behalfe   *And* yf he eftsones so offende then
for his seconde offence he shalle be shipped over to his M^r
withe letters under the staple seale declaring the cause of
his suche ablegation.

Ordenaunce agaynest playeng at cardes or
dice the xxvi daye of Maye anno xv^clxv.

It is ordeined that no manner of person of the fellowship
of this estaple shalle plaie at dice cardes or other unlawfulle
game for money within this toune of Bruges except it be
betwene the feast of Christmas and the xx daie of Januarii
next following *In which* tyme it shalbe leifulle to every M^r
and covenaunt servant to plaie and none other to plaie
And in suche case to plaie onely in the halle or parlor of
the staple howse upon paine that every personne doieng
the contrarie shalle forfaicte every tyme x^s   *And* he y^t so
doethe not having goods of his owne shalle at every tyme
be imprisoned x daies   Alwayes reserved that the heades
and governours for the tyme being shalle at theire pleasures
take suche sportes and recreations as them shalle please as
often as they wille and calle unto them suche personnes of
the fellowshippe as they shalle appoinct and none other

Ordenaunce for payement of thofficiers dueties

The xxvi^t daye of Maye anno domini xv^clxv it is agreed
concluded and ordeined that no fellowe of this estaple or
apprentice being atturney whiche shalbe indebted to any
officier or officiers of the same estaple shalle at any tyme
hereafter departe into Englond or fraunce before he have
contented & satisfied to the same officer or officers suche
debt or duetie as he owethe upon paine that whatsoever
fellow aforesaied shalle do the contrarie shalle paie to the
officer or officiers to whom he is so indebted doble that he
owethe to them according to tholde ordenaunces of this
estaple

Ordenaunce against taking of apprentices to boethe the fredomes towit of the staple and mercháuntes adventurers

fforasmuche as of late the companie of this estaple are placed within theise lowe countrethes where the companie of merchauntes adventures have of longe tyme ben by reson whereof not onely summe confusion of boethe the trades may hereafter growe But also suche desire wille ensue to be fre of the same companies as in tyme to come wille skant be founde any mere merchauntes of the staple to poursue and followe the sute of the companie whan any occasion shalbe as of late there was experience[1] *It is* therefore at a court holden the xxvi daye of Maye xv^c lxv ordeined ⟨29^d⟩ and enacted that from and after the feast of sainct Michaelle tharchaungelle next ensueng no person fre of this companie and of the merchauntes adventures shalle take to apprentice any person to enioe the fredome of this companie and of the merchauntes adventurers also by apprentishode But mynding to binde him for the staple shalle bind him to the same companie and not to boethe upon paine that the maister taking any suche apprentice contrarie to this order shalle forfaicte to thuse of the companie C poundes and for default of payement thereof the saied apprentice so admitted shalbe disfraunchised from the liberties of this estaple

Ordenaunce for mariages

fforasmuche as every brother of the companie of this estaple is bounde by his oethe to keape secret the commune counsailles of alle the saied companie and nothing to do that maye be derogation hurt or harme to the generalitie of the saied estaple. And for that also it apperteynethe to

---

[1] Presumably during the discussions which preceded the grant of the Merchant Adventurers' charter of 1564 (*vide supra*, pp. 55–6, 72–3), when the Staplers were afraid of the Adventurers' pretensions.

the court of the saied estaple to studie alle menes for the due
observation thereof and to take away alle occasions w^{ch}
might induce any brother aforesaied to commit the contrarie   The saied companie at this present court holden
the xxvi daie of Maie xv^c lxv have ordeined and enacted
that yf any brother of this companie aforesaied shalle
happen at any tyme hereafter to marry any woman not
being borne within the realme of Englonde or not borne
within any of the dominions thereof he shalbe bounde by
this present ordenaunce within two yeres next after the
daie of his suche mariage to remove his wyfe and his
familie into Englonde there to dwelle and inhabite as long
as she shalle be his wife upon paine the saied ii yeres
expired he not to be permitted or suffered to ship any
staple merchaundise to this estaple or to be attorney in the
same estaple at any tyme within the tyme of his continuaunce withe the same his wyf on this side the sees
Provided always that this ordenaunce shalle not extende
againest the mariage of any woman whose father is mere
englishe

Ordenaunce for a generalle serche

It is ordeined the v daye of June xv^c lxv that a generalle
serche shalbe yerely had one monethe before the first
shipping of the yeres rate of alle woulles and woullfelles
remayning in this staple at Bruges for the better observation of thordenaunce of rates in the saied estaple according
as was yerely used within the staple at Calles   And that
no fellowe set or put any staple merchaundise into any
howse or place to thintent the heade or heades or gouvernours of this estaple may not peasibly come to vieu and
se the same upon paine thesaied woulles or felles to take
no preferment of olde woulles or olde felles

Ordenaunce againest those whiche slaunderen any of the companie of this estaple or his goodes

Also whosoever of the companie of this estaple that slaundrethe any person of the saied companie or his goods to any merchaunt straunger whereby suche personne is impaired in his name or goods or els wrongfully maynteynethe any merchaunt straunger ⟨30⟩ against any fellowe by waye of action or otherwise and being thereof duely convicted shalle forfaicte to the court of this estaple for his first suche offence v^{li} for his seconde suche offence x^{li} for his thirde suche offence xx^{li} and for his fourthe suche offence to be discharged and crossed this place besides that shalle satisfie the partie for his dammage after the awarde of the court.

Ordenaunce for woulwinders

Where as nowe theise dayes hathe ben fownde as of olde tyme hathe ben fownde that no smalle lose hinderaunce and dammage hathe happened to the companie of this estaple and other buyers of woulles thoroughe the deceipfulle winding of woulles by the woullewinders wthin the realme of Englonde committed who albeit that they be sworne truely to exercise theire office of woullewinding wthout fraude or deceipt yet they desiring rather to content the myndes of suche persons as ben growers of woulles then tobserve thoethe by them taken for truely to winde the saied woulles do fraudulently and deceipfully winde the saied woulles contrarie to thorders of divers actes of parlement for redres of those inconveniences provided and established especially in the xxiii yere of king Henry the viii, withe this also the saied woulwinders do often tymes make the piles of those woulles by them wounde very deceiptfully laieng in the fore part of the pile the best woulle and behinde the course and wourst woulle besides that do convert woulles into the loke in the countrethe whiche ben

of baser nature whereby the buyer is persuaded by them
that suche woulles is better then in dede it is alle tending
to 'the great hurt circumvention and dammage of the
merchaunt buyers   *ffor* reformation of whiche thinges the
wardens of the companie of the woulle winders in London
have earnestly and instantly required the right wourshipfulle Maiour and companie of merchauntes of the staple
whome it touchethe muche and order mete and convenient
by them to be devised therein   *It is* therefore agreed concluded ordeyned and enacted at a court holden here the
vth daye of June anno xv^{c}lxv that whatsoever woulle-
winder or woulwinders at any tyme hereafter shalbe convicted before the Maior of the staple of Westminster or
before the Maior of the staple at Boston for the tyme being
of any untrue uniust and fraudulent winding of woulles
or deceiptfulle piling of woulles or of converting any
woulles in the growers howses into any higher sort then
the countrethe doethe proport, and wille not be refourmed
by the saied Maior but stille continuethe in his enormitie
That then thoffendour not being reconciliated befor the
Maior of the saied estaple for the tyme being for his suche
offences shalle have his name written in a table therefore
pourposely to be hanged up in the staple howse at Leden
Halle^{1} in London   *And* it is further agreed that what
brother soever of this saied companie that shalle set any
suche woullwinder to wourke his woulles after he shalbe
thereof warned by the wardens of the woulwinders of
London by lettre or otherwise shalle forfaict ⟨30^{d}⟩ for
every daye that he so doethe set him a wourke ii^{s} whereof
the one halfe shalbe to the presenter and thother halfe to
thuse of the wardens and theire companie of woulwinders

---

^{1} Leadenhall tended to become the centre of the Staplers' organisation in England, but it was not their property. It was rented from
the city, and the Staplers, subletting shops and warehouses there
(to Cockayne amongst others), were often in arrears with their
rents. (B.M. Add. MSS. 38170, fo. 353 and Staple Company
Minutes Book, 16 Nov. 1619; 9 Feb. 1619 (1620), 22 March 1619,
17 August 1624, *et passim*.)

aforesaied *And* yf any brother aforesaied be fownde culpable and doeth not fourthewithe paie the saied forfaicture of ii[s] per daie   That then the maior of this estaple shalle make payement thereof unto the saied wardens and thereupon shalle certifie unto the court of this estaple the name of him w[ch] so refusethe to make the saied payement *In* whiche the saied brother shalle paie to the court of this estaple the double to thuse of the saied estaple to be levied upon him and his gooddes at his next shipping to the same estaple and his childeren or apprentices not to be admitted to the fredome of this saied estaple before the saied forfaicture be fully contented and paied.

Ordenaunce for execution of ordonaunces

As vertue hathe no price except it be put in exercise so is the frute and benefite of good lawes blemished and baren withoute due execution of them   Therefore alle we the bretheren of this our wourshipfulle companie being assembled in ample nombre first in the name of almighty god secondly for the love and obedience we beare to the honor of our prince and countrethe and thirdly for respect of our honestie and commodite mynding to confirme our selves in quietnes concorde and obedience whereof shalle rise contentation to our gracious souveraigne ladie the Quenes Hightnes fame and praise to our naturalle countrethe credit and estimation to our societe and evin so enclyninge our selves to the perfourmaunce of the good orders and reasonable determinations made as althoughe it be verely to be hoped that it shalbe nedeles to devise paines for transgressours yet bycause continuaunce of tyme in greate assembles oft breadethe some inconveniences have by commune consent necessarely provided a rule of correction for the misbehavior of thoffendours yf any shalle happen desiring nevertheles and trusting to finde in alle and every brother of this companie suche uniformite in vertue and honest lyf that this order of execution of our

fourmer lawes and ordenaunces may seme hereafter to our
posterite rather adioyned to prevent vice and disorder
before it come Then to punishe faultes after they were
committed   *It is therefore* ordeyned that none ordenaunce
⟨31⟩ or act of this estaple made or hereafter to be made
by the Maior Constables and fellowship of merchauntes
of the same estaple shalbe altered abrogated dissolved or
dispenced withe alle by court of the saied estaple but by
consent aswelle of the right wourshipfulle maior of this
estaple for the tyme being as of alle the thre portes accustomed to ship hether to wit London Boston and Hulle
upon lettres to be sent to them under the places seele   *And*
in caas alle the saied portes do not agre in and about the
saied alteration or other the premisses yet yf two of the
saied portes withe the saied Mr. Maior and the court of this
saied estaple do agree in the saied alteration or othre the
premisses suche alteration abrogation dissolution or dispensation made in fourme aforesaied shalle stonde and be
as good and as effectualle as thoughe alle the saied iii portes
had condiscended thereunto. But if two of the portes
aforesaied withe the saied Maior and court of this estaple
cannot agre in or about suche alteration or other the premisses then no suche alteration abrogation dissolution or
dispensation shalbe made before the commyng over of the
saied Mr Maior and certaine personnes of the portes aforesaied to be called over for his assistaunce in that behalfe
pourposly to be appointed by court of this estaple. *It is*
further ordeined the vth daie of June anno xv^e lxv that yf
any parsonne of this estaple shalbe detected suspected or
presented to the head or heades of this estaple for the tyme
being of for or concerning any offence or act committed
or done contrarie to any of thordenaunces or actes of this
saied estaple nowe made or hereafter to be made and
stonding in force it shalbe leifulle to the Maior Lieutenaunt
or Constables of this estaple for the tyme being and to
every of them aswelle by themselves as by any othere
whome they wille put in trust whereof one shalle have ben

*no altera-
tion of
ordinaunces
w^thoute
Consent of
ye poortes*

and Mr Maior

*date of this
ordenaunce
5 June 1565*

Lieutenaunt or Constable of this estaple to examine serche
out and trie suche offence by thoethe of the partie so detected suspected or presented as by thoethe of any other
brother of this companie and other meannes and circumstances for the true knowledge thereof to be had   *And
every* suche parsonne aforesaied be he the principalle or
othere whiche shalle refuse to be examined in manner and
fourme aforesaied or that shalle not directly aunswer to
alle suche articles and interrogatories as shalbe ministred
unto him or them shalbe excepted and reputed as parsonnes
disobedient and forgetting his or their oethes taken to the
companie of this estaple and shalbe punished as followithe
towit the partie so detected suspected or presented shalle
for his first denialle or refusalle forfaict to the court of this
estaple fyfty poundes and so be quit for that offence and yf
he eftsones shalle offende and thereof being called to examination and shalle refuse to depose and directly not aunswer
as is aforesaied shalle forfaict for his seconde denialle one
hundrethe poundes and be quit for his seconde offence.
And for the third offence to be crossed the fredome of this
estaple   *And* every other brother aforesaied for his suche
obstinacie shalle forfaict to the saied court ten poundes
It is further ordeyned that whosoever of the companie
aforesaied at any tyme hereafter shalbe commaunded either
by the head or heades of this saied estaple for the tyme
being or by theire officer or by the places lettres to make
his apparaunce at tyme and place to him in that behalfe
to be ⟨31ᵈ⟩ appointed and denounced to make aunswer
to suche thinges as to him shalbe then and there obiected
for or concernyng the breache or violation of any act or
ordenaunce of this saied estaple and shalle make default
thereof shalle forfaict to the aforesaied court for his first
default xᶫˡst. and for his second suche default xxˡˡ   And
for his thirde suche default to be crossed the fredome of
this estaple and not to be thereunto readmitted under the
hans *Provided* alwayes that alle lawfulle excuses shalbe
allowed   *And* for asmuche as divers of the companie

aforesaied ben the bolder to offend in certaine ordenaunces
and actes of this saied estaple by reason that they ship not
to the same estaple nor intende to ship to the same at any
tyme hereafter it is therefore agreed and ordeyned that who
soever of this saied companie shalle happen to be condemned
by court of the same estaple in any penaltie for breache
of any ordenaunce or act here in this estaple stonding in
force and shalle have no gooddes in the saied estaple
whereby suche penaltie or forfaicture cannot be levied by
court yt then lettres shalbe sent unto him under the places
seele to make payement thereof to the tresourer of this
estaple for the tyme being in whiche caas yf he shalle not
make payement thereof according as he shalbe commaunded
his childeren or apprentices shalle not be admitted to the
fredome of this saied estaple untille suche tyme as the saied
penalties shalbe contented and paied   *It is* further ordeined
that yf the Maior Lieutenaunt or Constables of this saied
estaple for the tyme being do not withe as convenient
spede as he or they may within ten dayes after any com-
plainct or presentement made to them or any of them
secretly or openly of any offence or act done or committed
contrarie to any ordenaunce or act then stonding in force
procede to examine trie oute asmuche as in him or them
is the truethe of the matter withoute affection or displeasure
or do not in like manner w^th^in the tyme of his or theire
office publishe or declare to the court so muche as he or
they shalle finde by examination confession or witnes (yf
the matter be so far fourthe and ready to be published) to
thintent the person complayned on or accused may either
be clered or condemned according to his desert and the
equite of the cause or do not procede to iudgement of it
according to iustice in convenient tyme then every suche
Maior so offending shalle forfaict to the court of this
estaple C^l^, every Lieutenaunt C marks, and every
Constable xl^li^. *And* for the better administration of iustice
withoute affection or feare of any person it is ordeined
that upon the opennyng of any matter againest any brother

of this companie when the same shalbe opened and hard in court the partie, apprentice, atturney brother and partener shalbe voyded out of the court. And then suche personnes as have voice in court shalle declare theire opinions wether he be guiltie or not by a balle or button to be put in a boxe therefore provided. *That* is to saie yf he be guiltie then to put the balle or button into the boxe whereuppon guiltie is written and so econtra. And whosoever shalle attent the breache or violation of this ordenaunce or any braunche or article therein before the commyng over of the Maior or withoute the consent of the portes had in writing contrarie to the fourme abovesaied shalle incurre and forfaict theise following that is ⟨33⟩ to saie the lieutenaunt L^{li}, every Constable xl^{li}, and every fellowe xx pounds to be levied upon them and every of them offendours aforesaied and theire gooddes without grace favor or pardon *Provided* always and it is enacted that alle and singuler theise ordenaunces afore written made and established by court of this saied estaple sethens the commyng hether of the right wourshipfulle Sir Thomas Offley knight Maior of this saied estaple and his right wourshipfulle assistaunce with other of the companie of this saied estaple shalle take force strengethe and effect to be executed as followithe towit thordenaunce of hans from the daie of enacting thereof and alle othre ordenaunces aforesaied at and from tharrivalle of the next generalle flete and not before any thing therein conteyned to the contrarie in any wise notwithstonding And in the meanne tyme alle & every other fourmer ordenaunces before that tyme made shalle stonde in strengethe and vigueur and shalbe executed withoute impediment in as ample manner & fourme as thoughe none other ordenaunces had ben made to let thexecution thereof.[1]

margin note: consent of the portes

[1] The last twelve pages of the MS. are filled with a summary and index of these ordinances, and with summaries of such changes as were made up to 1785. These summaries epitomise the Minutes Book of the Company.

INDEX

Gigmill, 14, n. 2
Gilds, anticipate regulated companies, 89, 90, n. 1
   merchant, 1, 2
   restrictions on trade in Netherlands, 14
Gilpin, George, 51
Gloucestershire, 69
Glovers, 69
Granvelle, Cardinal, 43, 45, 46, 47, 48, 49, 50, 51, 54, 57
Gresham, Sir Thomas, 39, 48, 54, 56, 58
Guicciardini, 35, 44
Gyfforde, William, 105

Haddon, Dr Walter, 104
Hall, Edmond, 95, 104, 105
Hall, Thomas, 14, 15, 41
Hamburgh, 59, 65, 67, 68, 77
Hampton, John, 104
Hanse League, 54, 56, 59, 76
Havre, le, 36
Henry VI, King, 21
Henry VII, King, 21
Henry VIII, King, 10, 19, 21, 38, 46
Holland, wool trade of, 55, 61
   communal buyers of, 17
Horn, Count, 57
Huguenots, 36, 48
Hull, wool trade of, 22, 32 and n. 2, 52, 67, 96, 97, 98, 142, 144, 197
   Staple seal of, 96, 98, 200

"Increment" on wool, 22 *et seq.*
Intercursus Magnus, 17, 40, 61
Ipswich, 97, 142, 144
Ireland, 38, 44, 79, 81, 82, 83
Isell, 16
Isle of Man, 83
Isle of Wight, 83
Italy, wool merchants of, 7, n. 1, 8, 9, 10, 16, 17, 28, 29, 55
   wool trade to, 8, 68

James I, King, 78

Kendal, 81

Lead, 82
Leadenhall, 82, 99, 101, 195 and n. 1
Leghorn, 77
Libel of English Policy, 42, 43
Licences, for wool export, 8, 10, 19, 23, 24, 25, 61, 93
   for wool broking, 70, 77, 99
Lincoln, 66, 78, 82, 99, n. 3
London, 47, 50, 66, 70, 142, 144, 148, 188
   Common Council, 85
   position in Staple Company, 81, 82, 83, 95, 96, 97, 98, 99, 101, 174, 194

For EU product safety concerns, contact us at Calle de José Abascal, 56–1°,
28003 Madrid, Spain or eugpsr@cambridge.org.

www.ingramcontent.com/pod-product-compliance
Ingram Content Group UK Ltd.
Pitfield, Milton Keynes, MK11 3LW, UK
UKHW012347130625
459647UK00009B/609